ADOLESCENT GANGS
Old Issues, New Approaches

Publisher's Note

Chapter 6, *Energizing and Organizing the Community,* should include the following on Page 147:

Endnote
This chapter has been modified from the book *Gangs, My Town and The Nation* written by Norman D. Randolph, Ph.D., with Edsel Erickson, Ed.D. (Learning Publications, Holmes Beach, Florida, 1996). Used with permission.

ADOLESCENT GANGS

Old Issues, New Approaches

edited by
Curtis W. Branch

USA	Publishing Office:	BRUNNER/MAZEL
		A member of the Taylor & Francis Group
		325 Chestnut Street
		Philadelphia, PA 19106
		Tel: (215) 625-8900
		Fax: (215) 625-2940
	Distribution Center:	BRUNNER/MAZEL
		A member of the Taylor & Francis Group
		47 Runway Road, Suite G
		Levittown, PA 19057-4700
		Tel: (215) 269-0400
		Fax: (215) 269-0363
UK		BRUNNER/MAZEL
		A member of the Taylor & Francis Group
		1 Gunpowder Square
		London EC4A 3DE
		Tel: 171 583 0490
		Fax: 171 583 0581

ADOLESCENT GANGS: Old Issues, New Approaches

1 2 3 4 5 6 7 8 9 0

Edited by Edward A. Cilurso and Jean Anderson. Typeset by Cheryl Hufnagle. Printed by Hamilton Printing Co., Castleton, NY. Cover design by Joseph Dieter Visual Communications.

A CIP catalog record for this book is available from the British Library.
♾ The paper in this publication meets the requirements of the ANSI Standard Z39.48-1984 (Permanence of Paper)

Library of Congress Cataloging-in-Publication Data

Adolescent Gangs : old issues, new approaches / edited by Curtis Branch
     p. cm.
Includes bibliographical references and index.
ISBN 0-87630-923-6 (alk. paper). -- ISBN 0-87630-924-4 (pbk. : alk. paper)
  1. Gangs--United States--Case Studies. 2. Gang Members--United States--Rehabilitation.
3. Gang members--United States--Psychology. 4. Juvenile delinquency--United States--
Prevention. 5. Problem youth--United States--Case studies. 6. Social work with youth--United
States. I. Branch, Curtis W.
HV6439.U5A35   1998   98-50826
364.1'06'608350973--dc21   CIP

ISBN 0-87630-923-6 (case)
ISBN 0-87630-924-4 (paper)

CONTENTS

1

Welcome Home Boyz: Building Communities through Cultural Capital

V

5

**Youth Violence and Post-Traumatic Stress Disorder:
Assessment, Implications, and Promising
School-Based Strategies**

Lorita A. Purnell   **115**

6

Energizing and Organizing the Community

Norman Randolph   **129**

**PART III
MENTAL HEALTH INTERVENTIONS**   **149**

7

**Culture-Focused Group Therapy: Identity Issues in
Gang-Involved Youth**

Alice M. Vargas and Marina DiPilato   **159**

8

Youth Gangs, Cognitive–Behavioral Interventions in Schools, and System Change

William Carylon and Dion Jones   175

9

Pathologizing Normality or Normalizing Pathology?

Curtis Branch   197

PART IV
SUMMARY, CONCLUSIONS, AND
RECOMMENDATIONS   213

CONTRIBUTORS

Karim Abdullah
Juvenile Probation Department
Denver Municipal Court
Denver, Colorado

Curtis W. Branch, Ph.D.
New York State Psychiatric Institute/Columbia University
Columbia University Medical Center
New York, New York

William Carylon, Ph.D.
Department of Psychology
University of Southern Mississippi
Hattiesburg, Mississippi

Marina DiPilato, Ph.D.
Special Services Department
Rio Rancho Public Schools
Rio Rancho, New Mexico

Ann Doucette-Gates, Ph.D.
The Glendon Association
Santa Barbara, California

Ramon Gonzalez, M.Ed.
Teachers College
Columbia University
New York, New York

Dion Jones, Ph.D.
Department of Psychology
University of Southern Mississippi
Hattiesburg, Mississippi

Lorita A. Purnell, M.Ed.
School of Social Services Administration
University of Chicago
Chicago, Illinois

Afriye Quamina, M.S.
College of Engineering
MESA
University of California–Berkeley
Berkeley, California

Norman Randolph, Ph.D.
West Mifflin Area School District
West Mifflin, Pennsylvania

Alice M. Vargas, Ph.D.
University of New Mexico
Carrie Tingley Hospital
Albuquerque, New Mexico

PREFACE

This edited text is intended to contribute to the very sparse literature on clinical interventions with gang-affiliated adolescents. Specifically, it is designed to provide theory and practice-based experiences as a blueprint for others to follow in their attempts to find interventions, exclusive of law enforcement approaches, which have been shown to have promise in helping troubled young people who find themselves in gangs. It is different from other texts in the field in that it moves beyond simply describing the approaches and their merits. The unifying theme of the book is the fact that it is rooted in psychological theory that contends that adolescence is a developmental period which is characterized by exploration of multiple social roles and dynamics. Gang membership is a social role. The book does not, however, suggest that gangs in and of themselves are either good or bad. Rather, it accepts the fact that in some neighborhoods gangs are a part of the historical legacy and as a result are accepted by many of the residents as being a "given." Technically speaking, the book is interdisciplinary in scope. It opens with an introduction in which the author makes an argument for why this text is timely. The next section is an unusual feature. Gangs and related concepts are defined by the editor. The operational definitions that are provided are statements of how the other authors use the concepts, thereby eliminating the need for each author to spend the obligatory one or two pages defining key terms.

The origin of my interest in gang adolescents can be traced to my work with the Juvenile Probation Department of the Denver, Colorado, court system. It was there as a private mental health professional that I started to try to help families and adolescents understand the appeal of the gang and the ultimate effects it might have on their quality of life and familial relationships. The seemingly countless hours I spent in my office talking with young people who thought being in a gang was "no problem" taught me a lot about the quest for meaning in life and the multiple roads that are traveled in search of that often elusive goal. Perhaps what was most striking about that work was the tenacious way in which many of the young people defended the choices that they had made. From many of them I often heard that the were seeking "respect" and were willing to do whatever was necessary in order to obtain it. It should be noted that all of this was before the advent of gangsta rap and the youth culture which has now given a broad cross section of American culture a glimpse into their private psychological worlds. Therapy was a radical departure from the daily experiences of many of the young people with whom I worked. Or it was a revisit to some painful and unfulfilling experience they had suffered at the hands of a "shrink" in the penal system or public mental health system. Despite all of that background they kept coming to see me and in a lot of ways negotiating new frontiers in their lives without fully acknowledging what was happening. Now in retrospect I am eternally grateful to them for having shared their experiences with me. I only hope that they grew as much as a result of the experience as I did.

In the minds of many professional colleagues with whom I interacted, what I was doing was not effective or meaningful. Perhaps they were right, but there is the possibility that they were not. Evaluation of the effectiveness of mental health interventions is often not fully realized until months later. I sometimes think about the client who tracked me down after I left Denver to come to New York, verbalizing a host of bogus complaints about unfinished work but always leaving open the possibility of our "keeping in touch."

At the same time that I was learning tons of new things about how many troubled adolescents and their families try to cope with problems of living I was also learning a lot about how out of touch many agencies and programs were in their attempts, and often nonattempts, to work with gang-affiliated youth and their families. Standard, and often very outdated, research findings were routinely verbalized as justification for positions of benign neglect. Worse than that, deficit model thinking abounded in the minds of many helpers. Constructive dialogue about finding new ways of thinking about old issues was difficult, if not impossible, to create. Now several years later I offer this edited volume as a specimen of some new thinking about old problems. Hopefully it will become a catalyst for rethinking old research paradigms and theories. Let's hope the naysayers who appear to have an investment in continuing to pathologize all gang members, even when there is no objectively verifiable data to substantiate such behavior, will pause to consider some of the ideas articulated in this book.

I am extremely grateful to the contributors to this volume for taking the risk associated with departing from intellectual canons and suggesting that new ways of think and behaving relative to gang members and their families might move us in the direction of new outcomes.

ACKNOWLEDGMENTS

In life we can learn new things in every place and situation through which we travel. Truth comes in a variety of forms if we would but open our eyes and ears and receive it. The tremendous struggles that many of the gang youth and their families whom I have known over the past decade have taught me a lot about a variety of things. Perhaps the greatest lesson has been concerning the human spirit and the power of positive thinking. This combination, I'm convinced, is what has allowed some young people to salvage a life for themselves despite all of the negatives that have been heaped upon them by the worlds in which they live. They, too, sometimes have been unknowing accomplices in plotting their own defeat and impoverished existence. This book is devoted to the multitude of gang youth and service providers who are working with them. Let's hope that the day will come, even soon, when new ways of thinking will overtake us all and lead us into directions of new behaviors, ultimately producing new outcomes.

I am extremely grateful to the contributors to this volume who persevered and stood by this project, even as it underwent machinations that were out of my control. Thanks to Elaine Pirrone for encouraging me to take on this project. The valuable assistance of Rocky Schwartz and Gabriella, in getting the multiple versions completed and revised many times, is noted.

INTRODUCTION

This book is divided into four parts, three of which are devoted to a type of setting in which services are provided to gang-affiliated adolescents and their families: community-based interventions, specialized agency-based interventions, and mental health interventions. The final part offers conclusions. The first part is devoted to work that is most characteristically thought of as community-focused programs. The word community in the title suggests the residence of the gang members as the place in which the intervention work should occur, thereby not requiring the gang members to migrate out of their zone of safety as a prerequisite for getting help. Ramon Gonzalez's chapter, "Welcome Home Boyz," builds on the oft-repeated thesis that gangs are partially the result of a gross inequity in the spreading of economic wealth throughout urban communities versus suburban neighborhoods. He contends that one of the major factors motivating gang members is their quest for a piece of the economic pie. Consistent with that economic gain perspective, he suggests an approach leading to entrepreneurship as an intervention to help counteract the destructive behaviors of gangs.

"A Practitioner's Perspective" (Afriye Quamina) approaches community interventions from the perspective of anthropological and historical chronologies of gangs in neighborhoods as providing major insights into the behaviors of African American males within the school context. He suggests that educators should consider the observation that current teaching approaches are ineffective with a large segment of the population of African American males. He concludes that the pedagogical methods and underlying assumptions are not responsive to the psychological needs (i.e., affiliation, affirmation) of many African American males. His approach, much less direct and concrete than Gonzalez's, is seen as a valuable way to help program planners overcome their proclivity for typecasting gangs as homogeneous entities.

Ann Doucettte-Gates' chapter, "Hope: Sustaining a Vision of the Future," is a hybrid of developmental psychology research and sociological inquiry. She provides detailed data on the thinking of gang members and how it can negatively impact their ability to feel empowered enough to participate in any type of intervention that requires a delay of gratification, a skill that has not worked in their best interest, historically. Her chapter suggests that the absence of a sense of a future may be a direct causal factor in why many gang members may opt to participate in high-risk behaviors frequently. Implicit in her work also is the idea that depression may be an underlying dimension in the lives of many gang members. The section ends with a summary and a set of thought-provoking issues that may be facilitative of planning new types of community-based programs, programs that are sensitive to cultural differences but not apologetic in their approach to counteracting the destructive dimensions of gangs.

Specialized agency-based interventions, Part II of this text, concerns itself with the types of approaches that can be effectively mounted by probation departments and schools, in conjunction with other agencies. The overarching idea of this section is that no one single agency has the resources to completely take on the gang problem and be successful. Rather, a community-wide approach with different constituents providing different services consistent with their expertise is the method of planning of choice.

The impact of the probation department on the lives of gang members is discussed first, in the chapter "Denver County Court Probation Intervention with Gang-Affiliated Youth," by Abdullah and Branch, which identifies key ways in which the probation department can make a significant difference in the lives of families. They offer the idea of the court as a "super parent" and show how the dynamics of how families respond to authority figures is diagnostic and can be used to gain entrance into the ongoing dynamics of the family when they are not in crisis. Their work is a combination of psychoanalytically oriented observations and practical realities that exist within the world of courts and probation departments.

Lorita Foster's chapter concerns the behavior of gang members within the context of schools. She specifically addresses issues of how to engage gang members around academic tasks and how to harness their intellectual abilities for constructive purposes. The basis of her paper is her teaching experiences in a public high school within a gang-infested neighborhood in Chicago.

Norman Randolph thinks community inoculation against the disruptive impacts of gangs can be best accomplished by a high level of organization and vigilance. His chapter, "Energizing and Organizing the Community," proposes a plan for creating maximal community participation in the efforts to fortify itself. The school is central to such efforts.

Part III of this text is concerned with the provision of mental health services to gang-affiliated adolescents and their families. The section opens with a chapter on the use of group psychotherapy, with a cultural focus, as a way to help Latino adolescents resolve their identity crisis (Vargas and DiPilato). They offer specific suggestions for using a group model for reaching adolescents who have opted to join a gang. Inherent in their approach is the idea that affiliated and group orientation are features of these young people's behavior that can be harnessed by the mental health practitioner. Clinical case material is offered as supportive evidence. The model is sufficiently global that it can be adapted for use with a variety of cultural groups.

William Carylon and Dion Jones offer a research-based chapter that offers empirical support for the ideas articulated by Carylon and Jones ("Youth Gangs, Cognitive, Behavioral Interventions in Schools, and System Change"). Their central thesis is that the need for affiliation is so pronounced in adolescence that it often leads young people to engage in self-endangering and counterproductive behaviors as a way to win approval from peers and to give the appearance of acceptance.

Finally, Branch offers a chapter that undertakes the difficult question of whether treatments that have been offered to gang-affiliated adolescents have normalized pathology or if treatment as a mental health enterprise has pathologized elements of normal behavior that have occurred in conjunction with gang membership.

☐ Basic Definitions and Concepts

Scholars generally agree that the work of Frederic Thrasher (1927) was the beginning of social science's interest in the phenomenon of adolescent gangs. In the studies conducted in Chicago, Thrasher observed behavior and attitudes of 1300 street gangs. From his observations came theoretical postulates that continue to be held by many as being canonical. According to Thrasher a gang could be characterized as an interstistial group, originally found spontaneously and then integrated through conflict. It is characterized by the following types of behavior: meeting face to face, milling, movement through space as a unit, conflict, and planning. The result of this collective behavior is the development of tradition, unreflective internal structure, esprit de corps, solidarity, morale, group awareness, and attachment to a local territory (Thrasher, 1927, cited in Jankowski, 1991, p. 3).

Since the pioneering work of Thrasher, American society has changed dramatically. Despite the plethora of changes that have transpired in America, gangs continue to be a part of the landscape. In fact within the last

10 to 15 years there has been a significant increase in the rate of violence among adolescents; much of it is attributed to an increase in gang activity. The legacy of Thrasher has remained pivotal to scholars interested in gangs and the behaviors of their members. A large number of the scholars studying gangs continue to draw on the seminal work of Thrasher, but a small minority of scholars have noted serious limitations of Thrasher's work when juxtaposed against the social fabric of life in modern America (Doucette-Gates, this volume; Jankowski, 1991). Specific points of disagreement with Thrasher have been various, but the most fundamental is the question of definition: What is a gang?

The Thrasher definition has been the subject of modifications and complete reworkings. The question of definition among scholars is so pervasive that at one point the American Sociological Association sponsored a special edition of its official journal *The American Sociologist* and devoted it exclusively to the question of defining gangs. Needless to say the edition reflected a great divergence of opinions, each emphasizing different aspects of gangs (e.g., origin, structure, function, etc.). The absence of a widely agreed upon definition has made it very difficult for scholars to communicate effectively with each other. Likewise the general public has experienced confusion about understanding gangs as a social phenomenon and what, if anything, should be done about them. Ruth Horowitz (1987) thinks that the absence of a universally acceptable definition does not present an insurmountable problem.

It does appear, however, that individual scholars should be careful to state their operational definition of gangs and show how it informs and drives their work. In other words, noting the parochial definition of gangs one is using helps the reader know what assumptions and biases the researcher is using. Of course the more limited the definition the less generalizable are the results.

Of the plethora of recent definitions of gangs, the one offered by Jankowski (1991) is one which is the basis of the thinking about gangs offered in the current text:

> A gang is an organized social system that is both quasi-private (not fully open to the public) and quasi-secretive (much of the information concerning its business remains confined within the group) and whose size and goals have necessitated that social interaction be governed by a leadership structure that has defined roles; where the authority associated with these roles has been legitimized to the extent that social codes are operational to regulate the behavior of both leadership and the rank and file; that plans and provides not only for the social and economic services of its members, but also for its own maintenance as an organization; that pursue[s] such goals irrespective of whether such action is legal or not; and that lacks a bureaucracy (i.e., an administrative staff that is hierarchically organized and separate from leadership). (pp. 28–29)

The definition is comprehensive, commenting on origin, structure, activities, and implicit philosophy of gangs. It also addresses the old question of why young people join gangs. There are specific dimensions of the definition that merit further commentary.

Jankowski conceptualizes a gang to be quasi private and private simultaneously. By that strong dichotomy he is suggesting that there are features of gangs that are observable to "outsiders," but there are other facets of the gang (i.e., private) that are known only to members. This seeming contradiction is an important feature. It suggests that what we outsiders purport to "know" about gangs constitutes a small part of the whole picture.

The second condition for classification as a gang, as articulated by Jankowski, "whose size and goals have necessitated that social interaction be governed by a leadership structure that has defined roles" implies that there is an organizational structure for a gang, one that is clear and obvious to the membership. Perhaps the existence of this condition points out that in order to be a gang member one must be able to function within a set of structural parameters. To do so requires that the individual have the capacity to suppress his or her personal goals, agendas, and behaviors in deference to the superordinate canons of the group. At face value this appears to be a simple and basic trait of human beings. Such is not the case. Severely disturbed individuals who lack self-regulation often find it difficult to suppress their will for the will of the group. Instead, persons with poor self-regulation skills are frequently consumed by endless and out-of-control searches for ways to get their needs met. Finding ways to get their needs met, without giving very much to others in the process, is their constant preoccupation, as they show little or no regard for social conventions. Clinicians often characterize such individuals as narcissistic. They are notoriously poor candidates for gang membership.

An additional criteria of a gang, as postulated by Jankowski, notes that the authority of the group is legitimized to the extent that social codes are operational to regulate the behavior of both leadership and the rank and file. Gang members are expected to be able to accept the rules of the group. Highly individualistic and sociopathic persons have considerable difficulty satisfying this condition and as such are not likely to "fit" this demand characteristic of a gang. Likewise the gang has the capacity to manage its own affairs by planning and executing activities that are designed to take care of the group. The legality of the activities is irrelevant to the gang.

Consistent throughout Jankowski's definition is the idea that the goals and will of the group exceed those of the individuals. A good gang member must be able to accept the fact that he is "second" to the organization and that the organization has ways of taking caring of all of its members, even though the logic and wisdom of those ways may not be obvious at all times.

The latter condition requires an act of "faith," the member blindly believing that the group is able and will take care of him. Of course much of this is an idealism that an organization will respond to all of its members' needs. Cognitively this is equivalent to behavior exhibited by many latency age children (i.e., 8–10 years).

Perhaps the most poignant part of the Jankowski's conceptualization is that gangs represent an organization that is clearly structured in ways that can be described in concrete terms (i.e., leaders, rules, etc.). On this criteria alone many of the groupings that the media and general public have characterized as gangs would be reclassified as not meeting criteria.

The value of a definition rests in helping make certain that all parties to the dialogue are talking about the same entity. In generic conversations about gangs this is often not the case. Rather, images of gangs frequently range from a modern version of West Side Story type neighborhood gangs to auxiliaries for international terrorist groups, even in the same conversation. An ability to see gangs as having any dimensions other than being ruthless out-of-control sociopaths has also impaired some attempts to "understand" the gang phenomenon and its appeal to adolescents. The present text is an attempt to help expand the ways in which gangs are conceptualized. Jankowski's definition is the operational conceptualization that undergirds all of the chapters. The text provides "mixed coverage," commenting on "gangs" as organizations and gang members as individuals.

The concept of gang issues is used throughout this text. It connotes matters of interest to gang members and researchers studying gangs. Having subject matter covered as an issue does not connote it to be a "problem." For example, the question of gang membership (i.e., Who joins gangs?) is discussed often. From the perspective of gang members, being in a gang is not necessarily problematic. Likewise many community citizens would say that just being in the gang is not problematic; however, the things that usually occur as a result of being in a gang (i.e., violence, drugs) is problematic. The coverage in this text is an attempt to examine issues related to gangs from multiple perspectives and in so doing create a different type of mindset regarding the realities of gangs. Caution! Let's not race ahead and assume that the authors are attempting to negate the negative features of gang life or to make legitimate things that clearly fall outside of moral and civic codes of modern society. Rather, the present text is simply an attempt to look at some old issues in new ways. Hopefully the result will be that readers will move beyond longstanding positions of suppression and increased law enforcement efforts as a response to the reality of gangs in the lives of many young people. Perhaps an understanding of gangs, from the perspective of those who belong to them, will provide the reader with the beginnings of some creative thoughts about how to harness the human capital that is invested in gangs and fully develop and exploit its potential as a way to contribute to the common good of adolescents and communities. It is strongly hoped that the reader will come away from this text with the understanding that old ways of dealing with gangs have not been effective, evidenced in part by the continued proliferation of gangs and their increasingly violent nature. Some "new approaches" must be created. The exact look of those new approaches is not entirely clear. One thing that is clear, however, is that the new approaches will have to be diversified and include more than strong law enforcement and suppression philosophies.

☐ References

Horowitz, R. (1987). Community tolerance of gang violence. *Social Problems, 34,* 437–450.

Jankowski, M. (1991). *Islands in the streets: Gangs in urban American society.* Berkeley, CA: University of California Press.

Thrasher, F. (1927). *The gang: A study of 1303 gangs in Chicago.* Chicago: University of Chicago Press.

I

COMMUNITY-BASED INTERVENTIONS

The three chapters contained in this section represent an interesting cross section of views on how to work with gang adolescents and issues that should form the basis of the intervention. Gonzalez suggests that gangs are in the midst of redefining themselves. The transformation, he thinks, from outsider to responsible community members, has not been without problems. From his perspective, the most obvious evidence of the emerging change can be found in the names and classification (i.e., street organizations versus gangs) that many organizations are choosing for themselves. The reluctance to continue to use gangs as a self-descriptor appears to be related to the members recognizing that gangs have a pejorative connotation in the larger social context. It appears, based on this logic, that gang members have been listening to what others have been saying about them. To hasten their group identity transformations, street organizations are moving in the direction of being capitalists and active participants in their communities' economic life. Branch (1997) suggests that the concern about what others think of them drives much of the behavior of members of street organizations. Even in their states of disengagement with the communities in which they reside, gangs and communities have a dynamic relationship.

Doucette-Gates' approach to gang-affiliated adolescents, as represented in this volume, takes a bit of a traditional psychological approach. She explores the concept of future time perspective and how it influences decisions that gang adolescents make in the here and now. Implicit in her approach is the idea that gang adolescents have an inner psychological life to which they have access. The inner life is nurtured by the quality of the ecologies in which they function. Young people growing up in settings of economic poverty, poor quality education, and disjointed family life are at high risk for having limited vision of hopes of overcoming such adversities. The outcome is that they tend to live in the here and now, not being certain that they will live to have "a future." The overarching premise of the Doucette-Gates research appears to be that interventions need to be sensitive to the environs of the consumers, on a behavioral and cognitive level. She strongly suggests that perhaps the first step to making sustained interventions into the lives of gang adolescents and other at-risk youngsters is to get them to look beyond the here and now (i.e., dream, hope). Of course, that is no small feat but one which must be accomplished if there is to be any movement beyond current behaviors and thinking.

Issues related to here-and-now functioning among many urban African American males are articulated in Quamina's essay. The work is slightly different from its companion pieces in that it is heavily dependent on anecdotal data. The result is a decrease in objectivity and generalizability. Even with these limitations there is still value in the presentation. It articulates a set of questions concerning how and why African American males learn the scripts that they often display (i.e., emotional distancing, congregating in sets, being players). Quamina thinks that schools could play a vital role in helping young men explore other ways of being. His examination of the role of schools in fostering the patterns of behavior noted speaks to the issue of early socialization being the foundation upon which other patterns are built. From a developmental perspective, such an inquiry leads back to the question of what if the rudiments of prosocial developments never emerge. What then? Does the child simply exhibit arrested development and drop out of the larger society (i.e., withdraw into sets), or does he try to get his affiliation needs met by engaging in self-defeating self-destructive behaviors? Or, does he simply float along in life waiting for others to articulate his needs?

Three themes appear to emerge from these three chapters: time perspectives and how they influence the choices that young people make; questions of self-definition; and how do scholars or practitioners gather information about gang adolescents and for what purposes.

☐ Time Perspectives and How They Influence Choices that Young People Make

"Time" is a psychological dimension that is often neglected in understanding research. The concept, as used here, refers to time in the life of the subject (i.e., developmental moments); historic era (i.e., late 20th century); and point in an ecological maze which intersects the multiple systems of which the subject is a part, all simultaneously. Let me briefly explain this last idea.

Bronfenbrenner (1979) has suggested that all individuals are members of several systems at the same time. See Figure I.1. The point in time that cuts across all of the systems is what is being considered here. For example, an adolescent who is engaged in psychologically individuating from parents may be experiencing loss in the microsystems which involve parents while he is experiencing attachment and connection in microsystems involving friends and peers. Likewise mesosystems (i.e., school–church; home–community) may be represented with a mixed picture of positive experiences and negative or positive experiences or both). Figure I.2 gives a detailed representation of the hypothetical case.

The point here is that at any given moment in time an adolescent may be receiving a vast array of messages about himself and the worlds in which he functions. A partial determinant of what will be the nature of the messages delivered to the adolescent is where the point in time is located in the system in which it is occurring. Are the friendships in the microsystem just beginning or are they long-standing relationships? It seems to me that the exact location of time in the life of a systemic relationship determines to a large degree the type of message given and how important it will be

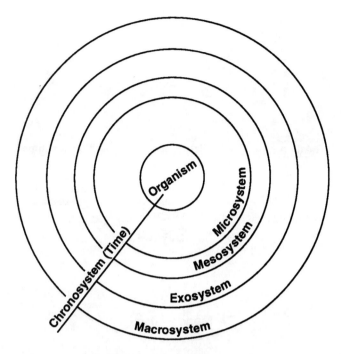

FIGURE I.1. Ecological Systems Map

perceived to be by the adolescent who is the recipient. The three authors represented in this section seem to agree that negative experiences from ongoing systems (i.e., neighborhoods, school) undoubtedly are important to adolescents, evidenced in part by the youths being very reactive to them. Remember that society has created an image of "gangs" that is negative and pejorative. Gonzalez suggests that because of that image, many of the groups so classified have opted to call themselves by another label. Quamina notes that the African American males whom he observed likewise are intensely affected by social images of them. The result is that they appear to drop out, in search of a place in which they will be viewed more positively perhaps. Doucette-Gates offers a similar observation. The critical difference in her statement and Quamina's is the consistency of message across time. The young men discussed by Quamina apparently received "the word" early on and made an adjustment in their behavior and attitudes which caused them to form their own subset. They could conceivably be thought of as dropouts who are still present. The youngsters in Doucette-Gates' study have received negative messages about themselves and their relationship with the larger society. Like Quamina's subjects they continue to attend school but clearly

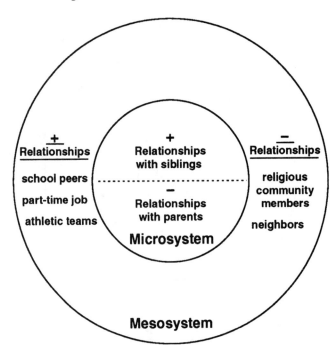

FIGURE I.2. Mixed Relationships Across Ecologies

are not as positively impacted by the experience as one would hope. Instead they internalize beliefs that suggest that there is no "future" for them. The "future" is "now."

Time, and timing, are critical elements in the lives of all of the subjects described in the first three chapters. The time in the lives of the subjects in which the messages about possibilities and the future are given is critical. The authors have suggested that the timing of negative messages to their subjects has significant implications for how they can potentially respond to the messages. Gonzalez notes that many of his subjects have responded by simply renaming themselves (i.e., gangs are now street organizations). Quamina's subjects appear not to be as creative. They do not redefine themselves; rather, they appear to internalize the messages given to them about themselves. The separation from the larger context in which they have been marginalized could be seen as an attempt to adopt behaviors that will allow them to continue to feel good about themselves but not believe what others (i.e., teachers) have said about them. In both cases it seems to me that the subjects are attempting to cope. They live in communities that they perceive to be less than supportive and affirming. In response to this interpretation they make some decisions about how they want to conduct themselves. Here time(ing) is all important!

If the negative messages occur early in the development of the individual such that he does not have the cognitive skills or political savvy to interpret the messages as negative, then he is likely to internalize them. The result of such behavior is often that the subjects come to see themselves through the eyes of someone else, all the while thinking that the vision is their own. Examples of such often occur with youngsters and their families who are overly reliant on the larger society and its major institutions (i.e., schools) for directions. Economically poor families are especially at risk for such behavior. On the other hand, if the negative messages about self are received by a young person *after* he has developed significant microsystems and mesosystems through which he evaluates the world, the outcome is likely to be very different. Consider again, for example, Gonzalez's subjects who are astute enough to critically appraise how others call them as valid and relevant to their lives.

In the same way that time is important for understanding the occurrences of events, it is also important for understanding how and when young people respond to socialization messages. Within the psychological literature, this is usually described as response latency or delay of gratification or both. Both of these concepts are particularly important for understanding the lives of gang adolescents and other at-risk youth.

The traditional literature on delay of gratification has suggested that young subjects and persons of color tend to exhibit a limited capacity for delay of gratification. Instead they prefer immediate rewards, even when they are small and of limited value, to delayed, more substantial rewards. Boys of multiple racial and ethnic groups consistently show less capacity for delay of gratification than girls. The delay of gratification research paragraph has usually required subjects to indicate whether they want a small reward immediately or if they opt to wait for a larger reinforcement later. Mischel and his colleagues (Mischel & Baker, 1975; Moore, Mischel, & Zeiss, 1976) showed that a revision of the typical delay of gratification dilemmas also produces patterns unlike those mentioned above. They have shown that involving the subjects in identifying the rewards and partial schedules of reward (as opposed to all or nothing, now versus later) also has an impact on results. These issues appear to be potentially useful in understanding the dynamics of the behavior of gang adolescents and their urge to acquire "things" (i.e., rewards) in a timely, perhaps even compulsive, fashion. Let me explain.

The quest for things, material and psychological, is what appears to drive the behavior of many gang adolescents. They want to be like others, as measured by level of social acceptance, indicated by having friends and all of the material things that others possess. Branch (1997) has shown that when asked to rate themselves on measures of values and sociability, gang adolescents were not different from nongang adolescents on the need or desire for social acceptance and related values. He reasoned that the marginalized status that many gang adolescents have thrust onto them does not diminish the gang member's need to be accepted. One way in which gang adolescents have attempted to force society to accept them is by acquiring and even flaunting the same material possessions that they assume to be emblematic of success in the larger world. The result is adolescents being obsessed with driving new and expensive cars and living life in the "fast lane." Now back to the issue of delay of gratification.

The gang adolescents who long to acquire the material symbols of success often have a big choice to make: work hard at socially sanctioned activities (i.e., doing well in school, being a superstar athlete or entertainer, etc.) and eventually acquiring the "good life," or engaging in illegal activities (i.e., drug trafficking, etc.), which may lead to immediate rewards. Inherent in this dilemma is also the gang member's sense of hope and tie perspective. Doucette-Gates (this volume) points out that for many adolescents, there is no hope because their past has been so bleak and impoverished. She suggests that such youngsters are only concerned about the here and now. Long-range goals such as going to college and playing on a professional sports team are nonsensical. For many of the youngsters described by Doucette-Gates, the future is now. All energies should be invested in acquiring all that they can (i.e., material things and psychological relationships) in the here and now. One might be tempted to interpret such behavior as a lack of a capacity for delay of gratification. Consistent with the historic articulation of the concept such an interpretation would be correct. However, it would only answer part of a very important and complex set of questions, namely, How did they come to internalize the values that they express? Why is it important that they are respected and accepted by others, especially the others who have marginalized the gang? What role does the social context in which the adolescents have lived play in shaping their delay of gratification response pattern?

The question of how gang adolescents evolve into who they are in the here and now has been largely ignored by scholars. Jankowski (1991) offers a brief exploration for gang behavior by suggesting that gang members express a high level of defiant behavior, which places them in conflict with the society in which they live. Many adolescents acknowledge that their families and communities reject them, partly because of their own defiant personality style. In order to overcome the rejections, according to Jankowski, many adolescents seek out others like themselves, which ultimately gives rise to gangs. While this explanation is believable, it still does not explain the "how" of the process. How do rejected adolescents decide that the "problem" is with others and not with them? How do defiant personality types decide that they really do want or need to be with others? And perhaps most important, how do adolescents move from familial and prosocial involvement to a position of acknowledging the gang, and all that it stands for, as being paramount in their lives? These questions are left unanswered by Jankowski's formulation. Despite its limitation as an explanation, Jankowski's theorem is the only one that recognizes the idea that most gang adolescents have had a period of growth and socialization before they joined the gang.

It is suggested here that the period of development before joining the gang holds valuable pieces of information about the inner psychological functioning of the adolescent, including their capacity for delay of gratification. Early socialization is generally regarded as being prognostic of later behaviors. The same is true of delay of gratification capacity. Individuals who acquire the capacity to delay during the early years of development are likely to continue to exhibit such ability later in life. Joining a gang is not likely to impact their capacity to delay gratification, as an individual. Becoming a member of a gang does create a layer of complexity in the lives of many young people. The question for them often becomes how their personal agenda is juxtaposed against the will of the group. This dilemma is often played out in situations where a decision concerning immediate or small gain or both versus delayed or large gain or both. It should be kept in mind that in many situations of choice the decision that is made reflects the will of the group, not that of an individual gang member. The relevance of group behavior as opposed to individual behavior in delaying gratification is significant.

Frequently a gang may find itself having to make a choice that has direct implications for its survival and "reputation." A delay of action may mean a missed opportunity which adversely affects the gang and its public image. Acting spontaneously, with no delay of gratification, may result in a poor quality decision that in the larger scheme of things may also negatively impact the gang but results in more press coverage and local notoriety. A distinction then needs to be made between delay of gratification ability as a group and delay of gratification as an individual.

The strengths that gang members develop before joining the gang do not disappear when they join the gang. Rather, they become pronounced parts of the behavioral patterns with the gang. Sometimes there is internal conflict about personal characteristics developed before affiliating with the gang and what the gang requires of them behaviorally. Indeed, the decision to join or not to join may be the source of emotional conflicts for some youngsters. While they are in the decision-to-join phase, some adolescents develop a high level of ambivalence about whether they *really* want to join the gang and the limits to which they will go in order to be accepted into the gang. These last-minute waverings are often observed in the form of gang recruits who fail initiations because they are unwilling to commit the ruthless acts required of them. It is suggested that such refusals may occur because the initiation acts conflict with the early socialization and morals of the new recruit.

An understanding of the concept of delay of gratification as it applies to the lives of gang members can also be accomplished, in part, by thinking about the issue of gang membership as one example of adolescents attempting to find validation in the eyes of others. For many, joining the gang serves as a source of social reinforcement at the hands of others whose evaluations are valued by the new recruit. Acceptance into the gang provides many members with a sense of belonging and value. Such a need for affiliation and belonging is developmentally appropriate for adolescents. It appears that the choice to join the gang and potentially win the approval and admiration of fellow gang members is avoided by a large number of at-risk adolescents. They, instead, choose to follow the more conventional routes of attending school and being prosocial members of the communities in which they live. From my perspective, it appears that the latter represents a delay of gratification choice, in anticipation of greater rewards later. The dilemma of to join or not to join also can provide valuable information about an adolescent's decisionmaking and the "process" that they undertake before affiliating with a gang.

It seems to be an untenable position to assume that the transformation from nongang to gang member is a spontaneous and all-or-nothing process. Rather it is probably the case that gang recruits slowly evolve into being fully committed to the "program" of the gang. The initiation act serves as an outward expression for an internal change that is assumed to be oc-curring. Unfortunately, there is a pervasive belief that because adolescents participate in the outward expressions of antisocial behavior, they are gen-uinely antisocial. Such is not the case. There is a small body of literature which shows that many gang-affiliated adolescents hold beliefs and values that are incongruent with their gang membership (Monti, 1994). Likewise, there is a significantly larger body of research findings that show that many delinquent adolescents are in a state of ambivalence, which vacillates be-tween outward antisocial acts and clinical depression (Branch, 1997). The existence of these two seemingly incompatible states may be thought of as a state of comorbidity; that is, they exist simultaneously.

Branch (1997) suggests that the transformation to gang membership sta-tus has the potential of triggering depression in many adolescents. He rea-sons that as the new gang members move away from their old identities (i.e., student, family relationships) toward the new gang membership, they expe-rience a sense of loss and depression. The relationships that are abandoned may have been longstanding and core dimensions of how the adolescents identify themselves. Because becoming a gang member is a process, it is important to explore how adolescents reflect on the question of identities. The question refers to identity before and after joining the gang. How do gang members define themselves, as individuals and groups?

☐ Self-Definition

The factors that adolescents use to define themselves are expressions of the contexts in which they function, not just any contexts but the contexts that the adolescent deems important. Most adolescents function in a multiplicity of settings (i.e., home, school, peer relations, part-time jobs, athletic teams, clubs, etc.). In each setting, they receive messages about their contribution to its functioning. Adolescents who are valued by others in the setting receive positive and laudatory messages. For example, adolescents who are above average in their scholastic achievements receive liberal amounts of positive reinforcement from teachers and other adults in school. They may even be the object of admiration for many other students who are reluctant to publicly express admiration for a peer who is a good student. Likewise, a student who performs marginally in school is likely to be negatively reinforced by school personnel and parents.

Because adolescents function in such a variety of settings, it is difficult to know exactly which settings have greater value to the adolescent. It is safe to say, however, that from each setting the adolescent gets a message about self-worth. The collective summation of those messages is what provides the adolescent with a basis for self-definition. It is almost as if a boxscore is being kept. Adolescents who receive overwhelming negative messages, across settings, are not likely to feel good about themselves. Contrary to popular belief, they are likely to look for a setting where they do feel that they are regarded positively. Their search often takes them to the extreme position of seeking acceptance by others who have also been outcast (e.g., adolescent gangs). This line of logic suggests that gangs are composed of marginal individuals who have not found high levels of acceptance and success in their communities of origin. Gonzalez (this volume) and Jankowski (1991) would strongly disagree with that position, insisting that many gang members are individuals with a reasonable history of social relations within their community of origin.

The first three chapters in this volume address the question of self-definition among gang adolescents in a variety of ways. Gonzalez comments on it most directly in his comments about self-labeling and organizational naming. His observation that many hitherto adolescent gangs are now renaming themselves street organizations is a very telling statement. According to him, the groups are staying away from calling themselves gangs because of the legacy of negative connotations associated with the term. This behavior suggests that the organizations are cognizant of what others (i.e., the larger society) are saying about them. What others are saying about them matters! There is an interesting paradox in some of this. Gangs often separate themselves from the larger communities in which they live but then spend significant amounts of time and energy being concerned about what that community thinks of them. Two important lessons are embedded in this. First, despite their frequently antagonistic relationship with communities, gang members need to be regarded positively. That need extends beyond the bounds of the gang into the host community. Second, the move toward a more socially palatable name (i.e., street organizations) affirms a need to be instrumental in dictating one's own identity, not relying on others. This pattern of self-determinism has been witnessed on another level in our society in the frequent name changes some ethnic groups have made over the last 20 years as well as to be active in determining how they will be defined (e.g., Black → Afro American → African American; Hispanic → Latino(a) → Mexican American/Puerto Rican/Dominican).

Gonzalez's chapter points out very clearly that even as gang members have been on the fringes of the larger society, they have been listening to what is going on in the larger society. Does this mean that larger society is the referent for the gang? Or does it mean that gang members too want to be regarded positively by others, even others outside of one's own sphere? Perhaps even more intriguing than the question of respect is Gonzalez's provocative suggestion that many of the values (i.e., economic stability, self-regulation, community building) that exist in American society at large are also pervasive among street organizations. Embedded in this observation is the idea that some gang members are similar to the rest of the world, in beliefs if not behavior, and that perhaps the common core of the two groups can be used as a basis for bridging the gaps that often make it difficult for the two groups to coexist.

Quamina's observations of African American males and their attempts to self-define are compelling but somewhat disturbing. He reports on his observations of young men who self-select groups that take them out of the mainstream of the educational and social communities to which they belong, in principle. They seem to drift away from their peers who are invested in school, opting instead to be a part of *sets*, which through the eyes of an outsider are directionless cliques. Quamina points out that his observations of the sets are an emic perspective that does not profess to understand the dynamics of the group. What is objectively verified by him, however, is that the young men in his study are connected only to each other. There is no level of involvement or valuing of school activities that could be observed by an outsider. Moreover, the young men appear to delight in living a life that matches the most negative stereotypes of Black men (i.e., shiftless, lazy, highly aggressive, etc.). In discussing his observation, Quamina raises several pertinent questions about how the young men came to develop such a behavioral repertoire especially in the face of hard-working and dedicated teachers' efforts. His discussion goes beyond blaming the victim to raising significant questions about educational policies and community involvement efforts. Nothing seems to have made a difference in the lives of the subjects. They persist in living what appears to be hopeless lives. What does all of this say about the young men in the study?

It is not clear to me what their behavior really means. Perhaps they are following a social script that is so compelling to them that they are helpless to resist it. Maybe they are creatively resisting being labeled as failures. They join the *set* where everyone else has social and educational experience like their own. In so doing they find acceptance and positive regard from a group of peers. Another possible explanation for their behavior is that they are simply pawns in a never-ending battle of social and economic forces. The real answer is, probably all of the above plus additional factors.

☐ Research Issues

The question of the utility of traditional research approaches with gang-affiliated youth is a very important one that is answered by Gonzalez, Quamina, and Doucette-Gates in very different ways. They answer the question in part by the methodologies they use to study the subjects whom they write about. The Gonzalez methodology can be described as participant observer with clinical interviews playing a critical role in the information gathering process. He uses archival research as a way to provide background information about the subject matter. It should be pointed out that even though he uses the background information to set the stage for understanding his current subjects, no qualification is made for the fact that the background information may have been gathered by methods that are alien to the subjects. That is to say, much of the information he uses as a conceptual foundation for understanding the gangs and the concepts associated with them may have had their origin in settings foreign to the gangs. At some level he recognizes this as he talks about the absence of an authentic theory of gangs that is rooted in the experiences of gang members. Instead, he notes that most of the theories of gangs are borne out of the intellectual curiosity of researchers who most often do not understand the lives of gang members. Doucette-Gates and Quamina raise similar points as they struggle with understanding the why and how of the behavior of the gang members.

Doucette-Gates formulates a basis for her inquiry by stating that future time perspective has a rich and importance legacy within the research paradigms used by behavioral scientists. Rather than concluding that it necessarily means the same things for gang members, she instead shows how their perspectives of time and the social contexts in which the gang members have been socialized are inextricably related. Inherent in her presentation is the troubling question of how are interventions going to be effective if those conducting the interventions cannot take at least an intellectual understanding of the lives of gang members with them. How can an understanding be accomplished if there is no mechanism for getting into the heads of the gang members? She offers a partial answer to this question by showing the utility of interviews along with more traditional research data, which can be obtained from standard approaches and devices such as questionnaires.

Of course, simply adding an interview does not guarantee that the information obtained will be any more reliable or valid. The reader is reminded that many of the subjects in Doucette-Gate's study and similar works have a long history of checkered, and sometimes overwhelmingly negative, relationships with researchers and others who represent the interest of the larger society. What would motivate them to be cooperative and disclosing of themselves one more time, especially to a system they have perceived as failing them? In the absence of a personal relationship between the researcher and the subjects, the only option available is for the researcher to try to make sense of the lives of the subjects from afar, precisely what Quamina appears to be doing.

Quamina's observations of the lives of African American males is from the perspective of an outsider. In cross-cultural research circles, this is referred to as an emic approach. It is a less-than-perfect solution to a difficult problem of understanding the life and motivation of another. The simple solution to this dilemma, of course, is to ask the subject to share his inner life with you so the need to interpret and draw conclusions is lessened. This all assumes, of course, that the subject will be willing to be cooperative. Experiences with delinquent adolescents and gang members are often anything but relationships of cooperation. On the other hand, some researchers have noted that gang members are very eager to tell their stories to anyone who will listen. In such situations, the researcher might do well to proceed with caution and consider the possibility of what they are being told is a wild fabrication and fantasy life at work. Now back to the Quamina young men and the use of observation and other qualitative approaches: The methods used by Quamina to try to get a better understanding of the youngsters with whom he was working have been shown to be highly effective by uncovering issues for further investigation. Qualitative approaches have also been known to simply elevate the researcher's personal views to new heights of importance. They are risky in that there is no way to systematically minimize researcher biases from entering the final conclusions as if they were facts. In some ways, these shortcomings are a painful reminder that the research enterprise as it currently exists is really experimenters trying to understand a phenomenon by subjecting it to too systematic examination. The process of systematic examination, even when touted as being highly scientific, is reflective of the values of the researcher. Quamina's work here is a reminder of that truth. In the search for objectivity, Quamina acknowledges the traces of his own agenda and values as he comments on the behavior of the young men.

The three authors highlighted here show a tremendous level of skill and poise as they try to illuminate the lives of young people who have often been marginalized by the larger society. Gonzalez points to the marginalization and how it comes to be central in the thinking of his subjects as they attempt to redefine themselves (e.g., street organizations versus gangs), suggestive that they have been listening to what others have been saying about them. The question is how to study gang members in a way that makes sense and is also reliable and valid. Other researchers have struggled with this issue with varying degrees of success. One of the most noted examples of the attempt to meet gang members on their turf but also to give some professional rigor to the work done with them is the controversial work of Martin Jankowski (1991). He joined adolescent gangs in Los Angeles, Boston, and New York. For several years he commuted around the country and wrote incredibly detailed notes about the life of the gang and its members. The final result was a book, *Islands in the Streets*, which became the object of much debate and consternation among scholars interested in gangs. Complaints about the book range from questions about the integrity of the author to disdain about the conclusions and theory articulated on the basis of findings. Branch (1993) reviewed the book and noted that it raises serious questions about how we have been attempting to understand the world and lives of others perceived to be unlike the research. The same can be said about the chapters presented here by Gonzalez, Quamina, and Doucette-Gates. They use a mixture of traditional approaches and idiosyncratic interviews designed to fully understand the world of the gang member. Does this really make a difference in the subject's level of cooperation with the research process? Or are the researchers simply deceiving themselves into believing that they have gained a unique glimpse of the gang member's inner life? The answer is probably not a simply either/or.

Last, the question of research with gang members raises an ethical question. For what purposes are research findings to be used? Much of the work with adolescents is accomplished by telling them that the results are to be used to help them. But is that what the researchers really have in mind? Helping the adolescent can be defined variously, depending on who is defining "helping." From the perspective of the researcher and other adults, the elimination of gangs and other youth collectives may be defined by the adult community as helping. It brings the adolescent into closer proximity with the adult community and increases the likelihood of a makeover of the gang member, even against his wishes. Helping the gang member has also often been synonymous with forcing a value system and behaviors onto him which he is not ready to accept.

It appears to me that there can be a middle ground on which researcher and gang member can coexist. It is illustrated in the three chapters in this section. Gang research is necessary to provide a factual basis for those who want to help the gang members become valued members of the larger society in which they reside. Gang research is also needed to give gang members a voice that is not marginalized or considered deviant. Having a voice may prove beneficial to gang members. They may learn to tell others (e.g., their family of origin, their community) what they want and need, psychologically speaking, and not have to resort to acting out. Perhaps the presence of an extensive and sensitive research literature on gang members will eventually lead others to conclude that the similarities between them and nongang members are not as extensive as we might believe otherwise. I remind the reader that much of the behavior of gangs is about gaining "respect." My experience with a number of gang adolescents over the years has been that they want to be accepted and valued. In the absence of such sentiments being forthcoming, the gang engages in defiant behavior that calls attention to them and their situation, developmentally much like the tantrum behavior of a three-year-old.

☐ References

Branch, C. (1993). Gang bashing. *New Ideas in Psychology, 12*(1), 103–109.

Branch, C. (1997). *Clinical interventions with gang adolescents and their families.* Boulder, CO: Westview Press.

Bronfenbrenner, U. (1979). *The ecology of human development.* Cambridge, MA: Harvard University Press.

Jankowski, M. (1991). *Islands in the street: Gangs and American urban society.* Berkeley, CA: University of California Press.

Mischel, W., & Baker, N. (1975). Cognitive appraisal and transformations in delay behavior. *Journal of Personality and Social Psychology, 31*(2), 254–261.

Monti, D. (1994). *Wannabes: Gangs in suburbs and schools.* Cambridge, MA: Blackwell.

Moore, B., Mischel, W., & Zeiss, A. (1976). Comparative effects of the reward stimulus and its cognitive representation in voluntary delay. *Journal of Personality and Social Psychology, 34*(3), 419–424.

CHAPTER

Ramon Gonzalez

Welcome Home Boyz: Building Communities through Cultural Capital

On March 30, 1995, over 800 activists led by the National Congress for Puerto Rican Rights (NCPRR), a grassroots Puerto Rican civil rights organization, staged a rally at 1 Police Plaza in New York City. The rally was a demonstration against police brutality in what the organizers termed "an outrage at the killing of our youth." According to the organizers, the rally's purpose was twofold: to commemorate the anniversary of a youth killed by a "gang" of White youths and to protest the historical abuse and murders of minority youth, more recently, Anthony Rosario and Hilton Vega, by a "gang of police officers" according to the activists. The activists were angered at public officials for ignoring the issue of police brutality in minority communities.

The most interesting aspect of the rally was not necessarily its stated purpose but those who attended. Besides the usual hard-core group of activists, this rally bore witness to the massing of members from four of the largest "street organizations" (what would colloquially be termed "gangs") in New York City: the Universal Zulu Nation (UZN), Almighty Latin King and Queen Nation, Los Netas, and La Familia. These street organizations cooperated peacefully with each other, college fraternities, and activists. This demonstration of street organizations' activism raises questions about the prevailing theories of gangs such as gangs/street organizations are antagonistic (Yablonsky, 1962) or apathetic in their communities (Thrasher, 1936) and are organizing to carry out illegal acts (Haskell & Yablonsky, 1982) and displays of turf control in their community (Miller, 1990). This nontraditional behavior also provokes discussions around modified theories of gang research as complex organizations involved in some aspect of their communities (Jankowski, 1991). Another interesting question that arose from the rally was why the NCPRR would involve street organizations in issues of community development and social justice. Is this an isolated incident or a planned strategy?

This chapter is a study of three New York City gangs and evolving intervention strategies used by three community organizations with the gangs studied. This chapter is broken into three components: a description of the gangs, a discussion of Coleman's "functional community" theory (Coleman, 1987), and an analysis of intervention strategies and approaches used by three community organizations in New York City. A description of contemporary gang structure and culture are necessary for us to understand why these certain intervention strategies are effective with these gangs. The intervention strategies are built on a premise that street organizations are integral parts of their local community and have developed skills, which will later be termed cultural capital, that can be used as an asset by their local communities to foster community development. This premise is discussed through an analysis of James Coleman's "functional community and social capital theory," which suggests that functional communities are built through intergenerational relations. A discussion of the theory of Coleman's functional community will help in understanding the philosophical foundations of the intervention strategies. The three community organizations seek to incorporate the organizational skills of the New York City street organizations studied into leaders of community organizations through involvement in community activism and networking with community members. The focus of this chapter is to steer current intervention strategies away from focusing on gangs as isolated communities toward a broader perception of gangs as integral parts of the community.

This study was based on two types of data collection: in-depth interviews and participant observations including attending "universals" (universal meetings are composed of all the chapters in a street organization). Interviews and observations were also conducted with three community and social organizations that use ecological intervention methods with these street organizations, and, finally, interviews were conducted with community residents and former gang members from East Harlem and the South Bronx, where most of the studies took place, to help contextualize these street organizations' behavior in the community.

Often the problem with gang research begins at the root of gang research, the attempt to define gangs. By defining gangs at an early stage of gang research, some researchers prematurely closed the debate and developed research from limited definitions. Ruth Horowitz suggests that we should not agree on the parameters of what constitutes a gang. The definition of gangs should remain open because, she writes, "it brings about a healthy discourse." She suggests that "looking at gangs in different ways allows for exploration of distinct aspects of gang experience" (Horowitz, 1990, p. 53). Gangs, like every type of human organization, change with the environment and local culture of the community. Street organizations refuse to be termed "gangs" because they feel it is a throwback to the seventies and films like *The Warriors*, a fictional and stereotypical portrayal of gang life in New York City. As will be discussed later in this chapter, street organizations see themselves more as a combination of social and fraternal organizations like local lodges.

The problem with a traditional definition of gangs is that it does not distinguish individual behavior from group behavior. As one youth explained, "When we do good it's an individual thing and when we do bad it is a gang thing." This raises the issue of distinguishing youth gangs from adult gangs (Spergel, 1995; Jankowski, 1991). In this chapter, after recognizing the dilemma of "labels," youth gangs or street organizations will be used synonymously and defined further as having a majority of members below 25 years of age.

☐ From Gangs to Street Organizations: A Look at the UZN, Latin Kings, and Netas

According to several community residents of the South Bronx and East Harlem, two areas where these street organizations are located, gangs have existed there since "anyone could remember." These areas would fall into what Spergel defines as chronic gang areas, "... areas that have historically been a breeding ground of gangs" (Spergel, 1995). From the Savage Skulls and Dragons of the sixties; Bachelors of the seventies; the UZN, Ballbusters, and Decepticons of the eighties; to the current groups, street organizations have continually developed in these areas. Today, members of street organizations seem more conscious of public backlash from the term "gang." According to Danny, a Zulu member, "the difference is that the term gang means negativity and we are positive, not like that shit from L.A." Members of the Latin Kings, Netas, and La Familia (derived from the West Coast version of the same organization) vehemently voiced this distinction: "L.A. shit is like ten years behind. What they are doing now, we did in the seventies. That shit is like Warriors; we believe in unity not killing each other," stated Yusef, a member of the UZN.

☐ A Glimpse of a Street Organization Meeting

Outside a local "universal meeting," at the old headquarters of the UZN, about 50 to 100 youths in groups of 6 to 10 met outside the meeting area, in the East River Housing Projects in the Bronx. Over 200 youths, a low turnout because of the rain according to one speaker, sat inside the meeting room in the local community center. The youths were Black and Latino. The dominant ethnic groups were African American and Puerto Rican. The room was organized like a conference hall with chairs in the front for guest speakers. The meeting started with an introduction by the UZN and a discussion about the 15 beliefs of the UZN. The speaker stressed "equality, freedom of religion, education, and truth" as the principles of the UZN. According to a Zulu speaker named Flex, "Everyone can be taught, but not everyone can learn. What you read may determine how you think. Your mind doesn't develop by what you read only but what you understand and therefore learn."

The next speaker was a member of the Nation of Islam. He stressed the need for Blacks and Latinos to come together and support Black and Latino businesses. He described how White owners traditionally made their money by opening stores in minority neighborhoods and then eventually retired, taking the money they had obtained out of the neighborhood. His speech was met by several responses of "teach, brother." He reiterated the point that Black and Latinos must support each other because, "Only we live in the South Bronx and neighborhoods like these, not them."

After two more speakers discussed African and Latino history and the need for unity, members of the audience were beckoned to speak. One chapter leader discussed the ongoing disputes with members of the Latin Kings. One youth asked members to bring their girlfriends to attend a fundraising party. Another chapter leader asked for help with dealing with the police. He stated that the police were stopping anyone with beads and "throwing us up against cars like punks being that we are organized." This statement led to a 45-minute discussion on police brutality: "White police officers need to feel superior by taking away our manhood, so know your constitutional rights," stated the current speaker T. C. Islam, the spokesman of the UZN. Someone yelled that the police were the biggest gang in New York: "They are more color coordinated and create more to harm our communities then the L.A. Crips and Bloods do to theirs." Everyone cheered.

The meeting ended four hours later. The organizers stressed to exiting members to restrain themselves on the trains home and not to wear their Zulu patches because, "Those oppressors [police] are at war with all people of color; they are looking for any reason for us to be locked down [incarcerated]." Throughout the interviews with street organizations, a common philosophy was developing: all members that were interviewed stated that cops were at war with them, and cops had purposely arrested them on trumped up (false) charges of weapon or drug possession. In response to the question of links between gangs and drugs as the popular media, some researchers and law enforcement agencies have suggested, Yusef, a Zulu member, stated, "That is full of shit because no family [street organization] supports drugs. That is against our beliefs and rules. If any individual sells drugs, that's on that individual, not on the organization. When Popo [street name for police officers] get accused by our people for police brutality, the mayor and everybody always say that is one bad cop and not representative of the police department. How come no one questions that, but we are always the bad guys no matter what!" King Louie, a high-ranking member of the Latin Kings, stated, "I can't tell a man how to make money because no one is hiring him due to his criminal record. I can only hope that he does it as an individual, not as a member of my family, but it is definitely not part of our philosophy."

After attending more chapter meetings and universals, and interviewing members of both the UZN and Latin Kings, common structural themes began to surface that seemed to explain the culture and behavior of street organizations. A description of those characteristics appears in Table 1.1.

Description of Characteristics

The structural leadership in these organizations varies. For example, the upper level leadership of the UZN is led by five of its oldest and most active members. The world council of the UZN is the decisionmaker of the national and international policies of the UZN. (The UZN claims chapters in Germany, Japan, London, and several other countries.) Local matters are addressed in the regional council, which is composed of chapter leaders. This is the central location of most of the power.

Latin Kings and Netas have a vertical upper level leadership. Jankowski discusses some of the traditional characteristics of gang structure, which he labels as vertical and horizontal structured organizations (Jankowski, 1991). Theoretically, Latin Kings have a vertical leadership structure from first crown (top leader) to the soldiers according to their constitution, although it was noted through these interviews that decisions that affect local matters are made on a local level and those decisions that affect national matters are made on a national level. The inconsistency between the Latin Kings organization's original structure and its current state was a result of the large number of leaders that are in prison and are denied access to members in the local communities. The Netas follow a similar format to the Latin Kings and share the same inconsistencies.

TABLE 1.1. Model: Street Organization

Characteristics	Zulu Nation	Latin Kings	Netas
Upper level leadership	world council	mixed	mixed
Lower level leadership	chapter council	hierarchical leadership	hierarchical leadership
Meeting structure	universal	universal	universal
Local level structure	chapters	chapters	chapters
Reason for being	"unity of urban nation under hip hop culture"	Latino prisoners' rights group and support Latino culture	Latino prisoners' rights group and support Latino culture
Turf oriented	no	no	no
Economic structure	entrepreneurial	entrepreneurial	entrepreneurial
Security structure	Shaka Zulu–parallel organization recruited from rank and file	"BGs"–bodyguards. Usually in pairs of two around leaders	not rigidly organized
Ethnic composition	Predominantly Black and Latino	Predominantly Latino	Predominantly Puerto Rican
Female components	yes "Zulu Queens"	yes "Latin Queens"	yes "Neta Queens"

There were several chapters of the Latin Kings that were interviewed that did not go to universal meetings as all chapters are required. Most of the decisions at these "rouge" chapters (as they were called by several of the leaders in the Latin Kings) were made without the consent of the leaders. They still associated with other Latin King members but made their own decisions as long as they did not conflict with the regional leadership. These chapters were another example of the inconsistencies with the perceived rigid structure of the Latin Kings.

Universal meetings occur when all chapters meet together and the council or horizontal leadership discusses organizational matters or holds cultural and history lessons. Universal meetings are arenas for discussion and exchange of ideas. Often visitors are asked to speak or share information that affects that particular street organization. These visitors are usually older inactive gang members or community activists.

Almost all researchers suggest that part of their gang definition consists of the group having a defined turf (Klein, 1971; Spergel, 1995). The three street organizations that were studied proved to be an exception. None of the groups maintain an exclusive turf. Two of the few theorists who have witnessed similar characteristics are Vigil and Yun (1990), who studied Vietnamese gangs and found that Vietnamese gangs were "roving" instead of static. The Latin Kings, Netas, and UZN members congregated in certain areas, such as the UZN members congregated often in the Bronx River Projects area of the Bronx, but it was not off limits to Netas and Latin King members. Mobility was key to all of the organizations. Many members had to travel outside their local areas to work and school. Leaders among the groups worked out a peace treaty so that all members could be guaranteed free mobility. This peace has evolved to a level were other street organizations salute one other with handshakes and other codes.

Traditional gang theorists suggest that gang members often have relationships with drug trafficking. Spergel (1964) found a relationship between drug use and drug selling with older members in his study on gangs. Spergel (1995, p. 47) also suggests that "much media and law enforcement reporting implies or states that sophisticated drug trafficking and street gangs, especially Black gangs, are closely associated." Economic survival is an important aspect of life for every youth in urban neighborhoods, and street organizations reflect that reality. Some members continue to sell drugs, but the current study witnesses several other prominent means of establishing an economic base among street organizations.

Influenced by a combination of the hip hop industry and the entrepreneurial philosophies of the Nation of Islam, the UZN has developed a strong entrepreneurial spirit. Members have included famous hip hop groups such as Tribe Called Quest and Ice Cube. Other major occupations are messengers, clerks, security guards, and artists. Some of the individuals in the UZN do participate in some form of an underground economy. Some members sell mixed disc–jockey-made tapes of the latest reggae, hip hop, and R&B songs to local stores, which sell the tapes at double the price to customers. The UZN, in the form of Shaka Zulu, also functions as a private security group, working security detail for many hip hop stars and local community organization functions. The UZN describes hip hop as a culture, and the writing component of that culture is graffiti as art. Several members of the UZN create signs and sell T-shirts and medallions with Zulu insignia to other members. Finally, members are supposed to give 10% of their profits from any business venture that has used the the UZN name to the world council for organizational expenses.

Latin Kings and Netas share similar systems of obtaining capital, although members of the Latin Kings and Netas do not have as extensive connections with promoters and artists as does the UZN. Members often worked as security guards, store clerks, and bouncers at local clubs. According to King Louie of the Latin Kings, "It is not part of our constitution to sell drugs, but I cannot tell a man how to support his family if no other options are available." King Sin stated, "Several of our members are parolees from prison, while others were picked off the streets. Who is going to hire us with a criminal record; what can some of us do?" During interviews no street organization member specifically stated that they had participated in drug trafficking, but it can be speculated that because it is against the rules and philosophy of the three street organizations interviewed and because interviews were often held around other street organizations members, none of the interviewees would admit to such behavior due to fear of reprisals.

As stated above, most of the organizations maintain a security component. The UZN maintains a security force similar to the structure of the Nation of Islam's Fruit of Islam. The security force is selected from volunteers obtained from various chapters and trained by the UZN "experts of security." Shaka Zulu is the name of the UZN's security force. Shaka Zulu is a quasi organization, operating almost exclusively for the world council and is subjected to suggestive opinions by the regional council. Latin Kings usually have two body guards (BGs) around their leaders. Their security resembles tactics of guerrilla warfare. According to members, children and women are used as lookouts and as stash spots. Some have hand-held communication such as cellular phones. The Latin Kings use such tactics because they believe that the police will do anything to arrest them. The security force is usually controlled by the top leadership. It is considered an honor to serve on the security force.

The ethnic composition of street organizations is extremely diverse. The UZN is predominantly African American and Puerto Rican, but there are also Dominicans, Jamaicans, Colombians, and some Italians. Latin Kings have traditional been thought of as Mexican and Puerto Rican (this belief is based on the Latin Kings of Chicago, which is considered the motherland of the Latin Kings in New York City). In New York City the Latin Kings were founded by individuals who were Costa Rican, Puerto Rican, Cuban, Dominican, and Spanish. During interviews with Latin Kings, ethnic identity of Latin Kings included Peruvians, Guatemalans, Colombians, Puerto Ricans, Dominicans, and Italians were noted. During interviews with Netas, African American members were also identified besides the spectrum of Latinos.

The females of these organizations have not displayed most of the traditional characteristics of females in gangs. According to Campbell, "In early writings girls were defined solely in terms of their interpersonal and structural relations to male gang members" (Campbell, 1990, p. 166). Female gang members had to be tomboys to be respected, or sex objects. Yet female members in these street organizations did not reflect these stereotypes. All of the female members in gangs must be viewed as equals. As King Dog stated, "my queen is a queen of the nation and must be honored as such—if you don't salute the queens, then you are not respecting the familia." One of the Zulu queens describes her role in the chapter: "A woman is as valuable as a man. Some are chapter leaders and some are head queens, but none are neglected because these brothers don't want to hear our mouths." It is a constant demand by Latin Kings and the UZN that the queens are integral parts of the nation and respected as such. Women in the UZN play a larger role in the power structure than women in the Latin Queens or Neta Queens. It can be speculated that the reason may be a result of greater numbers of educated women in the UZN as opposed to the Latin Kings, according to interviewee data, instead of a cultural issue such as machismo in Latino culture (since according to members of the UZN about half of the UZN is Latino).

Black and Latino gangs have existed separately in New York City for several decades, but within the last two decades they have slowly integrated. East Harlem and the South Bronx had several youth gangs including the Dragons, Viceroys, and Savage Skulls of the sixties. They worked in a much different economic and social environment than the street organizations of today. They were the stereotypical gang as described by Klein (1971). The Renegades and Black Spades were the gangs of the late seventies. They had been influenced by the sixties gangs but had also been influenced by the late sixties and early seventies "revolutionary gangs," as some community members describe the Young Lord Party and Black Panther Party. The Renegades and Black Spades were mixtures of both of these models combining stereotypical gang and social philosophical civic features. One of the members of the Black Spades, Afrika Bambatta, became the founder of the UZN. The Latin Kings developed from Chicago's Latin King, which has existed since 1936, and lately from the chapter of Latin Kings that had formed from New York's Rikers Island Correctional Facility in 1986. The newest organization, the Netas, evolved from the Netas of Puerto Rico's prison system in the early eighties. Thus, the UZN, Latin King Nation, and the Netas are a combination of a continuum of gangs in New York City, acculturated features of other cultural gangs, and a creation of new features that meet today's problems and issues. One of the goals of this chapter is to seek an expanded view about the current structure and culture about gangs in New York; the other goal is to expand the discussion on intervention strategy as well.

☐ Modified Theory of Functional Community and Social Capital

James Coleman and Thomas Hoffler's study on the performance of students at private, Catholic, and public schools helped develop the theory of functional community and social capital. The study found that Catholic schools outperformed private and public schools. Coleman and Hoffler postulated that parents of Catholic school students, brought together by the religious and rigidly structured schools, built a value community through their interest in their child's education. This value community created social capital through the interactions of the parents, teachers, and schools.

According to Coleman, functional communities are built around communities that were developed through intergenerational relations. These functional communities augment resources available to parents. According to Coleman, functional communities today have been severely hampered by the movement of families from communities due to economic stress and the role of the media within the values of the community. These conflicts cause dysfunctional communities to arise characterized by their lack of intergenerational closure. Coleman postulates that today's disadvantaged communities lack education, organizational skills, self-confidence, and "social capital"—the intangible, but very real, qualities consisting of "relations between persons." Because of working parents and communities that have become fractured or decayed, schools must re-create the "social capital in the community" (Coleman, 1988). Parents must come together to reinforce the norms of the school and support its goals.

Some of the problematic areas with Coleman's theory is that it leaves out the most affected stakeholder, the youth. It is assumed that the youth of these communities are passive receivers of values. Youth are active receivers of values and play a role in how those values are transferred in the community. Likewise, the theory also suggests that already social capital is absent in dysfunctional communities. Observations of street organizations and their meetings have revealed superior organizational skills, strong feelings for their spatial and cultural community, and various levels of political consciousness. These attributes can be described as displays of advanced societal group norms of behavior displayed by these youths. All of these attributes can be termed "native social capital." To distinguish the idea of native social capital, as opposed to social capital created or built by an institution, the term cultural capital will be used.

Gangs as active players foster and stimulate the collective cultural captive through youth and organizational culture. For example, various migrations of different ethnic groups are part of the cultural capital of East Harlem and the South Bronx due to a combination of economic migrations from Italy, Ireland, Caribbean nations, and institutional factors such as the large amounts of various Blacks and Puerto Ricans in East Harlem city projects. As active players, youth integrated through schools and sports despite the segregation that existed in the neighborhood. Hip hop culture in the early eighties, portrayed as rap music and graffiti, was the first major attempt of an integrated youth culture. Blacks, Puerto Ricans, Jews, and Italians all played roles in its early success. The UZN is considered one of the early creators of rap music. To understand the intervention strategy of Strictly Ghetto, National Congress for Puerto Rican Rights, and other community groups that work with gangs, is to understand the philosophy that every community and organization has cultural capital and the youth are active players in the development of this cultural capital. This modified theory of Coleman's social capital is the premise of these intervention strategies.

☐ From Street Organizations to Social Organizations: Intervention Strategies

Dynamics of Leadership, led by Charles Baron, usually hosts classes and workshops for schools and businesses on numerous components of leadership such as communication, public speaking, and organizing. Workshops were sometimes held free for the community. Baron and Hector Torres of Strictly Ghetto, an organization dedicated to working with youths in street organizations, worked out a deal that if Torres could have several youth attend the Dynamics of Leadership workshops, Baron would continue to offer free workshops, further develop leadership classes, and, after six sessions, a graduation ceremony would be held. The format of the class was an "interactive lecture" and discussion about an aspect of leadership. The class would then be split in two. Each class would have to debate opposing sides of an argument. Every person would have five minutes to debate the topic and be judged on their speech. Throughout the class about four youths led the discussion; two of those youths were Latin Kings. After the debate both Latin King members scored two of the highest scores. Their debate focused on the need to stop government aid in urban neighborhoods. According to Hector Torres, a former gang member of the Bachelors, a popular gang during the seventies, and the founder of Strictly Ghetto, "We target real brothers, who are in the street living it. We want brothers to make their own decisions." Part of Dynamics of Leadership and Strictly Ghetto's mission goals are to develop and foster leadership in the urban ghetto. On the issue of gangs, Torres states,

> I haven't found any gangs to work with, but I have found street organizations that have been demonized by others as being a gang. Very often language shapes people's thoughts and perceptions and by using the term gang, we have successfully demonized a whole sector of the community and separated them from their own people. The Ku Klux Klan wasn't named a gang but has many deviant individuals and it is perceived as a legitimate organization. I have problems with them.

According to Andre Rosa, an organizer in Strictly Ghetto, "You can't just come in and say, 'I want you to do this.' It is important to bond with them. You have to become one of their people who share similar experiences with them but with another perspective. Creditability must be established."

Another organization working in collaboration with Strictly Ghetto is the NCPRR. The NCPRR was created in 1981 and is considered by many grassroots organizations as the most prominent grassroots, mass membership Puerto Rican civil rights organization. It is composed of career activists, many of whom were part of the Young Lords Party, a grassroots militant political party that at one time was also considered a gang by law enforcement and popular media. NCPRR still maintains its militant stance attracting many gang members. The techniques that the Young Lords Party utilized to eventually control its image with the media and gain the support of the community are skills that NCPRR would like to impart to street organizations. Charlie Chan, a Zulu member, stated, "Panama Alba and Richie Perez (NCPRR's two most notable figures) have been where we've been. Many of them were Young Lords fighting against police brutality and the system even today." Several organizations have credited NCPRR as one of the few grassroots organizations who invite street organizations into their general body meetings and have held cultural and political workshops at the UZN and Latin King universals.

Traditional intervention strategy has relied heavily on suppression strategies favored by law enforcement. According to Spergel and Curry, who studied programs and activities of several organizations that deal with high-profile gangs, found that there were five major strategies of action. These actions consisted of community organization, suppression, social intervention, opportunities provision, and organizational development. According to their study, the most common or primarily used strategy of action was suppression (44%), followed by social intervention (31.5%), organizational change (10.9%), and community organization (8.9%). The least used strategy was opportunities provision, which consists of job training, job preparation, job development, and education of gang youth (Spergel & Curry, 1990). The study also found that, "Strategies of community organization and social opportunities were associated clearly and strongly with perceptions of agency effectiveness and a reduction in the gang problem" (Spergel & Curry, 1990, p. 308). Thus it can be stated that the most effective strategy is also the least used. All of these organizations share similar characteristics and intervention strategies. The premises of NCPRR, Strictly Ghetto, and Dynamics of Leadership intervention strategies with street organizations follow:

- Street organizations are integral parts of the community. They should not be isolated but embraced. They consist of the youth of our urban communities.
- Each street organization already has several skills and attributes that are positive. This cultural capital is the basis of any intervention strategy.

Tables 1.2 and 1.3 show the characteristics and strategies of each organization. The characteristics of NCPRR, Strictly Ghetto, and Dynamics of

TABLE 1.2. Community Organizational Characteristics

Organizational Characteristics and Philosophy	NCPRR	Strictly Ghetto	Dynamics of Leadership
Background of organizers	predominantly Puerto Rican grassroots activists	predominantly urban youth	predominantly African American activists
Background of leadership	career community activists, former Young Lords	urban adults	career community activists, former Black Panthers
Background of youth in the organization	progressive college and high school students and street organization members	progressive college and high school students and street organization members	progressive college and high school students
Organizational philosophy	"Civil rights and social justice for Puerto Ricans and all oppressed people"	"Development of positive urban youth"	"Development of leadership in communities of color"
Relation with law enforcement	distrust	distrust	distrust
"Should gangs be destroyed or embraced?"	embraced	embraced	embraced

Leadership are noted because they show a consistency across all three organizations. The leaders of these three organizations have "been there," as street organizations like to term having similar backgrounds of hardship and urban life. Richie Perez, Panama Alba, and several other prominent members of NCPRR have been community activists for over 25 years. Charles Baron of Dynamics of Leadership is a former Black Panther who has continued to work with Perez and Alba since the early seventies. Hector Torres of Strictly Ghetto was a gang member and former member of the notorious Bachelor's Club, one of the major drug gangs in the mideighties. Members of these three organizations have strong community ties and have built strong intergroup relations. The three organizations have strong grassroots membership and strong community relations. They all believe in developing leadership in "our communities," suggesting that street organizations are part of that community. They all share a belief that street organizations

TABLE 1.3. Intervention Strategies

Cultural Capital	NCPRR Strategies	Strictly Ghetto Strategies	Dynamics of Leadership Strategies
Leadership	Foster leadership development through meetings, discussions, critiques, and hands-on experience	Foster leadership development by providing opportunities to showcase leadership	Foster leadership development through workshops, seminars, and discussion
Organizational skill	Foster organizational skills through organizing social justice campaign around community issues such as police brutality campaign	Foster organizational skills through organizational critiques, discussions, and community development	Foster organizational skills through workshops and discussion
Self-esteem	Foster organizational skills through organizing social justice campaign around community issues such as police brutality campaign	Foster self-esteem through public speaking on radio program, interacting with activists who are respected by street organizations, and interacting in discussion with college students	Foster self-esteem through workshops and discussion
Networking	Foster networking through collaboration between college students, street organizations, and career activists	Foster networking through collaboration between college students, street organizations, and career activists	Foster networking through collaboration between college students, street organizations, and career activists
Racial/ethnic pride	Supportive of racial/ethnic pride but also discuss important alliances based on common interests such as social justice issues	Supportive of racial/ethnic pride of urban youth	Supportive of racial/ethnic pride of all African Diaspora and oppressed people

(*continued*)

TABLE 1.3. (*Continued*)

Cultural Capital	NCPRR Strategies	Strictly Ghetto Strategies	Dynamics of Leadership Strategies
Motivation	Foster motivation through commitment to social justice, respect of community residents, and street organization	Foster motivation through commitment to social justice, respect of community residents, and street organization	Foster motivation through commitment to social justice, respect of community residents, and street organization

are part of the solution, not the problem. Richie Perez states, "even if we were to get rid of every gang and criminal off the streets, in ten years there will be just as many criminals and gangs; they are products of society that is pronounced in low income communities." According to Torres,

> We work with what these street organizations bring to us and not hold them to our standards and not rob them of what they come with; what they come with is beautiful. If you could articulate what they come with then that is great. They have been told that their behavior is antisocial and we tell them, no, that behavior is not antisocial. What others may seem as disruptive, we see as leadership. It is how that behavior is interpreted and being one of them, we are not threatened by their behavior; we understand it. And we work with that and utilize their skills that they have, and show them how their skills can parlay to other areas.

The intervention strategies that these organizations utilize with street organizations stress common techniques and sharing of resources. They have established strong collaborative relationships and they form to combine three organizational strategies, community organization, social opportunities, and social intervention, into one effective mechanism. These three strategies in detail cover job training, educational classes, providing role models, leadership development, networking, mobilizing the community, building community trust, and educating the community. Each organization acknowledged that the foundation to foster these areas already exists in the cultural capital of the street organizations.

Examples and purposes of the strategies follow:

- Job training: Currently Strictly Ghetto is developing a telecommunications company and security company. The immediate goal is to teach these skills to street organizations and use the business, network, and organizational skills each street organization has developed to achieve these business goals. Richie Perez has often stated that the problem with the urban ghetto is the lack of jobs and opportunities. Hector Torres states, "street organizations need an alternative to other means of operation that are not productive for the community." Job training fosters self-esteem, motivation, and ethnic pride.

- Education classes: All three organizations have either led cultural, social, and political classes or have attended the universals and participated in such classes. The purpose is to make street organizations' members directors of their destiny and not reactors to decisions made, according to Torres. Torres states that street organizations have always had cultural classes: "We want them to turn their minds to positive solutions that use their skills." Currently, members of the NCPRR are devising a voter registration strategy that utilizes the attributes of the Latin Kings: their speaking abilities, public relations, organizational structure, and discipline in fulfilling a directive to register voters. Education classes foster leadership, organizational skills, self-esteem, and motivation.

- Role models: Speakers from the three organizations are invited to participate in the universals and small discussions with street organization members, and street organization members are invited to participate and interact in each community organization. Role models exist in each organization and are defined by their pursuit of knowledge, passion, and commitment to their goals. There is a mutual respect that is earned from participation in community events. Praise in community organization is awarded through dedication to a task and networking. Street organizations want the respect of their neighborhood and thus are willing to dedicate themselves to any task. At a recent demonstration, the Latin Kings and Netas were praised for their late night dedication to calling community residents. The rally turned out 2000 people. These events foster networking and self-esteem.

- Leadership development: A recent example is a Latin King by the name of Wells. Wells was clearly outspoken in several classes at Dynamics of Leadership. Torres challenged him to take that energy and discuss the plight of Latinos on Al Sharpton's *Youth Action Network* radio show. After some initial pushing, according to Andre Rosa of Strictly Ghetto, "he talked so much we almost had to pull the mike away from him. That successful outing will build his self-esteem and he will share that experience with his nation [street organization]." All three community organizations seek to provide leadership opportunities in real situations with real consequences. Mistakes are made, but what is learned from the mistake provides leadership development. Dynamics of Leadership facilitates workshops and seminars to organization members on listening, time management, organization, and public speaking. NCPRR uses a different method. They call their strategy "apprenticeship in struggle." It is a strategy they have used with other interested individuals such as college activists. It often includes helping to organize, facilitate, and execute a justice campaign around a community issue such as environmental racism, police justice, and prisoners' rights. Discussions before and after the event are important because they help create accountability, self-critiques, and foster organizational planning. Strictly Ghetto often facilitates between Dynamics of Leadership, NCPRR, and the street organizations. Besides leadership, this strategy develops self-esteem and motivation.

- Networking: Working with several community organizations, college students, and career activists creates networking. Often in these situations, experiences are either transferred or shared as in the case of Mystic, a Latin King who went with a young filmmaker, Sonia Gonzalez, from NCPRR to see Shakespeare in Central Park. In group interaction, they realized they shared a similar interest, and a network outside their immediate community was formed. Currently, Mystic is looking toward acting as a possible career alternative. According to Mystic, his interactions with Sonia and theater have been "eye opening." Through the interaction with NCPRR in its various justice campaigns around community rights, street organizations have networked with various lawyers, teachers, and business leaders. The street organizations are beginning to take advantage of the networking. Ron Kuby, a famous community lawyer has decided to work with the Latin Kings on protecting the civil rights of members. Besides networking, members interact with other role models and develop ethnic pride.

- Mobilizing the community: The initial observation at the beginning of this chapter was one of the events in which street organizations learned how to make press releases, motivate an audience, work the media, and develop a database in the interest of the community. The issue was police brutality and racial violence. The lesson that was learned from the event is the need to know how to mobilize the community and fight for your rights in a positive and effective way. NCPRR and Dynamics of Leadership want members to become activists in their local community, through classroom and hands-on training, that put the members of these street organizations' skills to work for the community. In addition to gaining leadership and organizational skills, street organization members develop civic, racial, and ethnic pride through these events.

- Building community trust: Latin King members have been working with the NCPRR helping to organize conferences on political prisoners, Puerto Rican youth, the need for more minorities in American films, and supporting community events. "Because of their consistent commitment to community events," according to community members John Parado, a resident of East Harlem, "the Latin Kings seem to have evolved from a gang to a social organization." The Latin Kings have previously worked on the campaign of State Assemblyman Nelson Denis and other local politicians. King Tone stated, "leaders have made mistakes in the past; we are trying to move beyond those mistakes." Most of the Latin Kings and Netas have created strong links with community activists through their work on prisoner rights.

- Educating the community: According to Henry Merchado, "In large part to the consistent attendance of Latin King and members of Strictly Ghetto, a small gathering of forgotten political intellectuals has turned into a popular community class about Puerto Rican History at 116 Street." Latin Kings and Netas have participated in various community panels and have spoken at various youth conferences about identity, most recently at Muevete, an annual Puerto Rican youth conference sponsored by Aspira of New York and the National Latinas Caucus.

These intervention strategies seek to incorporate all of the characteristics of street organizations into fostering and developing the skills and characteristics of future leaders and community organizations. The intervention strategies use the cultural capital of street organizations as a foundation to develop more social capital through the increasing interaction of street organizations, community organizations, and the interests of the community. All of these organizations use strategies that incorporate street organizations into the community. According to Charles Pineda in his discussion of the Federation de Barrios Unidos, a federation of Latino barrio residents, it saw the importance of having "opportunities to do something in the community which met the basic psychology and needs of the gang barrio member (care, acceptance, love, achievement, recognition, responsibility, self-esteem, and self actualization)" (Pineda, 1974, p. 42). Pineda's statement could be extended to include all members of inner-city communities. Coleman has suggested that urban communities need to build intergenerational relationships to develop functional communities. These social relations build social capital and create avenues of resources that communities are able to utilize and sustain social, economic, and educational development. It has been further expanded that street organizations also have social capital that is supported and fostered by their street organization, which has been termed cultural capital. This premise of cultural capital is the foundation upon which NCPRR, Dynamics of Leadership, and Strictly Ghetto base their intervention strategies in helping urban youth. According to Torres,

> We have to do this freestyle (look at the cultural capital in each individual group) because every situation is different. If they are a macho crew, we convert that into a different channel such as knowledge. Instead of defining macho as guns we define macho as knowledge. Instead of saying who has the

prettiest girl, they challenge each other by saying, "I bet you don't know what year did El Grito de Lares take place." Instead of wrestling, they wrestle with their minds.

It is interesting to note that it has never been part of the goals or platforms of any of the community organizations to target street organizations. Unlike previous street-gang outreach programs of the sixties and seventies, NCPRR and Dynamics of Leadership are geared to community leadership development, not development or direct intervention in gangs. Klein (1971) has suggested that street-gang outreach programs in the sixties and seventies groups failed because of a lack of a strong plan and confused goals. The intervention strategies that are used with NCPRR and Dynamics of Leadership are geared to all youth that participate in these community programs. Without the street organizations, all three community organizations will continue with their regular programs. It is this consistency, community reputation, and longevity of these that make them respected and attractive to street organizations.

☐ Conclusion

What has risen from this study of street organizations in New York City are the several innovative intervention approaches that are being developed and the need to expand the current discourse on gangs by stressing the need for a "true community approach," an approach that is grounded in the premise of community building that members of gangs are integral parts of a community. Gang members have brothers, sisters, parents, and partners who may not be in the gang but are indirectly affected by what happens to the gang, and this in turn affects the community. So before we decide to support a "take back the community" approach, such as isolating the gang and rescuing a few members through a suppression policy or obliterating the entire gang, we should understand the ramifications of such a strategy.

Coleman's social capital theory suggests that stronger communities are built through intergenerational communication. A modified theory of Coleman's social capital suggests that everyone contributes to a community social capital, including youth. This "native community capital" or cultural capital further suggests that gangs as active participants in their community generate, foster, and transfer that cultural capital through their interaction with gang members, other youth, and other communities.

The premise that the intervention strategies that NCPRR, Dynamics of Leadership, and Strictly Ghetto are grounded in is that street organizations are part of the community and have skills gained through organizational and community interaction that are important for community development.

These community organizations seek to embrace gangs into their programs of community development. Leadership and community development skills already exist in urban areas, in street organizations as well as outside. These intervention strategies develop and reinforce that existing cultural capital into pride in both the spatial and cultural community.

Previous theories of a community approach have always stressed law enforcement agencies' interaction with grassroots, tenant, and local community approaches (Spergel, 1995). Interestingly, the reason that street organizations and these community organizations initially worked together was a result of police brutality. New York City police enforcement agencies are not trusted by the street organizations and community organizations that were studied. It would be very difficult for such an intervention strategy to work in East Harlem and the Bronx. Tensions between police and local communities are great. Another interesting aspect of the community approach favored by traditional theorists is that it leaves out the youth as active participants in solutions to gang problems. Youth are not seen as part of the solution but part of the problem that adults can solve. It is this lack of communication and trust among a community's youth that creates a situation where youths look toward gangs to solve their problems.

NCPRR, Dynamics of Leadership, and Strictly Ghetto's intervention policy differs mainly from prevailing theories by suggesting that communities can solve their own problems through their biggest asset, their youth. The community organizations invite the street organization members to solve the problems of all the participants' local communities. Their ideas and views are given equal weight with other participants, regardless of their background, in the discourse to find a discussion solution to a community problem. Community organizing strategies are discussed with street organization members and are executed by street organization and other community members. Street organization members are seen as an integral part of the community.

Traditional urban youth have been taught that the only way to advance in society is by leaving their community; therefore, there is very little reason for these youths to want to invest in their urban neighborhoods. The strategies used by these community organizations with street organizations augmenting the local community's cultural capital suggest alternatives to the out-migration of youth and the isolation of youth who participate in traditionally "deviant" behavior such as gangs.

As suggested by the movie *Boyz in the Hood*, we must reanalyze what is happening in urban communities and reject these traditional definitions of gangs that are not in the interest of the community. We need to develop a way of welcoming "the boyz" into the community by increasing interaction between "the boyz" and other segments of the community, especially its elders. These "boyz" are the future of the urban community. Members of the community, community organizations, and institutions must understand that intergenerational relations create and develop communication.

Street organizations are a means of socialization for some urban youth and an arena to develop among peers. Youth develop a culture that interrelates with the general culture of the community. Street organizations have skills that communities often overlook. What we can learn from these intervention strategies besides intervening in the deviant behavior of gangs is how to rescue our communities through our youth. Street organizations have been in New York City since the turn of the century. Where the Boy Scouts are afraid to venture, street organizations fill that vacuum. Street organizations voice the culture, attitude, and fears of urban youth; it is up to communities to listen to and talk with their children.

This chapter has been concerned with members of street organizations *after* they have made the decision to become members. Issues concerning the process of deciding to join have not been addressed directly. Not commenting on the "why" and "how" young men and women evolve into full-fledged street organization members should not be interpreted as a statement of the relative importance of the topic. In reality the question of "why" young people join street organizations is a complex question. There are probably as many different reasons as there are members. Less daunting, however, is the issue of when young people are at risk for such membership. In the next chapter Quamina discusses observations he has made of African American males, which seem to directly place them at risk for being societal failures and prime candidates for socialization into subcultural groups (i.e., gangs, street organizations, cults). The reader is cautioned not to make leaping conclusions about other ethnic groups based on his findings. Rather, think of his findings as representing work with a very narrowly defined group, which may have value in identifying patterns and histories unique to other ethnic groups who are significantly represented in gang cultures.

☐ References

Campbell, A. (1990). Female participation in gangs. In C. R. Huff (Ed.), *Gangs in America* (pp. 163–182). Newbury Park, CA: Sage.

Coleman, J. S. (1987). *Public and private schools: The impact of communities.* New York: Basic Books.

Coleman, J. S. (1988). Social capital in the creation of human capital. *American Journal of Sociology, 94* (Supplement), s95–s120.

Haskell, M., & Yablonsky, L. (1982). *Juvenile delinquency* (3rd ed.). Boston: Houghton Mifflin.

Horowitz, R. (1990). Sociological perspectives on gangs: Conflicting definitions and concepts. In C. R. Huff (Ed.), *Gangs in America* (pp. 37–54). Newbury Park, CA: Sage.

Jankowski, M. (1991). *Islands in the street: Gangs and American urban society.* Berkeley, CA: University of California Press.

Klein, M. (1971). *Street gangs and street workers*. Englewood Cliffs, NJ: Prentice–Hall.

Miller, W. (1990). When the United Sates has failed to solve its gang youth problem. In C. R. Huff (Ed.), *Gangs in America* (pp. 263–287). Newbury Park, CA: Sage.

Pineda, C. Jr. (1974). Chicago gang—Barrios in East Los Angeles Maravilla. Sacramento, CA: California Youth Authority.

Spergel, I. (1964). *Slumtown, Racketville, Haulburg*: Chicago: University of Chicago Press.

Spergel, I. (1995). *The youth gang problem: A community approach*. New York: Oxford University Press.

Spergel, I., & Curry, G. D. (1990). Strategies and perceived agency effectiveness in dealing with the youth gang problem. In C. R. Huff (Ed.), *Gangs in America* (pp. 288–309). Newbury Park, CA: Sage.

Thrasher, F. (1936). *The gang* (2nd ed.). Chicago: University of Chicago Press.

Vigil, J., & Yun, S. C. (1990). Vietnamese youth gangs in Southern California. In C. R. Huff (Ed.), *Gangs in America* (pp. 146–162). Newbury Park, CA: Sage.

Yablonsky, L. (1962). *The violent gang*. New York: MacMillan.

2

Afriye Quamina

Adolescent Gangs:
A Practitioner's Perspective

I've been pounding the educational pavement for nearly 25 years searching for the educational Rosetta Stone that promised to unleash the best-kept secret of all time: those precise principles and reliable teaching and learning methods that consistently work in favor of African American boys' academic achievement. I knew that there was something out there in the educational community that worked, and I wanted to know.... I had to know!

I started this journey somewhere in my first professional year, teaching fifth and sixth graders, where the schism so nakedly stared me in the face. It horrified me to witness African American boys (i.e., young brothers) struggling academically. They could barely read, write, or calculate and they had been allowed to graduate to an upper elementary educational program. And I quickly learned that this wasn't simply an issue I faced but one of national concern. How did this happen? How were these handicaps formed? Yes, handicaps. They were not polite or politically correct "challenges" but glaring handicaps. These handicaps were not recent developments in the lives of these students. They had been there for quite some time—like way back when, like at the starting gate. To have these young men here at this juncture begging for a preschool interpretation of the alphabet, when they should be clamoring for an understanding of life and its intricacies, is criminal. The other young students could. Why not African Americans? Why not them? That question was about to send me over the cuckoo's nest, and I hadn't been in the educational war but a few months.

I was not only concerned about their learning processes, within the history of irresponsibility, neglect, and denial, but I was also deeply concerned about the effect of this on their lives and the continued development of these young men over time.

Children come to school to gather skills and an acute, yet sensitive, awareness of life that eventually should lead to their personal liberation. They may not know this, but, ideologically speaking, education is the principal transformer in that process. In the liberating process, their particular lives, and the life of their resident community, should also benefit from their dedicated participation. Each community should accurately feel and observe the significant and natural growth changes in each of its children. The elder should visibly witness the light in the children's eyes glowing beyond proportion, dramatically reflecting the deepening of their social character forming. That should be a natural expectation, because education is a healthy and healing process. It has long been a healing art form, similar to that of a holistic medical art form, a psychological therapeutic art form, and all other fine and refined art forms. It is also a field dedicated to assist all humans, and especially children, to new levels of self-awareness and to also act as a lever to improve each student's overall physical, psychological, mental, cultural, and economic well-being.

Young African American boys are not succeeding, and as a result are leading and living lives of noisy hopeless desperation. They spend time in the academic setting either sitting alone in the midst of activity; roaming the halls; or hanging outside either on the grounds, bleachers, in the stairwells, or out on the corner, while others their age are searching the cosmos, tapping into cyberspace, renewing relationships with man's beginning, refining their life's understanding, or finely cultivating their nation-building skills. Could it be that their "moving" to the outskirts of focused activity is a response to the receipt of personal and group indignation? Could it be that these young men, to preserve and protect themselves, both culturally and psychologically, have "moved" to distance themselves from a formalized learning that has sought to remove their souls? Could it also be that they seek refuge to a life-giving and maintaining ritual that acts as an identity restorer to reconstitute their original selves and serves to heal and give them a foundation for cultural growth? It is very reasonable to think that if someone did not want you to be close, he or she would find very simple, yet complex, ways of moving you away from himself or herself. We know when we are not wanted or there exists no interest on our behalf. It is only natural to go to a place of welcome or rejuvenation, where someone or something cares, truly cares.

As a teacher, I found it necessary to go beyond my principal specialty and to research what was so peculiar about these young men and hopefully discover through this effort the actual nature and learning process of the young African American male.

There were several things I knew prior to embarking on such a perilous journey. First, young men tend to gather in groups or age sets and establish their own curriculum for learning. This emerges as a street version of rites of passage identifying sex, violence, money, drugs/alcohol, and music as its top-of-line features (Johnson & Gipson, 1996; Perkins, 1987; Quamina, 1996). These elements are nonspoken areas of knowledge taught and modeled by young African American males finding the learning from outside the school classroom more invigorating an experience than the in-school curriculum. Second, these young men also tend to reside or "stay" in the same geographical location or have been raised in that location and, therefore, share a common root origin (Quamina, 1996). These age sets or "sets" travel or "hang" together and develop bonding relationships that began shortly following five or six years of age. Third, most were hostile toward education, since the identification of success was not reflective or representative of their community values and was compounded by their own personal unsuccessful attempts at academic achievement. It was extremely difficult for these boys to see themselves honored in any way through the educational process. In other words, the community was not seen in the school, and the school was certainly not seen in the community. The school generally closed its doors to the community directly following the school day, even when the school directly resided within the walls of the community. When the school door closed, it deliberately meant nonfunctioning; shut down; barren; empty; final; and more symbolically, dead. Some interpretations also indicate that shutting down represented a snubbing of the community and hinted at some inherent school–community antagonisms. (When the students leave, theoretically the life of the school is drawn and is rendered impotent. It simply appeared as an edifice for the brothers to view with disdain.) Forth, irrespective of sociology, the intricacies of learning and school for most African American boys have always been an educational challenge. There are some true cultural underpinnings most educators and educational systems have refused to regard. With the overwhelming evidence that high percentages of African American males do not succeed in line with the current pedagogy, then reason would direct that change would take place and other considerations made to eradicate the problem. There is a uniqueness about this population that has not been adequately researched, magnified, and made available to both learner and teacher. Further, the role of culture and the attendant world view both of the school and the learner need further exploration to realize the areas of confrontation, parallel, and fit.

☐ **The Journey**

American society has charged most of young urban African American males as gang members and labeled their coming together as criminal and violent. They have been characterized as wanton killers, hoodlums, lusters for death, warriors for turfdom, reckless and uncaring, familially insensitive, irresponsible, and largely incorrigible. I live in Oakland, California, once touted as a youth gang capital and have spent countless hours with young African American males. I have constantly searched and re-searched for clues to disrupt the cloak of misconception of gangs and gang life. I have sat and eaten with so-called gang leaders and the roughest of gang participants. I have also visited with families of these young men and consulted with close relatives. I have found jobs for them. I have talked with their girlfriends and wives. I have talked to those who were in jail, some serving long, seemingly unfair, sentences, and those who were in juvenile halls for a mere overnight stay. Some needed to be away from their community to allow for reflection and atonement. In some cases, it was definitely necessary. I have consulted with judges, probation officers, psychologists, health practitioners, counselors, directors of many youth programs, police officers, and social workers. I have argued with authors and researchers, teachers and teachers' aides, administrators, academicians, and educational specialists. I have even spent countless hours with notable healers and those who used various healing practices to assist in the human transformational process. I have looked at the culture created by young Black males and adopted as a legitimate lifestyle within the American fabric. I have literally looked at this phenomenon backward and forward. I have read and read and studied and studied until I do not want to actually read another sentence. I am tired, and I find that no one clearly knows, and strangely they should not. Somehow, we all want to kindly cage this phenomenon into a comfortable time period or category so we can look at it like a disease, a Black social disease that will infect all of society unless we hurriedly inoculate the young. We just do not know what to do.

The brothers see themselves as forming families rather than any form of gang, unit, group, or set of violent actors. They use fictive names to refer to each other, for example, "family," "folks," "people," "homes," "cuz," "brother," "blood," etc., and to build close connected relationships. These young men gather together for what a family sees itself as maintaining a sense of purpose, camaraderie, psychological and emotional support, entertainment, and economic well-being. As a family, they look after one another with respect to their abilities, age, and length of time in the "family" and position in the family. They have grown to be trusted friends and acquaintances and have some intrinsic point in common that serves to tie them together. They hang together "cuz they be brothers" and it just "be's like that." They like being identified with each other, especially as somewhat related. They enjoy this connectedness. "We be down for each other, cuz it's what we do." Nothing more than that. Family is simply family. Family never has to apologize for being family. It just is. It is the nature of things. It is an old anthropological story. Its beginnings are found way back in the African hinterland, long before the advent of Jesus. Men hanging together because it is what they do—myth make; share stories; counsel; heal wounds; conjure; plan; solve life equations; ritualize relationships; experiment with perspectives; test physical, mental, and social strength; work; build; challenge; laugh, and laugh, and laugh; teach, teach, and teach; and dare each to outgrow the other. Historically, this seems to be a natural process for all males, irrespective of ethnic origin. Yet men of African ancestry, males of various ages, irrespective of geographical and social reference, choose to authentically participate in this fictive family development as a cultural beginning, in the process of developing as men.

As with most families, there are many and varied models. So it is with sets. There is no specific standard of how sets are created, what individuals are which specific personality types, or actually how long they live. They are designed like most human phenomena to simply provide a cultural shelter for those who have something in common, something that connects them. Environmental concerns, psychological supports, or human ecological connectors seem to be the main source of relationships.

☐ Gang Bangers

Some sets are unfortunately violent or do violent things. They are extremely small in number. They may perform criminal acts, for example, gang banging—or jumping on other young men who perhaps live in the same or different parts of the city. They protect the community from potential marauders or "enemy" that would have as their mission to penetrate beyond the supposed compound boundaries. In other words, these sets almost see themselves as players in a militaristic or quasi-militaristic type organization with the principal aim to protect their identified territory or turf. There is no set number that compose this type of set, nor is it really clear as to its life. Some of the young men are initiated through a violent process of "jumping in" and continue this tradition of violence long after the initiation period. They sometimes fashion themselves as combatants or gladiators of a particular community. They have created an urban stronghold to defend, whether it is known broadly or narrowly with young men within their resident community. They further see themselves as *GangStars* and continue to glorify their patroling and their perceived need as a necessary function for warriordom and excuse their violent acts as a requirement for survival. Their educational attainment is generally marginal, and their educational careers are often spotted with insincerity, very little, if any, personal regard, a challenge of the relevance of literacy and the position of gathered knowledge other than for the practical function of satisfying their needs as abstract and unnecessary. This set unfortunately has a short life focus, because jail, death, drugs, or long-term disability resulting from injury is the prognosis.

☐ Players

Some sets are complete with young men known as "players" who very aggressively seek out young women to use for fun, pleasure, and small-scale economics. Some will put indeterminate hours into making themselves "look good" and to appear as a "player," a "gigolo," a "mack daddy," or a "sweet daddy," who has honed life to various erotic interactions with women. They keep themselves physically sanitary or "clean" and often refuse any direct contact with physical work. Their world has been glamorized by various media or advertising, cinema, and novels. The "cool papa" persona wooed the women and served to exploit a methodology exposing underground living, complete with drug and alcohol usage, and various illegitimate income styles. Today's young players are invested in the glorification of women bashing, open and proliferated sex, and extreme self-absorbed behaviors. These brothers see themselves as "cool" and highly knowledgeable of street life. These young men say they are "getting their hustle on" as a way of demonstrating their entrepreneurial skills. Their "hustle" is principally directed to the development and maintenance of an underground economy that purports to function as comprehensively and as extensively as the above-ground tax-based economy. Their use of language and knowledge of various human behaviors suggests a keen intellectual understanding. School was utilized as a social network and the development of refined speaking and writing skills in most liberal arts areas of study. School, therefore, had meaning since they could position themselves, academically and socially, as articulate, knowledgeable and, consequently, attainers of power. School became a facility that fostered high self-esteem and helped to shape their self-concept. They knew the inner workings of success and its payoff. Last, they were keenly aware of leadership and how it could be used for manipulation or influence. Players are sharply aware of the benefits of manipulation and can recognize how it affects even areas of children's play. Children who keep score and choose who will participate in the play arena carry wholesale power and are customarily seen as in charge. They may not maintain a physical presence, but they certainly exercise control for social leadership. Schools, similar to the street, are complete with people, who are manipulatable, dependent, and enjoy a good heartfelt story.

☐ Just a Group of Brothers (JAGB)

Recently there is a sizable group (sets) of young men today who are strangely nomadic, not by nature but through a sociological and psychological imperative that has started to emerge. "Being at home" just does not fit. They feel very awkward living "at home." They really do not live in any one place but find themselves "staying" at a friend's, relative's, or new acquaintance's residence or temporary quarters. They gather in groups and travel from one location to another "looking for something to do." They hang out in parks, on various unmarked or "untagged" (graffiti-drawn) street corners, recreation centers, vacant lots, during any unscheduled hour of the day. They interact very seldom with school or with any specific structure other than with each other and on occasion with the local police. In their travels, they come into contact with other groupings of young men who are also looking for the same level of activity. Sometimes they clash, and sometimes they coalesce and share their experience(s). In that effort, they expand their acquaintanceship and hence their set. Their blending or confrontation is determined by the corresponding levels of respect deferred between and among each member of the groupings. Some agencies refer to these young men as outcasts or on the street they are known as "set jumpers" or "set hoppers." They are essentially transient. We found their academic experiences were unfortunately bland and nonsupportive. School was hard work and filled with disappointment. Somehow they never "fit," yet they always desired to ideally group with those young people who did. These brothers were the principal focus of "being capped on" by their social peers. They were always perceived as a little different, and no one really knew why.

☐ Small-Time Hustlers

Some sets who behaviorally resemble players, yet prefer working strictly with other young men, are made up of young men who specifically hustle. They hustle small con games, deal drugs, rob or even burglarize, steal, "jack cars," or resort to petty thievery or commit other small crimes or participate in all these activities. "They be doin' their business" and consider their acts as equivalent to "work." It takes highly developed acumen to grow at hustling. Some develop high functioning skills at trade, barter, and purchase. They are actual street merchants constantly on the move, creating and closing business. At one time, the local juvenile halls housed more of this population than any other. Most have biological family relationships and live primarily with one of their relatives. These young men form an understanding of what it means to "be slick" and expect to "game" on anyone and everyone. They would rather work at convincing others that life is much easier when you expect something for nothing. Additionally, they view most people as prey and they are the self-ordained vultures. Their aim is to "get over" and bask in the ability to keenly entertain with their fast hands and quick talk. This set is composed of independent entrepreneurs who use the set as a consortium to tell their stories and gather referrals. Their issue with themselves is the same that most have with them: trust. As exciting as they appear, trust disallows any real long-term commitments.

☐ Sports Jocks

There are some sets that are composed of sports jocks, who have strong interest in basketball, football, baseball, swimming, soccer, or some other form of popular sports competition. They spend the majority of their time playing "ball" and hanging around courts, gyms, or fields or all these places. These boys have combined interests with talent and learned skills to reach further into the world of sports. Sports have worked for years as a method for creating sets, places where boys who have not succeeded in social and academic domains can distinguish themselves. Often, sports work to cultivate added desire to achieve academically. Seeing themselves as expressing acclaimed competencies, boys sometimes transfer these experiences to school where they can more than appropriately leverage themselves. Those who are environmentally and culturally connected to peers who have low to no inspiring educational experiences, on the contrary, could disintegrate any spark of educational pursuit. One is either compromised and thus rendered hopeless or challenges these areas of relationship and stubbornly determines to remain focused. Prior to early secondary education, these boys use school simply to congregate, talk, and play sports. Sports become their principal meaning in life.

As they age, there are many young sports jocks who play at the local parks and gyms and negotiate their acumen into a way of hustling (i.e., gathering income through their playing against other individuals or teams). Some of these young men blend the aforementioned themes and find a path through life living off a reputation created by their supposed sports history.

☐ The Achievers

And last, the most misunderstood of all sets are those who are composed of boys academically or career focused, African centered, or immersed in some form of spirituality. This is the most diverse of all sets. These groupings meander in and out of relationships with other established sets. They seem to maintain a similar hanging out pattern of group behavior due to their principal connection with the prevailing cultural sense of what males do who are African American and are connected. As they appear academically focused and adroit, the members of other sets encourage their personal and group achievements as long as they remain "real" or continuously conducting their development as African Americans and do not get lost in the world of "white education."

☐ The Hustle

In each of the sets, there are several themes that link to one another. The predominant, and most often misunderstood, theme is the idea of the "hustle." Young African American males are highly inventive and prolific and will challenge an absent environment by creating something from nothing. They have had to be. (One would simply need to research the hundreds of recorded and patented inventions of African men upon their release from enslavement to identify the history or epistemological base for such a phenomenon.) This is an area where the community and set agree. Each person is told, and sometimes taught, that to succeed in this American environment, it is necessary to create a "way," a specific style that best expresses you, that best represents your understanding, that is your hustle. You apply your whistle to whatever it is you do. It is not meant derogatorily but complementarily and encouragingly. It is an artistic expression of self and self-knowing. Schools have definite structures and inflexible systems employed for learning. Evidently, Black boys do not adjust as rapidly as others in the application of their hustle. Something happens to unseat their learning style that is revived in the set (or gang?) of young males when they gather.

African American males are genealogically connected with Africa. There is a direct human link to that world and the way that world works. When the newly enslaved left the shores of West Africa, they were taken principally to the Caribbean and to the South and North America. Each knew Africa was their home. Anthropologically, each also knew they were from the same or similar families. Each had left a culture that grouped children by age sets to formulate educational strategies to maximize the extension of learning a cultural contextualization. Education began at the time of birth and ended with death. The child had to pass through various stages of age groupings with a system of education that was defined for every status of life (Kenyatta, 1965). Boys were brought together to experience cognitive and social development with boys of the same age and like developmental accomplishments. When the various societies neglected to organize learning by groups, they found that boys were aimless, vandalized, committed low-grade crimes, and were largely disobedient (Sjonsberg, 1989). The idea that young males should spend as much time together learning and experiencing life under the guidance of an elder lends itself to a structure similar to a rites-of-passage tradition as found on the continent of Africa. This offers the opportunity for learning in this special relationship to parallel what happens in the real world. It also extends a pathway to higher and more advanced areas of understanding as the young male ages. All learning is age appropriate and developmentally structured to stimulate and strengthen the cognitive, emotional, spiritual, and physical areas.

☐ The Street Curriculum

The young male is exposed to a curriculum that sometimes draws high interests and involvement as early as primary grades and carries through well beyond high school graduation. This curriculum prepares young men how to conduct themselves as hustlers, players, and malcontents. This curriculum exposes young boys to an unhealthy understanding of daily and cultural life that is far removed from nature or experiences in applicable ethics and moral development. The street curriculum has been active in the African American community prior to the historic Emancipation Proclamation, where it could be found active in various areas of the free north where it was used to assist unemployed former slaves to garner an income. The curriculum has changed drastically over time. The current curriculum consists of sex, violence, money, drugs and alcohol, and derogatory forms of music. Young men are taught either by other young men or an "O.G." (elder or original gangster) in the ways of life on the street. Young men employ many methods to attain or utilize one or more of the curriculum areas to improve their status in the street community. They develop skills and refine them to a level of high functioning so they can actively compete to achieve top status in that community. Those who accomplish such status are revered by those on the street and are well known to those off the street. These people have a large influence on the ideals of young boys. As school becomes more of a challenge, or as continuous thrusts of indignation occur, a young boy may see the street life as a viable option. In that regard, it is often said that he was "pushed out of school" to struggle and make a way on the street. Although misperceived as a viable option or an option at all, the life on the street is fraught with definite serious consequences or endings. Death is a daily reality, as is jail, prison, violence, sickness, mental illness, alcoholism, drug addiction, homelessness (see Doucette-Gates, this volume) and a road of no return and life filled with emptiness and hopelessness. Young African American boys with low academic skills are highly susceptible and vulnerable to this life and lifestyle.

☐ The Cultural Pattern

A person's world view, how they picture others, and essentially how they view themselves is a result of culture. Additionally, culture is that human cement that virtually draws and ties people together. An economy is developed, friendships are made, relationships are formed, families are built, rituals are performed, religions are practiced, customs become traditions, and people have created ways of determining what has value, holds principle, and formulates histories. The inner world of culture is forever moving and attempts to give direction to living.

Young African American males come together because some element of culture encourages them to gather. On basketball courts, street corners, barber shops, pool halls, gas stations, gyms, church back rooms, college plazas, in cars, in hallways, in stairwells, state houses, hospitals, boulevards, park benches, bars, dance halls, courtrooms, outside liquor stores, inside wash houses, and wherever the energy draws African men, young and old, of so special and significant an ancestry, time stops and life is recolored. It is like a way station—a setting in the middle of where and nowhere to allow for cultural refueling. Hanging out is not as mindless or superficial as it appears to the onlooker. Hanging out is a male spiritual life dimension for "being there" and being connected and being one and connected through their male identity. Each one is bringing his all to converge on this location. Being there is for complete histories to be brought, quantified, and qualitatively undivided.

African American males are guided by a variation of two overriding and currently intersecting spiritual cultures. Christian-based, semi-individualistic, blue collar, Southern lifestyle influenced ways of life of that of highly African-centered, family-oriented, upwardly mobile, spiritually focused, familial hierarchical, but child-centered, communal experiences. African American males' view of life and the world is as varied as the mixture. As these two spiritual cultures silently, yet demonstratively collide, the children are finding few long-lasting connectors to either.

Each are fully comprehensive, yet the children are having great difficulties accepting the monolithic orthodoxy that each seems to demand. A solid mass seems to reject both and substitute a reliance on themselves for cultivation of an underground and seemingly exciting and highly rebellious way of life. They flaunt sexuality, cast off old timeless values and traditions like useless and formless clothes, flip fingers at societal laws and mores, and denigrate their self-proclaimed humanity. Notwithstanding echoes of time past of each generation's evolution from adolescence to adulthood, this continuous and snowballing Americanized rite of passage has created a no-turning-back, "in your face," drop-kick culture. Young brothers in the wake of this renewed concentration on remaining young, hip, and money oriented at any cost are continuing to lose. They are going to age and be faced with what they did not preserve that was rooted in the past, structured, and had weathered all climatic conditions.

The brothers say that education is empty, and that school is a waste of time, and teachers do not really care, not really. Teachers say they do, but they do not act like it. It is *all* mouth: *"they be running hecka game—straight up gafflin' brothas and we ain't goin' fo' it . . . not no mo'"* (Anonymous, 1995). Teachers who are sincere often offer shocking comments, which graphically demonstrate the importance of culture. Currently, the hip hop culture is fun, exciting, and fast-paced, but is not really meeting the needs of the masses of young men. They know academics are an integral part of their lives and they cannot continue to ignore the benefits. So many teachers offer insights and personal experiences that they hope will be helpful to the young men with whom they are working. The freedom provided by hip hop is wholesale fantasy, commercialized, and inner-self-stripping. The young men know that, but it presents the American ideal of anything goes, Horatio Alger in blackface, and highly unethical and vigorous competition. The more and greater the compensation, the more activity and more fallout, often unseen fallout. There are constant reminders when we hear insidious declarations that "every man is out to get his" or "I'm out for mine," which negates the reality that there are no individuals in a cooperative culture, where the effort is for all to be successful through a collective approach. This new glossy and magnetizing culture is very powerful and has a luring effect on young males. They witness others who physically and culturally resemble them as representatives of what this culture offers through hard work, persistence, violence if necessary, open sexual display, female disrespect, mockery of family values, elevated value of drug and alcohol use, and a complete personal renaming away from one's ancestry and sacred traditions. The world that is established through the lens of this culture demonstrates how young men are again ignored and used as chattel to serve the arms of the industry. Again, they lose; however, we now know what is available to assist young boys to levels of advancement.

☐ The Resident Communities

The communities that give birth to these young men are variegated both vertically and horizontally. African American communities are complex and yet are very simply structured. Economically, most African American communities comprise a continuum of people within five economic strata: (1) those with very little to no income with no "visible" means of support and can be homeless, but it is a choice, because relatives and community family members are available to help them; (2) families on welfare; (3) families who work every day in blue collar jobs; (4) professional families who achieved a modicum of high social status, yet continue to reside in a predominantly African American community; and, last, (5) those who upwardly migrated to a more ethnically diverse community with a greater possibility of integrated marriages and relationships that more aptly represented their professional or work community profile.

Generally within the context of culture (i.e., mixed culture) neighborhoods seem to flow together but form a distinct and unique subculture within that block or area. What happens on one block may not affect the normalcy of another. The villageness of their lives has become more strained over time and offers very little monitoring and social investment in the development of the neighbor's child or children. Even the contact among adults is peripheral and of short duration. News even travels slowly because the cultural connection that once was is no more or is rendered extremely limited. There is also a good chance that the next-door neighbor has been living there for just a few months, and they are following in the footsteps of those preceding who "stayed" just a few months. We see high transience vis-à-vis any sizable degree of permanence. The culture of the neighborhood, although at one time very powerful, had the ability to determine by its intimidation (1) how people related to each other, (2) how people conducted their daily business of familymaking, and (3) how support among a community was provided and distributed began to shift. This shift, unfortunately, saw men leave their homes, mothers uphold households, and boys rendered fatherless. It seemed the more families became urban, the more they experienced separation, both internally and externally. The young males found their lives governed so frequently by what happened in the street; on the way to play, on the way to the store, on the way to lessons, and on the way to school that their home culture became less and less the significant force that prepared them for various stages of youth development or deterred them from forming a world view representative of what was "outside" rather than inside. This was now their community and the environment of the community was in charge. Young males learned so ardently from each other that it was literally difficult to pull themselves apart. As innocent as one's view of child's play was, it has long been considered a preliminary activity for the formulation of relationships, exchange of ideas, and development of character. It is exciting and learning is continuous, yet approaches to learning and learning "styles" are also created. These styles seem to run counter to the pedagogy of American education and serve the poor development and academic demise of black males. The transient nature of many communities also negatively impacts efforts to enlist the community in attempts to neutralize the disruptive influences of many gangs (i.e., community organization strategies), as described by Randolph (this volume).

Am I the only one who has observed the aforementioned patterns of isolation and disengagement that are so frequent among African American adolescent males? Or does it appear that way because of my visceral and passionate concern about these issues? Of course I'm not alone in these observations or my concern about African American males. Frequently it feels as if I am an isolate, and that's not good. In trying to understand some of these behavioral patterns and how they adversely impact the educational experiences for these boys I have searched the human development, pedagogical, and psychological literature feverishly. The results are that I have discovered several scholars who offer insights into the issues and implicit suggestions for educational practitioners like myself.

The issue of parental supervision and its impact on African American adolescents is commonly discussed. Wilson, Kastrinakis, D'Angelo, and Getson (1994) show that a high level of parental supervision significantly impacts sexual attitudes, knowledge, and behavior of urban Black adolescent males. The researchers report that in their sample of 241 urban adolescent Black males, parental supervision and use of condoms were positively correlated. A similar finding, more relevant to the issues at hand, is reported by Ensminger (1990) and Wasserman, Miller, Pinner, and Jaramillo (1996). Ensminger reports that parental supervision is causally linked to range and types of problem behavior reported by Black urban adolescents. Boys with more problems and greater severity of problems (i.e., substance abuse problems) have lower levels of parental supervision. Wasserman notes that lack of parental supervision seems to be a constant theme among those with conduct disorders whom she studied. Monitoring of free time, networks of friends, and television watching are behaviors that are subsumed under parental supervision in both studies. Concerning the oft-reported negative impact of television watching among Black children and adolescents, Stroman (1991) concludes that the relationship is not linear or as obvious as is often assumed. Her work examines television's role in the social development of Black children, including television use, socialization context, potential antisocial and prosocial effects, and television as an educator. Stroman concludes that "television is a significant player in the socialization (cognitive and social) of Black children with positive and negative impacts."

These findings cause me to feel better in that they suggest that socialization among adolescents is an outcome that is caused by a multiplicity of factors. That doesn't, however, tell me much about what happens in schools that could partially help explain or remediate the outcomes that I have observed. More searching led me to a few scholars who have directly commented on the social self in the educational setting. Taylor, Casten, Flickenger, and Roberts (1994) suggest that African American adolescents' school achievement is negatively influenced by their perception of a discriminatory "job ceiling" affecting their employment opportunities. Taylor et al. also report that the more aware of discrimination African American adolescents are the less important they perceive academic achievement to be. The result is that they become less engaged in their school work. Is this active sabotage of self or creative saving of face? Clark (1991) takes another approach to this issue of school competence. She observes that students who persist (i.e., are resilient) in school are those who possess attributes that help to build social identity, friendships, and social support networks, all which contribute to school competence and good academic performance. Parental involvement, cultural sensitivity, and small group learning, she believes, all contribute to resilience.

Fuller (1992) introduces an element of caution in thinking about student performance in school. He administered the Children's Depression Scale to 27 African American adolescents in a public school for severely emotionally disturbed adolescents and to 51 junior high school regular education African American students. Findings indicate that the maladaptive students manifested higher degrees of clinical depression than did the adaptive students. Could it be that some of the social dropping out and isolation that I am observing is depression, undetected and undiagnosed, at work? An older study by Hendricks, Montgomery, and Fullilove (1984) echoes similar sentiments. In her study of 98 Black adolescent males it was found that those who do not believe they have control of their destiny (i.e., external locus of control and helplessness) are more likely to be school dropouts than others. Helplessness is a hallmark of depression.

Perhaps the greatest confirmation and validation of my observations can be found in Taylor et al.'s (1994) discussion of disengagement of African American youth. Taylor argues that many such youth adapt to their problematic environments and slowly acquiesce to a lifestyle characterized by antisocial behavior.

☐ Conclusion

Working with young, low-achieving African American boys can be a very demanding and challenging endeavor, especially when applied to a fixed

Western pedagogical style. Approaching learning without a well-understood consideration of the student's full culture is a mistake and as a consequence is fruitless. The goal is that both student and teacher optimally learn from any learning experience that allows either to reflect, learn, or relearn a skill or methodology, and to apply this learning to an immediate life experience. The thread that weaves through all sets and groupings of young boys is, fortunately, within the obvious. The dynamic of connectedness is a demonstration that they want to come together, and the added element of discourse or sharing of the experience allows them to bring their manifold histories to bear upon a situation. They bring themselves without censor. They bring all that they know and are open to use their inherent methodology and communication style to collaborate with their peers. Boys yearn for structure, a tight envelope that bears safety, security, and stability. Their set is familiar, a place they know, and encourages them to be themselves while learning. Schools do not. Schools require that they change learned community-based behaviors for new school-oriented behaviors that suit the schools' program needs and requirements. The behaviors that are adopted are often not necessarily those that will give the greatest benefits to one's set or community. Who can argue that education is not useful and ideologically necessary for achievement and advancement in society? Absolutely no one! Education is a requirement for freedom and participation in civilized life. Overall, it sounds harmless and beneficial. The problem, however, is that young African American males are not surviving in this system, and there is something very detrimental going on. Sure, there is responsibility on both the school and the student; however, the student brings his native self to receive that which is supposedly good for him, in a process that reflects his best interests. To that end, his culture, his past, his present, and his future must be respected, and not admonished. The problem is in the process of learning, not in the essence. It is how these young men are approached, recognized, honored, and humanly encouraged to learn that makes the differences. Otherwise, it does not work. Their culture is alive and their style for living and learning has worked for tens of thousands of years. Black males will educate and have educated themselves when no one else would. There is a way of succeeding and it is known. These young men learn how to street hustle, socially hustle, sports hustle, economically hustle, and, some, academically hustle. Schools need to follow these simple yet highly rewarding suggestions to maximize the education of African American males:

1. Honor their spirit as complete learners, irrespective of what academic deficits they hold. No one comes to an educational facility complete; otherwise, there is no need for one.

2. Be open and give respect for the world they live in. They are not absent of culture or a world view. Learn and insist on the life of the culture in their learning.
3. Have them work in groups with timed tasks that also have requirements for studying outside of the classroom.
4. Spend credible time to learn from them what makes them excited and retains their glow for living. They are children, not machines.

Perhaps a shift away from a completely cognitive focus to one that is concerned with cognitive and behavioral domains of the student, as suggested by Carylon and Jones (this volume), might be helpful.

The foregoing observations of African American males in school settings present some unsettling dilemmas. Who is to be implicated for perpetuating a system in which young minds can be shut off so early in their developmental process? Does the creation of sets among these students represent a creative attempt to create a system that affirms them as "good people"? Or do the patterns discussed in this chapter indicate a pervasive sense of helplessness and despair? When the future time perspectives and visions are extremely short sighted and negative, as described by Doucettte-Gates in the next chapter, dropping out of the school scene and into sets probably represents a way to save face. In the next chapter, data which may partially explain some of my observations are presented. Doucette-Gates utilizes a combination of ethnographic and quantitative data collection procedures. The result is a rich and insightful glimpse into the private inner worlds of a group of inner-city students who sometimes choose the gang as their only hope in an otherwise hostile and unconfirming world.

☐ References

Clark, M. (1991). Social identity, peer relations, and academic competence of African American adolescents. *Education and Urban Society, 24*(1), 41–52.

Ensminger, M. (1990). Sexual activity and problem behaviors among black urban adolescents. *Child Development, 61*(6), 2032–2046.

Fuller, T. (1992). Masked depression in maladaptive black adolescents. *School Counselor, 40*(1), 24–31.

Hendricks, L., Montgomery, T., & Fullilove, R. (1984). Educational achievement and locus of control among black adolescent fathers. *Journal of Negro Education, 53*(2), 182–188.

Johnson, R., & Gipson, C. (1996). *Visions: A career guidance/life management workbook for African American males*. Sacramento: California Department of Education.

Kenyatta, J. (1965). *Facing Mount Kenya*. New York: Vintage Books.

Perkins, E. (1987). *Home is a dirty street: The social oppression of black children*. Chicago: Third World Press.

Quamina, A. (1996). *Three to one program: An evaluation*. Oakland, CA: Alameda County Office of Probation.

Sjonsberg, E. (1989). *Change in an African village*. West Hartford, CT: Kumarian Press.

Stroman, C. (1991). Television's role in the socialization of African American children and adolescents. *Journal of Negro Education, 60*(3), 314–327.

Taylor, R., Casten, R., Flickenger, S., & Roberts, D. (1994). Explaining the school performance of African American adolescents. *Journal of Research on Adolescence, 4*(1), 21–44.

Wasserman, G., Miller, L., Pinner, E., & Jaramillo, B. (1996). Parenting predictors of early conduct problems in urban, high-risk boys. *Journal of American Academy of Child and Adolescent Psychiatry, 35*, 1227–1236.

Wilson, M., Kastrinakis, M., D'Angelo, L., & Getson, P. (1994). Attitudes, knowledge, and behavior regarding condom use in black urban males. *Adolescence, 29*(113), 13–26.

Ann Doucette-Gates

Hope: Sustaining a Vision of the Future

Will the future ever arrive? . . . Should we continue to look upwards? Is the light we can see in the sky one of those which will presently be extinguished. The ideal is terrifying to behold, lost as it is in the depths, small, isolated, a pin-point, brilliant but threatened on all sides by the dark forces that surround it; nevertheless, no more in danger than a star in the jaws of the clouds.

Victor Hugo, *Les Misérables*

During the early 1990s, the media was saturated with coverage of the limited life expectancies of racial/ethnic minority males, especially African American males. The popular media's use of demographic statistics brought to the forefront the realities that incarceration was more likely than a college education for a significant proportion of African American males. Data (1979 to 1995) reported from the National Center for Health Statistics indicate that early death due to homicide for African American males between the ages of 15 and 24 was seven times more likely than for their White male counterparts.[1] Administrative data from the early 1990s in New York City revealed that every 28 hours the life of a young person between the ages of 14 and 24 was lost to violence. African American males accounted

---

[1] Data are from the Mortality (Compressed) dataset, Office of Analysis and Epidemiology, National Center for Health Statistics, Centers for Disease Control and Prevention (CDC). Homicide death rate is based on an age adjusted death count for Caucasian and African American males between the ages of 15 and 24. Data are available on the CDC WONDER/PC Data File System.

for the majority of these deaths. *"There ain't nobody at this school who doesn't know somebody who's got shot,"* reports one 17-year-old African American male from New York City.

The prevalence of this media coverage raised concern regarding the *hope* of racial/ethnic, inner-city youth for future expectations. Youth were highlighted in media giving testimony to the grim prospects of the future. With a grim or limited vision of the future, the promises of career payoffs for educational effort and achievement and the anticipation of rewards and social mobility for hard work may have restricted motivational capacity to encourage these youth to behave according to the *conventional* mainstream expectations.

> When you are poor and you are just a little kid and you always see the guy with the BMW and the Benz and the stuff you don't have, and you see how much attention they get and you want that attention and you try to be like him and you start doing things, hanging out with the wrong people and you start doing the things that he does. You want the stuff and you take the risk.... Yeah, you could get popped (shot), but that ain't too bad. [What about the risk of dying?] You gotta think it won't happen to me, that's all. (17-year-old African American male)

☐ Inner-City Life: The Impact of Social Adversity

Research suggests that the growing sense of joblessness (Wilson, 1987, 1991) and resulting difficulty for youth in assuming traditional and meaningful adult occupational roles are primary predictors of youth violence and crime. Although we tend to think of work as a means of securing needed and desired resources, work also serves as a reference point in organizing and scheduling our lives and, additionally, as a source of social identity. While we preach the "promise of the future" and opportunities for good jobs, many youth find that these are not grounded in their social reality. The values, beliefs, and promises promulgated by mainstream society are not confirmed in many adult lives in their neighborhoods.

More often than not, the individuals identified as inner-city youth are overrepresented by African American, Latino, and recent immigrant populations. Under the banner of *equal opportunity*, many inner-city youth live impoverished lives in a media-exploited world of perceptible plenty. They experience failure in comparison with the expected success of their White suburban counterparts.

Inner-city neighborhoods are often isolated and characterized by a consolidation of poverty, crime, joblessness, and a lack of perceived prestige and power. Because of this consolidation, those living in these inner-city areas tend to be avoided by individuals in the mainstream culture. The

reception of inner-city students by the families of their suburban counterparts during the implementation of Civil Rights legislation (desegrega-
tion, busing, etc.) is an illustration of such avoidance. The consolidation
of adverse social conditions strengthens the boundaries separating minority
groups living in at-risk inner-city neighborhoods and mainstream dominant
groups.

Little is known about the impact of these adverse social conditions on
childhood and adolescent constructions and interpretations of society and
the functions of the economic system on occupational possibilities (Bloom-
Feshbach, Bloom-Feshbach, & Heller, 1982). Research often fails to consider
that outcomes may differ as a result of exposure to varying degrees of
social adversity or the experience of social adversity in the midst of those
living in more favorable conditions. In a Canadian study by Paulter and
Lewko (1987), subjects exposed to the negative economic factors of family
unemployment and community hardship had distinctly pessimistic and even
cynical occupational outlooks. This study failed to indicate whether the
subjects were living in a community where their economic standing was
similar or distinct from others living in the same community.

☐ Beyond Thrasher: Characterizing Gangs

For many inner-city youth, gang and youth subcultures provide the advantages that mainstream society promises but fails to deliver. Gang membership offers the promise of social (collective) identity, respect, potential economic mobility, and protection that many inner-city youth believe society
cannot provide. Although criminality or delinquency has been historically
identified with gang activity, research indicates that this is a relatively new
phenomenon. Early research reports that gang behavior was characterized
by hanging out, although some crime did occur (Thrasher, 1927). Thrasher's
(1927) classic study of more than 1300 gangs in Chicago during the 1920s
asserts that gangs stole what they needed and often sold what remained to
area residents for prices they could better afford. Currently, criminal and
delinquent behavior appears on the rise. The current behavior of gangs has
been generalized to the past, obscuring the reality that for many inner-city
gangs crime is a new enterprise, perhaps a result of changing economic
times during the past decade. It is important to note that crime is not the
only function of gangs, nor perhaps is it the most important.

Gang and youth subculture membership may be one response for inner-
city youth to the adverse social conditions they encounter. Gangs today are
typically perceived as by-products of troubled neighborhoods. It is important
to note that contemporary gangs do not fit the *West Side Story* stereotype,
and that not all youth subgroups are gangs.

Gangs are typically characterized by group defined organization, group determined membership and initiation criteria, neighborhood boundaries, racial/ethnic solidarity, allegiance to common goals, and in many cases entrepreneurial opportunity (Padilla, 1992). Nationality, once a deciding factor for White immigrant gangs, is less a concern for membership in today's White contemporary gangs. Perhaps the single most significant change in membership structure is the formation of independent gangs of young women. These young women are no longer relegated to the status of auxiliary members of male gangs. Little research exists on the presence of gang-like membership or organizations in more affluent communities.

Other youth groups such as *crews, networks,* and *homeboys* resemble and are sometimes incorrectly assumed to be formal gang organizations. The distinction among these groups, although important to study, is not the primary focus of this paper. There are often overwhelming barriers that inner-city youth face in securing emotional and social support, safe environments, material resources, and economic opportunities.

Little is really known about the ties of gang members to community institutions (see Vargas and DiPilato, this volume). Weakened community ties would help to explain the exploitation of community institutions, the drug trade, which provides profit and encourages violence and fear among community residents (see Gonzalez, this volume).

☐ Broken Promises: Anyone Can Grow Up to Be the President?

The limited access opportunities of inner-city life for racial/ethnic minorities constrain behavioral choices. Often the behaviors of inner-city youth are considered to be an unwillingness to adhere to a White middle-class work ethic rather than a reflection of adverse social conditions, cultural discord and misinterpretation, or constrained developmental opportunities. When Larry, a 17-year-old African American male, was asked to reflect on his options for the future and potential for success, he responded,

> Success—you could be a nobody out there in the streets. There is so many homeless people out there in the streets and in the subways and they is gifted and some of the people I see in the schools they ain't all that smart or intelligent. I look at them and say that is a shame. People in the subways making music out there I can't express the way I feel about that. They probably strived out there to get a job, but it is hard out there and they probably quit and they stopped—it is too rough. Nobody wants to see you or recognize you. Success is a person living a positive life; you don't have to be rich, just a nice home, a nice family, a legit job, and a positive attitude.

The belief in equality, opportunity, educational access, and the economic returns of hard work is not supported for Larry's inner-city environment and the lives he witnesses on a daily basis.

While we promote education as the link to a *good job*, the conviction diminishes among inner-city youth that school functions to teach the fundamental values and attitudes that support the economic system, along with the necessary skills and competencies that will make the system work. Many inner-city youth lack access opportunities and the needed credentials that are essential for meaningful employment, economic mobility, and, perhaps, more important, social identity. *"It's hard to look at school as a way out. We fought so hard to get in school and there is not one Black person I know who wants to go to school. I don't go to school—those people (school) are holding me back,"* asserts Jerome, an 18-year-old African American.

☐ Looking toward the Future?

The ability to envision the future and make plans is intuitively perceived as important for a successful adolescent transition to adulthood. The ability to look toward the future with some sense of promise adds an important dimension to behavioral motivation in terms of planning and setting goals and objectives (Nuttin, 1984). It seems plausible, given the recent media attention illustrating a bleak future for many inner-city minority youth, that the ability to consider the future consequences of present behavior might be somewhat compromised.

The role of the future has not been generally accepted in behavioral science. Science has difficulty accepting the fact that not-yet-existing events are already active. Future time was introduced to psychology by Tolman (1932) through the notion of anticipation and expectancy. Tolman defined anticipation and expectation as a concern with the succession of events which happened in the past to predict the future. Lewin (1931) described this as a notion of temporal extension.

The temporal dimension of behavior is often overlooked in its motivational capacity. Behavioral action happens in the present; only those variables that are active at the moment affect and explain the behavioral action. Lewin (1935) calls this the principle of contemporaneity. Nevertheless, psychologists stress the fact that future and past events in the frame of the individual's time perspective codetermine behavior through an instrumental relationship, linking past and present experience with the probability of positive or acceptable outcomes in the future (Estes, 1972; Nuttin, 1984, 1985; Raynor, 1969; Raynor & Entin, 1982, 1983).

The concept of time perspective refers to one's attitude toward time—having a more or less positive or negative outlook regarding the past, present, and future. Time perspective also focuses on the extension and the level of substantive reality given to thoughts of the past, present, and future. For example, are thoughts of *hoped-for* future outcomes based on a perception of reality or fantasy—dreams that are unlikely to occur? Last, time orientation implies an overall orientation or focus or both on the past, present, or future.

Time perspective has a cognitive dimension as well as a focus on temporal location (past, present, future). The objects of an individual's cognitive representation are not tied to the present moment at which the behavior takes place. For example, the class a student may be thinking about right now may be the class he or she took last semester or the one he or she hopes to take during the summer session. The object itself is the essential element of the representational act; thinking, remembering, and planning are impossible without an object that constitutes the intentional content of the cognitive act. The object of the representational act is actively present, but the temporal location may be the past or future. Temporal perspective has impact on present behavior to the extent that it is present on the cognitive level of behavior.

Future time perspective may be important in explaining successful academic outcomes, the ability to link educational efforts to career goals, and, conversely, interpreting adolescent engagement in risk-taking behaviors without apparent consideration of future consequences. The student who sees his or her studies as instrumental for a future career has a realistic perspective of the relationship between school and occupation as well as an integrated perception of the present and future with regard to the activity of school. A Scandinavian study of school-aged children and adolescents demonstrated that positive affective evaluations of the future were related to the likelihood that anticipated goals would be realized (Nurmi, 1989). It is in the future that the goals achieved through effort and study are realized.

Many anthropological and sociological studies reveal a restricted future time perspective among individuals living in unfavorable psychological, cultural, or socioeconomic conditions (Cottle & Klineberg, 1974; Klaus, 1987). For example, it may be more adaptive for clinical patients to abandon the future and live in the present, as was evidenced in a Russian study of adolescent alcoholics (Khomik & Kronik, 1988). Likewise, it may be more realistic for some socioeconomic groups to make no plans or behavioral projects for the future, given what may be witnessed in their day-to-day experience.

Extended time perspective stimulates long-term goal setting and long-term projects to work on. Distant goals are more motivating to individuals with longer future time perspective. It has been shown that achievement motivated students perceiving an instrumental relation between present academic study and distant careers are more motivated to study than are others not perceiving this relation (Nurmi, 1989; Von Klemper, 1980). Motivation is more fully channeled to the instrumental act (present study habits) when the instrumental relation is perceived.

The dynamic aspect of future time perspective is formed by the inclination to ascribe high valence to goals in the distant future. The cognitive aspect is formed by the tendency to grasp the long-term consequences of actual behavior, as reflected in the concept of instrumental value of the behavioral act. The motivation invested in the instrumental act can be both positive and negative. If the characteristics of the present instrumental act are strongly aversive, for example, studying, attending school, or maintaining conventional social norms, the motivation for accomplishing the distant goal such as graduation, attaining a promising career, avoiding the juvenile justice system, will be limited (DeVolder & Lens, 1982). If, on the other hand, the distant goal is stronger than the aversive features of the instrumental object, for example, studying and staying in school or avoiding *underground economies*, the individual will likely persist in studying and going to school and avoiding illegal activities:

> It depends on the situation you have in selling drugs. Your family depends on the situation you have in selling drugs. Your family might not be all that well-off financial and you might need money and it might be hard for you to get a job, and you go out there and sell drugs and after a while you start using your own product. (Ron, 17-year-old African American)

Although intuitively many people believe that youth subcultures are not planful and pay little attention to the future consequences of deviant behavior, research indicates that the adverse conditions of the day-to-day lives of family members and other adults in the neighborhood may convince these adolescents that the future they envision is even less promising than the present (Doucette-Gates, 1992). *"I don't have no time to think about the future, having all those pressures coming up, worry about somebody knocking you off or worrying about whether they come to rob your house or hurt your family,"* states Jose, a 19-year-old Hispanic male.

This paper examines the associative relationships among adverse social conditions and temporal attitude and perspective about the past, present, and future conditions in thinking about gang-affiliated behavior. The data presented integrate a qualitative and quantitative approach shaped largely by the voices of inner-city adolescents living in New York City.

Participants for this study were drawn from a larger pool of students who participated in a survey study across a network of four New York City alternative high schools. The students within this network of alternative schools describe themselves as predominantly Hispanic (50%) and African American (42%) and other (8%: 3% Asian, 5% Caucasian), and are for the most part economically disadvantaged. School officials report 76% of the students are eligible for the free breakfast and lunch programs. A compari-

TABLE 3.1. Distribution of Subjects by Age and Race/Ethnicity

Race/Ethnicity	Mean Age	Age Range
African American ($n = 26$)	17.41	16–20
Hispanic Origin ($n = 21$)	18.0	16–19

son using subjects' postal zip codes and demographic census data confirmed the school's report of the proportion of students described as economically disadvantaged (Doucette-Gates, 1990).

For this study, one school within the network was randomly selected. A sample of 50 male students who attended classes 50% or more of the time during the previous grading period was randomly selected from the student roster. Forty-seven students from a New York City alternative high school served as the actual subjects of this study. The original sample included 28 African American and 22 Hispanic males between the ages of 16 and 20 years of age (see Table 3.1). Three of the subjects disclosed during the interviews that they had been sent to this particular high school as part of a drug treatment program, so were not included in any of the analyses (African American, $n = 26$; Hispanic, $n = 21$). Eleven participants (23%) reported active membership in gangs, six participants (13%) indicated ongoing intermittent association with gang members or activities or both, and the remaining participants (64%) indicated no gang association or affiliation or both. Data regarding gang affiliation were collected as part of a self-report on the survey instrument. All research participants were compensated in the amount of $15 for their time. Participating adolescents were given the opportunity to sign assent. Parental concert was obtained passively.

All participants completed the following:

Demographic Measures (self-report)

Subject age

Family composition

SES indicators: parental education and occupation

Race and ethnicity: subject self-report

Psychological Scales (intact scales–survey)

General Well-Being (GWB) Scale: (Ware, Johnston, Davies-Avery, & Brook, 1979)

Anxiety Scale (GWB): (Ware et al., 1979)

Depression Scale (GWB): (Ware et al., 1979)

Self-Esteem Scale (RSE): (Rosenberg, 1965)

Psychological Scales (constructed scale–survey)
Victimization: subject's self-reported experiences of victimizing
    incidents
Drug and substance use: self-report of drug and alcohol use
Time (Attitude and Temporal Extension) Scales
The Time Attitude Scale: Semantic Differential Scale (TAS—Nuttin, 1985)
Motivational Induction Method (MIM): Sentence Completion Task
    (Nuttin, 1984, 1985)
In-Depth Interview

Survey: Scale Construction.   Scales were constructed by summing across
individual items. The Likert type item response choices permitted additiv-
ity without transformation for all scales (Likert, 1932). Survey items were
reviewed for directional consistency before the summation of scale items.
Reverse direction recoding was used in two instances: (1) to make all items
in a scale consistent for direction, either all positively worded or all negatively worded, so that individual items did not cancel each other out when
summed, and (2) when it was possible to scale items so that higher values
on the total scale reflect positive or more frequent aspects of the construct.

For the purposes of scale construction, the treatment of missing data on
individual items was as follows: (1) a subject was required to have valid
data on more than half the items in a scale to receive a score for the scale;
(2) the mean of valid values across scale items was multiplied by the total
number of items in the scale to arrive at scores for each subject within the
total range of the scale, with the subject's mean for valid values assigned to
any that were missing.

Association between Items and Scales.   An additional criterion was
imposed for constructed scales. When items factored into more than one
distinct scale, the association between the items had to approach orthog-
onality. Varimax rotation provided the initial conditions for meeting this
criterion. Items that straddle factors in the unrotated factor matrix cannot
always be clearly assigned to distinct factors after rotation and therefore
must rely on conceptual assumptions.

Scales were rejected if their correlation approached a ceiling calculated as
the product of their internal reliabilities ($R_{12} < \alpha_1\alpha_2$). This was to avoid the
problem of collinearity when scales are included in regression equations.
This will improve the stability of analyses involving scales factored from a
single pool of items.

Reliability for intact and constructed survey scales was measured using
Cronbach's Alpha as an estimate for internal consistency (Cronbach, Gleser,
Nanda, & Rajaratnam, 1972). Reliabilities for these scales ranged from .64
to .92.

The Time Attitude Scale (TAS). The TAS (Nuttin, 1985) is designed to measure both general and affective attitudes toward time. The TAS is composed of nine items measuring affective attitude toward time.

From time to time, reflection on the past and future invade our thoughts. It is assumed that remembrances of the past and expectations of the future have either positive or negative affective influence in our lives. A subject with an optimistic future orientation is more likely to pursue the goal and increase its probability than a subject with the same goal and a pessimistic orientation. Optimism is likely to intensify the subject's incentive to realize the goal. In addition to affective assessments of the past, present, and future, subjects are likely to experience other perceptions such as control or lack of control, excitement or boredom, freedom or boundaries when thinking about the past, present, or future.

The Affective Time Attitude Scale, based on Osgood's (Osgood, Suci, & Tannenbaum, 1957) semantic differential rating technique, uses nine bipolar pair of adjectives referring to the subject's motivational and affective attitude toward the past, present, and future. Each bipolar adjective pair corresponds to a seven-point scale ranging from very positive to very negative. For example, for the adjective pair *"hopeful–hopeless,"* the seven-scale points are *very hopeful, hopeful, rather hopeful, neither hopeful nor hopeless, rather hopeless, hopeless, very hopeless.* Subjects were asked to indicate on the scale how they spontaneously experience their past, present, and future. The past, present, and future stimuli were randomly ordered to control for the effects of presentation. In all, subjects completed three measures of the Affective Time Attitude Scale (past, present, future). Reliability for the TAS was measured using Cronbach's Alpha as an estimate for internal consistency is reported as .91, .90, and .88, respectively (for the past, the present, and the future). The Affective Time Attitude Scale required approximately 15 to 20 minutes to complete.

Motivational Induction Method (MIM): Sentence Completion Task. Future time perspective is measured using Nuttin's (1985) MIM sentence completion task. The MIM measures motivational or goal objects and their temporal location within the subject's lifespan. The MIM is composed of 30 sentence stems (motivational inducers) which include verbs expressing a tendency, an effort, desire, intention, activity, etc., for example, "I will be happy when . . . , I am doing my best to . . . , I hope. . . ." The subject responds by expressing an object of personal motivation. Inducers are both positive and negative. Subjects are asked to think of all the things they are interested in and told that grammatically correct sentences are not necessary. Each inducer is printed on a separate page to prevent the subject from comparing statements. The sentence stem completion task took approximately 25 minutes to complete. Table 3.2 provides examples of the sentence stems and some participant responses.

TABLE 3.2. Selected Participant Responses: Time Perspective Sentence Completion Task

I hope to
   graduate from high school, be successful
   be successful in a career
   become man of dreams working person, have a nice family
   make it good in life and be happy
   be rich
   go on to a better life
I intend to
   get myself straight off the drugs
   work, get married
   find myself dozing—getting high
   be like Donald Trump
I am striving (to or for)
   a Maxima car, going to work, taking son to school
   gold/platinum album, be a recording artist
   a chance in the real world
I will do everything possible to
   not get shot
   protect my family
   keep promises I make
   give my child a better life than I had
   destroy xxx's reputation
   go and retire and live life after I get married and have a family
I would not want
   to be a dropout
   a baby
   my life to end so soon
   anyone to steal from me
   to die of someone stealing from me for drugs
   to die
   the world to stay like this
   my Mother to die before I make it to the top and help her out
   total annihilation
I would not hesitate
   to break the law to get what I want

Coding Scheme for the MIM.   Responses were coded, as defined in the *Manual of Motivational Content Analysis* (Nuttin, 1985, pp. 133–176), for the object content and for the time frame in which each object would most likely occur in the lifespan of the subjects. The temporal localization of motivational objects is based on an average estimate for when the object or goal would likely occur for the subjects as a group. There are two components in establishing temporal location: (1) the time period in which the subject is presently located (adolescence) and (2) the time period in which the goal, aspiration, or desire would most likely be accomplished. For example, if the subject expressed, "*I will be happy when I graduate from high school*," the temporal distance is measured from the subject's present location, presently a high school student, to diploma completion, which for these subjects is expected within one to two years.

Temporal Extension.   Temporal extension, an overall disposition to focus on the past, the present, or the future was calculated as the *proportion* of motivational objects in the present social and immediate social future to the number of objects in the distant social future. Participant responses referencing life periods after the high school period were summed and coded as more distant future. Subject responses expressing the high school period and calendar periods up to a year were summed and coded as present and immediate future. Although some participants did respond to the sentence stems with references to the past, most responses focus on the present and the future. This is consistent with reported studies using this instrument.

Sometimes the motivational object cannot be explicitly located within a social period. Some subject responses were vague and unable to be precisely coded for specific life periods. For example, the following responses reference a motivational object that is expected to continue throughout the remainder of life, "*I hope to succeed in life*" or "*I wish to be happy*." Responses that are unable to be coded as specific social life periods, such as those mentioned above, are coded as *open-present*. Open-present responses were not included in the calculation of the proportional index of temporal distance.

Motivational Objects: Future Time.   In addition to temporal extension, the MIM offers four overriding broad categories to code motivational objects referenced in the sentence stem completions of each participant. These categories are as follows:

(1) *Self*: physical, personality, psychological, social characteristics, career goals
   Example: ... to be independent, ... to be happy
(2) *Social contact—other people*: referring to interpersonal contact and reciprocity between the subject and others
   Example: ... to marry my girlfriend, ... to have a lot of friends
(3) *Natural and man-made material objects—possessions*: the role and importance these objects have in the subject's life circumstances
   Example: ... to be able to travel and see new things, ... to have a new BMW
(4) *Cognitive and conceptual realities*: cognitive, career skills, ideological, political, religious activities, values, justice, independence
   Example: ... to find the meaning of life, ... to understand things better

Motivational objects can also be coded for specific properties of the objects themselves. Although aggressive and destructive inclination are seldom expressed in the literature (Nuttin, 1985), they were evident in the data yielded by this study. Codes were developed for motivational object responses that expressed destructive motivational objects, as well as for motivational objects of a conflicting and avoiding nature. Examples of these coding categories with actual participant responses are provided below:

(1) *Destructive Objects*: expressed aggressive and destructive tendencies of a volitional nature. Aggressive tendencies can be directed toward the self or at others.
   Example: I would not hesitate to break the law to get what I need.
   Example: I will do everything to destroy xxx's reputation.

(2) *Conflicting Objects*: expressed objects that are in opposition.
   Example: I very much hope to win the lottery, even though I don't buy tickets.

(3) *Avoidant Objects*: expressed avoidance, for example, instead of expressing, "I hope to succeed," the subject states, "I hope not to fail."
   Example: I hope not to fail the math test. I want to not be without money in this world.

The interrater reliability for the coding of motivational content and estimating temporal location using the kappa coefficient was .92 and .79 for coders A and B, respectively. These kappa coefficients indicate acceptable reliability across coders.

The MIM is not designed as a motivational test or as a measure of the strength of motivational tendencies. It is intended to generate a sample of representative objects for a group of subjects that initiate or influence behavior (Nuttin, 1985). The MIM assumes that subjects are able to know and express concrete goals and aspirations, and that goals and aspirations affect behavior (Allport, 1961). This is not to deny the possibility that subjects might express the direct opposite of what they are able and willing to do (Argyris & Schön, 1978).

Socially desirable responses are a consideration in any research study when the researchers are perceived by the subjects as potentially more powerful or socially and culturally different or both. It is, however, reasonable to believe that the same inhibitors preventing the subject from saying what he really wishes, desires, etc., might in reality prevent him from acting on those wishes or desires (Nuttin, 1985). Social desirability is in itself a motivational aspect of behavior. Validity of the MIM should therefore not be solely judged on the strength of the correspondence between goals, desires, aspirations, and actual behavior. Furthermore, as this measure is not intended to disclose the psychodynamic properties of expressed motivational objects, the assumption that verbally expressed goals and aspirations impact behavior serves as face validity for this measure.

Internal consistency serves as a reliability measure of the MIM. If sentence stems are designed to generate motivational objects, then consistency in completing different sentence stems in the task is a reasonable index of the measurement accuracy of the measure. As the subjects receive only one measure, the 30 sentence stems were divided into two equivalent halves. Particular attention was paid to the intensity of the verbs and the direction (positive or negative) of the sentence stem inducers. Reliability estimates from single test administrations, in which equivalent halves form the units on which an analysis is based, have increasingly used an analysis of variance approach (Thorndike, 1982). Internal consistency for the MIM motivational objects and temporal location was determined using this approach. After dividing the sentence stems, a two-sample median nonparametric analysis of variance test (appropriate for frequency data) was used to determine the consistency or homogeneity of the measure. No significant differences in response distribution across categories were found for the motivational objects or temporal periods.

The hypotheses for this study are expressed in terms of the strength of association, the degree of relationship among the variables under investigation. An initial examination of the variables revealed unimodal distributions. No extreme skewness was noted. Overall, *future time* orientation was measured as a proportion. The data was arc transformed to stabilize the variance associated with proportional data, prior to any analyses (Box & Cox, 1964; Carroll & Ruppert, 1984).

The nonsignificant Chi-Square indicates that gang affiliation/association and future time perspective for this sample are independent. There is no significant relationship between temporal perspective between gang-affiliated and nongang-affiliated youth (see Figure 3.1). It is interesting to note that the highest proportion of participant responses centered around immediate (up to the next three months) and near future (more than three months to the end of the high school period) time periods.

It was assumed that more positive *temporal attitudes* toward the past, present, and future would be associated with extended time perspective. The relationship between the attitude toward future time and future time perspective for positive psychological functioning has been documented in the literature (Blakeley, 1991; Khomik & Kronik, 1988; Melges & Bowlby, 1969). Contrary to expected results, temporal affective attitudes were not significantly related to future time perspective (see Table 3.3). The correlation between attitude toward past time and future time perspective approached significance (γ_{12} $-.2191$) in a negative direction raising the question of whether unpleasant memories of the past may in fact promote an individual to look toward the future.

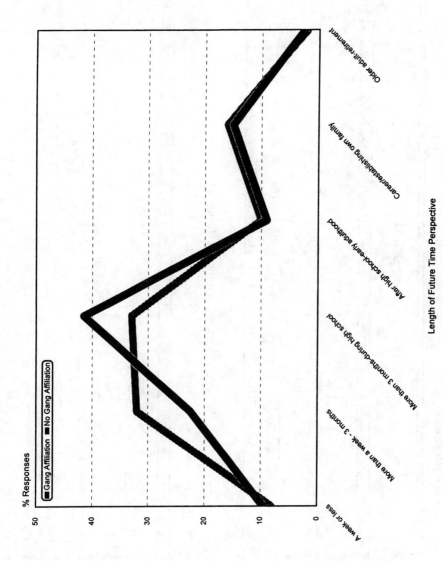

FIGURE 3.1. Future Time Perspective Profiles: Gang and Nongang-Affiliated Youth

TABLE 3.3. Correlation Coefficients

CORRELATION COEFFICIENTS

	GANGSR	SETOT	DEPRESSN	ANXIETY	VICTIM	USER	PAST	PRESENT	FUTURE	GENPAST	GENPRES	GENFUTRE
GANGSR	1.0000											
SETOT	-.1108	1.0000										
DEPRESSN	.2231	-.5814**	1.0000									
ANXIETY	.1735	-.3970*	.7341**	1.0000								
VICTIM	.1100	-.3467*	.3967*	.5610**	1.0000							
USER	-.1879	.1691	-.4321**	-.4736**	-.6583**	1.0000						
FUTURE	.2663	.2323	-.0146	-.0123	-.5134**	.3047	-.2499	-.9140**	1.0000			
GENPAST	-.2795	.3336	-.4046*	-.3245	.0671	-.0526	.0771	.1887	-.2191	1.0000		
GENPRES	-.0715	.2934	-.3536*	-.2374	-.0676	-.1019	.0727	.1050	-.0624	.2399	1.0000	
GENFUTRE	.0505	.3790*	-.5579**	.3768*	.2048	.0265	.0280	-.0738	.0321	.2494	.6017**	1.0000

*. Signif. LE .05   **. Signif. LE .01   (2-tailed)

PARTIAL CORRELATION COEFFICIENTS

Controlling for... GANG Membership

	SETOT	DEPRESSN	ANXIETY	VICTIM	USER	PAST	PRESENT	FUTURE	GENPAST	GENPRES	GENFUTRE
SETOT	1.0000										
DEPRESSN	-.5778**	1.0000									
ANXIETY	-.4094*	.7193**	1.0000								
VICTIM	-.3083	.3798*	.5882**	1.0000							
USER	.1311	-.3462*	-.4444**	-.6736**	1.0000						
FUTURE	.2353	-.0203	.0011	-.5418**	.3538*	-.3328	-.9417**	1.0000			
GENPAST	.2776	-.2694	-.1652	.1727	-.2207	.1864	.2265	-.2573	1.0000		
GENPRES	.3325	-.5654**	-.3953*	-.0830	.0276	.0326	-.0056	.0019	.3189	1.0000	
GENFUTRE	.4042*	-.5961**	-.3970*	-.2242	.0208	.0241	-.0525	.0245	27.69	.7957**	1.0000

*. Signif. LE .05   **. Signif. LE .01   (2-tailed)

Shading indicates change in strength of association.

SETOT: Self-esteem; DEPRESSN: Depression; ANXIETY: Anxiety; VICTIM: Victimization; USER: Drug Use; FUTURE: Future Time Perspective; GENPAST, GENPRES, GENFUTRE: Temporal attitude toward the past, present, future.

Associations between Future Time Perspective, Adverse Social Experience, and Mental Health.   Adverse social conditions were assumed to be inversely correlated with future time perspective and positive temporal attitudes. Furthermore, adverse social conditions were assumed to be associated with conflicting or destructive motivational objects.

The victimization and drug use scales contained in the survey were used as approximate measures of adverse social experiences. These survey scales query subjects concerning the frequency of their experience of theft, sexual abuse or harassment, physical attack, perceived threats to their person or property, and personal use of controlled substances. Two subjects expressed the following:

> It hasn't been going too well, but I been shot once already this year and it threw me off course and I lost a lot of weight and you know things haven't been going too good but maybe next year, you know after the summer goes by and I can set my priorities and I can come back here and make the grade as people would say. (Michael, a 16-year-old African American male from New York City)

> The schools are really fucked up and the security guards too. Right now they are trying to get rid of all the security guards to bring in new ones 'cause the old security guards let certain types of kids do certain kinds of things that they had to do to earn money in the school ... you know what I mean, weapons and drugs ... they just let them go. (Joey, a 19-year-old Latino male from the Bronx)

The victimization and drug use scales are coded as follows: higher scores indicate increased exposure to violence, assault, crime, and threats, and more frequent drug use by subjects. As expected, future time perspective was negatively correlated with victimization (τ_{12} −.5134, $p < .01$). Specifically, subjects with less frequent exposure to victimization (threats, violence, harassment) expressed higher frequencies of extended future time. This relationship remains constant when controlling for gang affiliation/association (τ_{12} −.5418, $p < .01$). Drug use approached but did not reach significance at the .05 level (τ_{12} .3047) for the total sample. However, when controlling for gang association drug use was positively associated with temporal perspective ($\tau_{12.3}$ .3538, $p < .05$) indicating that gang-affiliated youth with more extended future time perspective were more likely to use drugs (see Table 3.3).

Mental health measures of depression and anxiety were included in this study because gang affiliation is often considered from a model of psychosocial pathology in terms of social deviance and coping skills. Mental health status was measured using the depression and anxiety subscales of the General Well-Being Scale (Ware et al., 1979) and the Rosenberg (1965) Self-Esteem Inventory. It is important to note that the depression or anxiety scores for both gang and nongang-affiliated youth did not fall within clinical ranges. Consistent with other reported studies, depression was negatively associated with attitude toward the past (γ_{12} $-.4064$, $p < .05$). When controlling for gang affiliation, this relationship, although in the same direction, was no longer significant ($\gamma_{12.3}$ $-.2694$). Depression was also positively associated with anxiety independent of gang affiliation. The comorbidity of depression and anxiety is strongly cited in the adolescent mental health literature. The experience of victimization also had significant correspondence with depression for all participants, indicating that depression increases with increases in the experience of victimization. Interestingly, drug use is inversely associated with depression (γ_{12} $-.4321$, $p < .01$; $\gamma_{12.3}$ $.3462$, $p < .05$), indicating that youth reporting increased levels of depression are also reporting higher levels of self-reported drug use. This leaves open to question whether drug use offers some anesthetizing protection against depression. This relationship, although still significant, is less so for gang-affiliated youth.

As expected, self-esteem was significantly associated with lower levels of self-reported depression and anxiety, as well as more positive attitudes about the future. More exposure to the experience of victimization significantly decreased self-esteem for nongang-affiliated youth (γ_{12} $-.3467$, $p < .05$). However, this relationship was no longer significant for gang-affiliated youth (γ_{12} $.3083$), suggesting that gang membership may offer some protective psychological strategies for managing the experience of being victimized.

Associations between Nonpositive Motivational Objects and Future Time Perspective and Adverse Social Experiences. Adverse social experiences were assumed to be associated with higher frequencies of destructive and avoidant motivational objects expressed in the sentence completion task measuring future time perspective. Destructive motivational objects were found among the subject responses in this study, even though they are not typically expected responses as noted in the literature (Nuttin, 1985). Three significant relationships were found. Positive temporal affective attitude toward the future was significantly correlated in a positive direction with frequency of destructive motivational objects (γ_{12} $.7197$, $p < .001$). This is an interesting and unexpected finding, implying that for these research participants, temporal affective attitude can have both a negative or positive motivational consequence. In other words, the ability for subjects to perceive the future in no way dictates the value placed on the future or the expected outcomes. Optimistic futures may not be grounded in the social reality of many of these subjects. A significant Chi-Square ($X^2 = 6.2276$, $df = 1$, $p = .0126$) indicates that the expression of destructive motivational objects and gang affiliation/association for this sample are not independent (see Figure 3.2). The likelihood of a subject falling into a given

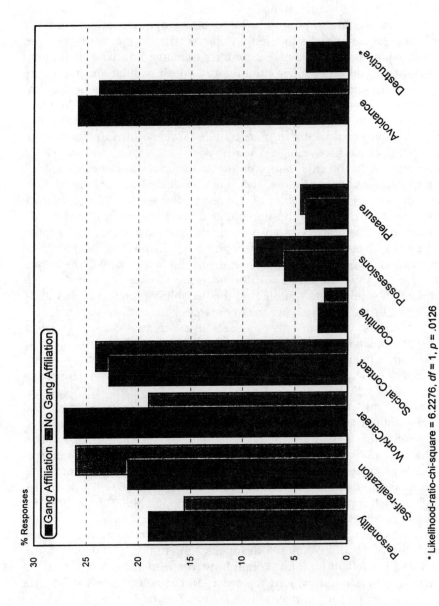

FIGURE 3.2. Motivational Objects: Future Time Perspective

* Likelihood-ratio-chi-square = 6.2276, $df = 1$, $p = .0126$

cell (race/ethnicity × family composition) is a product of the relationship between gang affiliation and destructive motivational objects rather than of marginal probabilities. Avoidant motivational objects and gang affiliation were not significantly correlated.

It is also interesting to note that the highest proportion of the sentence stem completion responses focused on objects that were related to career, self-realization, and social contact. Contrary to many intuitive beliefs about gang-affiliated and other inner-city minority youth populations, the desire for possessions and pleasure (having fun, etc.) were among the least mentioned motivational objects. Cognitive objects were least likely to be mentioned. This is not surprising since most of the participants described several experiences of school failure in more traditional schools before enrolling in this network of alternative high schools.

In keeping with the exploratory nature of this investigation, metric scaling (multidimensional scaling—MDS) was conducted to examine the relationships among the variables of interest to the study and the salience of these relationships for both gang-affiliated and nongang-affiliated youth. MDS arranges data points (variables) in geometric space so that the distance between two data points has the strongest relationship. For example, two points closest in geometric space have strong similarity, while two distant points are dissimilar in nature. MDS models are typically two or three dimensional. It is important to note that the variables of interest to this study (temporal attitude, temporal perspective, depression, anxiety, victimization, drug use, self-esteem, destructive motivation) are treated as a set of objects.

For these analyses, gang affiliation was dichotomized. Youth reporting strong gang affiliation and some youth reporting some association with gang activities were combined. Replicated MDS (RMDS) was conducted using matrix data for gang and nongang-affiliated youth. The basic assumption of this statistical procedure is that both data matrices (gang and nongang-affiliated youth) are the same except for error associated with systematic response bias. A two-dimensional and three-dimensional solution was ALSCAL (SPSS—Norusis, 1990). The fit indices indicate that the three-dimensional model fits somewhat better than the two-dimensional model (three-dimensional model: S-stress = .03386, Stress = .06835, R^2 = .98816; two-dimensional model: S-stress = .05042, Stress = .08007, R^2 = .98413). The model fits the data fairly well but not perfectly (see Figure 3.3).

An examination of the stimulus coordinates indicates some difference in the salience of the three dimensions for gang and nongang-affiliated youth. Dimension 1 is salient for both groups; however, Dimension 3 is less salient for youth with gang affiliations. Likewise, Dimension 2 is less salient for youth reporting no gang affiliation (see Figures 3.4 and 3.5). Figures 3.4 and 3.5 illustrate a two-dimensional representation of the salient dimensions for both gang and nongang-affiliated youth.

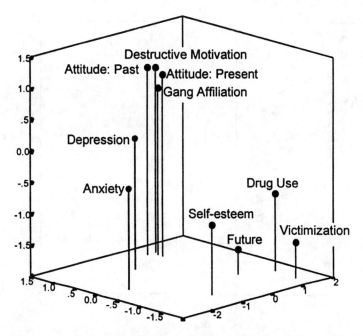

Fit Indices: S-stress = .03386   Stress = .06835   RSQ = .98816

FIGURE 3.3. Three-Dimensional Stimulus Space

Figure 3.4 illustrates the close proximity of the desire for destructive objects and attitudes toward the past indicating a high degree of similarity for
gang-affiliated youth. The lack of distance suggests that for gang-affiliated
youth, temporal attitude toward the past and present and the desire for destructive motivational objects are closely related. Gang involvement may be
mediated by early adverse experiences and that intervention may be more
effective if directed at prevention rather than ameliorating the outcomes of
gang participation once the youth are involved. There is greater distance between depression and present time perspective. One way to interpret these
data is to consider that gang affiliation may support psychological needs for
youth in adverse environments.

Figure 3.5 depicts similar patterns for nongang-affiliated youth regarding
the proximity between temporal attitude toward the past and the desire for
destructive objectives. Temporal attitude toward the present is less proxi-
mate to attitude toward the past and destructive objectives for nongang-
affiliated youth. There is also a notable increase in the distance between
anxiety and future time perspective for nongang-affiliated youth. There is
also a notable increase in the distance between anxiety and future time

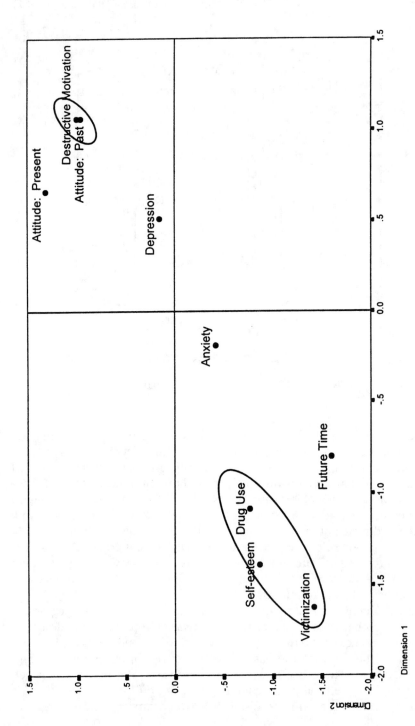

FIGURE 3.4. Salient-Dimensional Space: Active Gang Affiliation

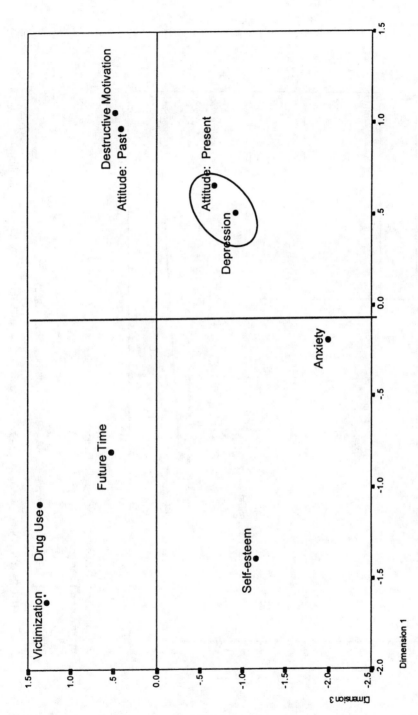

FIGURE 3.5. Salient-Dimensional Space: No Active Gang Affiliation

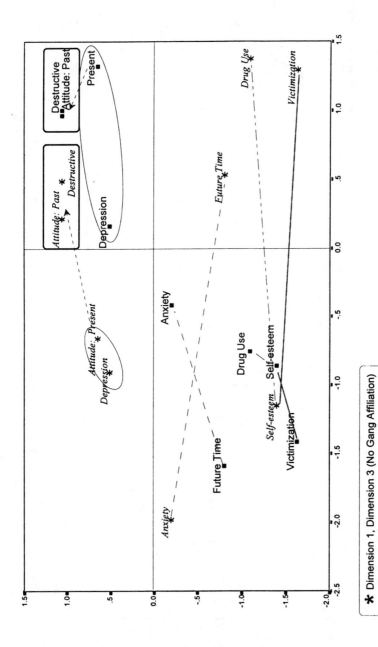

Fit Indices (three dimension): S-stress = .03386   Stress = .06835   RSQ = .98816

FIGURE 3.6. Dimensional-Space Overlay: Active Gang Affiliation—No Active Gang Affiliation

perspective for nongang-affiliated youth than for their gang-affiliated counterparts. Interview data reveal that for gang-affiliated youth concern regarding retaliation and random violence is considerable—"*You can't trust nobody. They all want what you got,*" states Ron, a 17-year-old African American. Additionally, given the increased potential for violence associated with initiation processes, expressions of gang loyalty, and intergang rivalries, it is reasonable to consider that anxiety levels might be somewhat higher for gang-affiliated youth.

Figure 3.6 illustrates the overlap plot of Dimension 1 and Dimension 3 (nongang) and Dimension 1 and Dimension 2 (gang) coordinates. It is interesting to note differences in distances between gang and nongang-affiliated youth for specific sets of variables. For example, Figure 3.6 illustrates relatively little distance between self-esteem and drug use for gang-affiliated youth, but much greater distance for nongang-affiliated youth for these variables, leaving open to question the role of drug use in maintaining self-esteem for gang-affiliated youth. These is considerable difference in the proximity of self-esteem and the experience of victimization for nongang-affiliated youth as compared with the closeness of these variables for their gang-affiliated counterparts. Interview data from this study and statements from gang-affiliated youth in the media often reflect a significant value placed on receiving respect. The correlation between self-esteem and the experience of victimization is significant for the entire sample but is no longer significant when controlling for gang membership. This finding implies that gang affiliation may support a sense of self-esteem in the presence of victimization, in that other gang members are likely to retaliate against suspected perpetrators of indiscretions against individual members of their gang. Another interesting difference noted in Figure 3.6 is the increased distance between depression and temporal attitude toward the present for gang-affiliated youth compared with their nongang-affiliated counterparts. As suggested previously, gang membership may provide psychological support for youth experiencing adverse social conditions.

☐ Conclusion

Little has also changed concerning remedies for gang organization and behavior. Gangs continue to be perceived as by-products of troubled neighborhoods. Interventions continue to take two strategies: socialization and removal (see Abdullah and Branch, this volume). Socialization interventions are best illustrated by community outreach workers and athletic and cultural programs. The focus is on the gang members as an attempt to save the gang participant from himself or herself. Our continued focus of the deviant youth without consideration of the surrounding social environment will not move our efforts to support youth in a productive direction. Youth growing up in neighborhoods with little opportunity for meaningful and engaging work have no *conventional* referent point for organizing and scheduling their lives and limited means of achieving self-supported adulthood.

An ecological approach (Bronfenbrenner, 1979) is needed to begin to understand the cumulative effects of exposure to adverse social conditions. Community-based programs must begin to replace the remedial approach of outsiders trying to fix inner-city neighborhoods. Research needs to focus on how various aspects of gang membership and youth subculture are filling psychological, emotional, and social needs of inner-city youth. A focus on resilience as well as longitudinal designs are also needed to adequately inform our thinking on youth behavior and gang membership. Perhaps most important, youth must be given a participating voice in working toward more adaptive and positive solutions.

The second strategy sets out to remove the gang organization or as many members as possible from the community. The Federal Weed and Seed program—*weed* component is perhaps the best example of this tactic. Emphasis is placed on police surveillance and community education. Despite the Federal government's commitment to Weed and Seed, little is known of its effectiveness across diverse communities. If we believe that gang identity and solidarity is strengthened by conflict with outsiders, surveillance tactics may have the unintended effects of reinforcing the very behaviors and activities we wish to ameliorate.

Little attention is focused on the supportive structures gang membership may offer in the midst of social adversity and grim futures (see Gonzalez, this volume). Often, the links between interventions focus on literacy, career development and training, neighborhood clean-up activities, and community-level economic development and are not acknowledged as target attempts toward preventing or ameliorating or both the problems associated with youth violence and gang affiliation.

Although admittedly there is much to learn concerning gang membership and organization, more attention needs to be directed toward an appropriate mixture of quantitative and qualitative methodologies. Researchers have approached gangs as aberrant and pathological groups, as well as, although admittedly with much less intensity, legitimate forms of human association that demonstrate resiliency in the midst of social adversity. We tend to associate prevention and intervention successes with demographic statistics reflecting the level of community violence in terms of youth homicides, felony crimes, and number of incarcerated youth. A focus on more subtle relationships such as truancy, school attendance, increases in grade performance, and their relationship to increased community employment in nonsecondary labor markets might better serve as a barometer of success—success that might be replicable in some or many dimensions.

There is inconsistency regarding our fear of youth gangs and our willingness to capitalize on their commercial value. The social isolation of inner-city neighborhoods and the current commercialization of gang culture is an example of this interesting dichotomy. Although gangs are considered an organization to fear, to remedy, to remove, etc., they are also strongly associated with contemporary mainstream commercial activity (see Gonzalez, this volume). Gang members purchase silk-screened T-shirts, jackets, and embroidered emblems and customize and stylize automobiles, etc. They rely on neighborhood merchants and in some instances provide substantial income to these vendors.

The cultural products of gangs have been appropriate by mainstream commercial industries as well. Examples are homeboy lettering appearing on rock album covers during the 1980s and 1990s and gang graffiti appearing in rock videos. MTV has bridged gang culture with national television audiences. Rap and hip hop music represent further commercialization of gang culture. A recent rap CD by Kool Moe Dee featured a BK monogram (athletic shoes—British Knights) standing in front of a jeep with the front tire resting on a red bandanna. Within the gang culture, one could interpret this symbolism as disrespect to the Bloods, a well-known and established gang. The BK monogram can easily be interpreted to signify "Blood Killer." The hand signals of Los Angeles and other southwestern gangs are taken from the deaf alphabet. Graffiti and gang cultural artifacts may well serve as a barometer of gang activity and furthermore as an indicator of changing patterns of allegiances.

While we struggle to create policy to control gang activity, we simultaneously celebrate its commercial appeal. The statement of Larry, a 17-year-old African-American male survivor of gunshot wounds, who states, "*Nobody wants to see you or recognize you*," is inconsistent with the commercial prosperity of gang culture—a culture we at the same time attempt to assuage.

If left to their own cognitive resources many inner-city adolescents, like those described in this chapter, would say they have no future beyond the present. The long history of failures and complicated social demands that stretch beyond their personal and familial resources attribute to such feelings of a lack of self-efficacy. Schools often contribute to this feeling of pessimism in a variety of ways. Helping hopeless and depressed young people develop a new approach to their relationship with the social systems is an enormous task. It is, however, a behavioral objective, which means offering some level of resocialization with enough success that schools continue to be invested in the process. Social agencies (i.e., schools, courts, community organizations) must be committed to this type of interaction if there is any hope for overcoming our current problems with gangs and violence among adolescents.

The next section of this book is devoted to specialized agency-based interventions. A number of viewpoints, some at variance with others offered in this volume, are presented. Perhaps the greatest position articulated by these chapters is the idea that a multifaceted approach (i.e., educational, social service, law enforcement) is necessary because the gang problem is multidimensional.

☐ References

Allport, G. W. (1961). *Pattern and growth in personality*. New York: Holt.

Argyris, C., & Schön, D. A. (1978). *Theory in practice: Increasing professional effectiveness*. San Francisco, CA: Jossey-Bass.

Blakeley, T. A. (1991). Orientation in time: Implications for psychopathology and psychotherapy. *American Journal of Clinical Hypothesis, 34*(2), 100–110.

Bloom-Feshbach, S., Bloom-Feshbach, J., & Heller, K. (1982). Work, family and children's perceptions of the world. In S. B. Kamerman & C. D. Hayes (Eds.), *Families that work: Children in a changing world*. Washington, DC: National Academy Press.

Box, G. E. P., & Cox, D. R. (1964). An analysis of transformations revisited: Rebuttal. *Journal of the American Statistical Association, 17*, 209–210.

Bronfenbrenner, U. (1979). *The ecology of human development*. Cambridge, MA: Harvard University Press.

Carroll, R. J., & Ruppert, D. (1984). Power transformation when fitting theoretical models to data. *Journal of the American Statistical Association, 79*, 321–328.

Cottle, T. J., & Klineberg, S. L. (1974). *The present of things future: Explorations of time in human experience*. New York: The Free Press.

Cronbach, L., Gleser, H., Nanda, H., & Rajaratnam, N. (1972). *The dependability of behavioral measurement: Theory of generalizability for scores and profiles*. New York: Wiley.

DeVolder, M., & Lens, W. (1982). Academic achievement and future time perspective as a cognitive motivational concept. *Journal of Personality and Social Psychology, 42*, 566–571.

Doucette-Gates, A. (1990, December). *The urban adolescent: Influences on the formation of occupational identity*. Paper presented at the Annual meeting of the American Vocational Association, Cincinnati, Ohio.

Doucette-Gates, A. (1992). Concept of self as learner and temporal perspective: Associations with school failure among racial and ethnic minority male high school students. (Doctoral dissertation, Columbia University). *Dissertation Abstracts International, 53*(09), 4974B.

Estes, W. K. (1972). Reinforcement in human behavior. Reward and punishment influence actions via informational and cybernetic processes. *American Scientist, 60*, 723–729.

Khomik, V. S., & Kronik, A. A. (1988). Attitude to time: Psychological aspects of early alcohol addiction and deviant behavior. *Voprosy Psikhologii, 1*, 98–106.

Klaus, A. (1987). Die Fahigkeit zur lebensplanung schuljugendlicher [The ability to plan for life in young students]. *Psychologie fur die Praxis*, (Supplement), 66–78.

Lewin, K. (1931). Sachlichkeit und Zwang in der Erziehung zur Realitat. *Die Neue Erziehung, 2*, 99–103.

Lewin, K. (1935). *A dynamic theory of personality*. Selected papers. New York: McGraw–Hill.

Likert, R. (1932). A technique for the measurement of attitudes. *Archives of Psychology*, No. 140.

Melges, F. T., & Bowlby, J. (1969). Types of hopelessness in psychological process. *Archives of General Psychiatry, 20*, 690–699.

Norusis, M. J. (1990). *SPSS for windows professional statistics release 6.0*. Chicago: SPSS Inc.

Nurmi, J. E. (1989). Planning, motivation, and evaluation in orientation to the future: A latent structure analysis. *Scandinavian Journal of Psychology, 30*, 64–71.

Nuttin, J. (1984). *Motivation. planning, and action: A relational theory of human behavior dynamics.* Hillsdale, NJ: Erlbaum.

Nuttin, J. (1985). *Future time perspective and motivation: Theory and research method.* Hillsdale, NJ: Erlbaum.

Osgood, C. E., Suci, G. J., & Tannenbaum, P. H. (1957). *The measurement of meaning.* Urbana, IL: The University of Illinois Press.

Padilla, F. (1992). *The gang as an American enterprise.* New Brunswick, NJ: Rutgers University Press.

Paulter, K. J., & Lewko, J. H. (1987). Children's and adolescent's views of the work world in times of economic uncertainty. *New Directions in Child Development, 35*, 21–31.

Raynor, J. O. (1969). Future orientation and motivation of immediate activity: An elaboration of the theory of achievement motivation. *Psychological Review, 76*, 606–610.

Raynor, J. O., & Entin, E. E. (1982). *Motivation, career striving, and aging.* New York: NY: McGraw–Hill.

Raynor, J. O., & Entin, E. E. (1983). The function of future orientation as a determinant of human behavior in step-path theory of action. *International Journal of Psychology, 18*, 463–487.

Rosenberg, M. (1965). *Society and adolescent self image.* Princeton, NJ: Princeton University Press.

Thorndike, R. L. (1982). Applied psychometrics. Boston, MA: Houghton Mifflin.

Thrasher, F. L. (1927). *The gang: A study of 1303 gangs in Chicago.* Chicago: University of Chicago Press.

Tolman, E. C. (1932). Purposive behavior in animals and men. New York: The Century Co.

Von Klemper, B. S. (1980). Formal thought, future time perspective and planning (Doctoral dissertation, Rutgers University–The State University of New Jersey, 1980). *Dissertation Abstracts International, 41*, 04A.

Ware, J. E., Johnston, S. A., Davies-Avery, A., & Brook, R. H. (1979, December). *Conceptualization and measurement of health for adults. In Health Insurance Study: Vol. III, Mental Health* (Report No. NOR-1987/3-HEW). Santa Monica, CA: The Rand Corporation.

Wilson, W. J. (1987). *The truly disadvantaged: The inner-city, the underclass, and the public policy.* Chicago: University of Chicago Press.

Wilson, W. J. (1991). Studying inner-city social dislocations: The challenge of public agenda research. *American Sociological Review, 56*, 1–14.

PART

II

SPECIALIZED
AGENCY-BASED
INTERVENTIONS

In this section, four authors have explored issues relevant to the development of intervention programs to help gang-affiliated adolescents. The approaches used by the authors draw on their expertise as practitioners in educational and correctional settings. Each of the presentations talks about specific issues unique to the work setting in which the author functions as a professional.

The first chapter in this section by Abdullah and Branch comments on the history of the Denver Probation Department and its efforts to provide services to the juvenile court in the interest of gang-affiliated adolescents. The brief history of gangs as they exist in Denver seems to point out two types of gang legacies. The first concerns outside influence and how it has migrated and permeated the Denver community. Because of the arrival of Los Angeles-based gangs, many members of the community were at a loss as to what could be done to stymie the proliferation of gang activity. Some have interpreted this lack of action early in the expansion of the gangs into the Denver community as evidence of denial. Specifically some writers and activists noted that as gang graffiti started to appear in the Denver community, many individuals were reluctant to accept this as a prognostic sign that gangs from other locations were starting to relocate to the city.

Abdullah and Branch suggest that the proliferation of gangs in the Denver community happened so quickly that agencies charged with providing corrective and preventative services to adolescents and their families were ill-prepared. In the chapter contained in this volume, they also note that the arrival of gangs from other communities meant the introduction of ethnic cultural norms in a hybrid form that did not exist in the Denver community. Such an introduction created a sociological problem that further compromised the ability of local agencies to deal with the gang problem.

The second type of gang activity noted to have occurred in Denver over the past 10 to 12 years is a variation on the local gangs, primarily in the Latino neighborhood, that have existed in the community for a number of years. While the gangs have existed in the community as a part of the social fabric of the community, they have not, until very recently, been identified as a major disrupter to the otherwise harmonious relationships that are perceived to exist within the city.

In talking about the influence of outsiders and the mutations on local culture that have presented themselves as local gangs, Abdullah and Branch note that often the gangs are divided by themselves and others along racial and ethnic lines. This pattern of self-selection and division is one that is noted throughout much of the sociological and criminology literature on gangs. It has been noted by some writers that gangs organize themselves along racial and ethnic lines as a way of fortifying themselves against outside influences, even within their local community. Perhaps the most noted example of such purification or setting of limits to keep others out has occurred among the skinheads. They are committed to racial purity and have as a major objective the elimination of all people of color and gay and lesbian individuals. It is interesting to note also that in commenting on the racial and ethnic theme among gangs, Abdullah and Branch do not specifically address the issue of skinheads. However, in another publication, Branch (1997) notes that it has not been until very recently that skinheads have been considered by the Denver media and law enforcement community to be a gang. Rather, historically they have been identified as a "loosely knit organization of young people." It seems that such selective nonuse of the term gangs, especially when the behavior in question clearly matches gang-like behavior, is another example of denial.

In their chapter, Abdullah and Branch briefly discuss the range of services that have been provided by the probation department in an attempt to help the juvenile court effectively provide services to gang-affiliated youth. Programs that have been organized by the probation department include a boot camp, a family intervention project, and ongoing intense supervision of adjudicated adolescents. This range of services represents an interesting array of approaches to the "gang problem." The more traditional boot camp approach, militaristic in nature, seems to have grown out of a belief that what gang adolescents need is some sense of firmness and rigidity of boundaries. It is interesting, if not troubling, that what many planners of such programs have failed to acknowledge is the absence of structure and consistent requirements in the lives of gang adolescents as being a major causative factor for their problems in the here and now. It seems somewhat naive to believe that simply introducing structure and high levels of demands will help troubled adolescents overcome their proclivity for antisocial behavior. This approach also is predicated on a belief that the problems many gang adolescents experience are the result of willful acts in which they disregard prevailing social conventions. Overlooked in this approach is the possibility that many of the adolescents involved in gangs are experiencing internal psychological problems that perhaps would be most responsive to another type of mental health or socialization orientation other than "tough love."

The Family Intervention Program described by Abdullah and Branch represents another orientation that has found expression among probation department workers over the years. It is predicated on a mental health model of multiple family therapy. This incorporation of mental health services within the probation department was a revolutionary and bold act at the time that it occurred. The work completed during the Family Intervention Program was done by local mental health providers who consulted with the court and probation department about what types of things needed to happen for families after their initial involvement with the program. Abdullah and Branch note that, in the early stages, there was much skepticism among probation and court personnel regarding the Family Intervention Program. Those who were opposed to this approach argued that the court and probation departments were charged with rendering justice and supervision, not providing supportive services that more appropriately should be handled by mental health and social work personnel. However, the creation of the Family Intervention Program did stimulate some discussion among individuals working with families and gang members regarding the limits of what can and cannot be included in programs sponsored by the justice system. This discussion and resulting reexamination of the roles of the probation department were seen as being highly instrumental in recognizing the limitations of a very linear and narrowly defined approach to working with families.

The final approach that Abdullah and Branch describe is one of intense supervision. This approach requires that members of the probation department are involved with gang members on a rather frequent basis. Supervision in this case means monitoring of all of the young person's activities, school and community, in an ongoing way. This approach is somewhat different from the more distal involvement that probation departments have historically had with gang adolescents. Central to the intense supervision approach is a monitoring of a young person's attendance and participation in school or employment activities or both. The relative importance of school in the lives of delinquent adolescents has often been diminished by professionals because of an unfounded belief that delinquents, more specifically gang members, are not interested in educational pursuits. There is, however, a small body of literature that suggests such to be not the case. Branch and Rennick (1996) have shown that in a suburban school district there was heavy representation of gang adolescents. They note that the individuals who voluntarily identified themselves as gang members attended school at roughly the same level as other students in the school and could not be easily identified by outsiders based on their behavioral and educational profile.

The work of the Denver Probation Department with gang adolescents and their families appears to be multifaceted. This inclusion of diverse approaches suggests that the planners are aware that there is no unidimensional program that can meet most of the needs of adjudicated adolescents. Indeed, the variety of programs discussed by Abdullah and Branch also suggests that there is a flexibility among program planners in the Denver Probation Department who note the need for new directions periodically as the manifestations of gang behavior also take new directions. Last, the range of services offered by the Denver Probation Department suggests that the department itself has been engaged in some level of self-evaluation and is continuously flexible regarding what it needs to do to increase its effectiveness with the young people whom it serves.

The role of the school as a social institution in the lives of gang adolescents and their families is nowhere more apparent than in the chapter by Lorita Foster. She begins by commenting on the impact of deaths on the lives of young people. Foster offers a personal revelation in commenting on students and former students who were killed in a brief period from 1990 to 1993. She notes that the loss of each of these students had a profound impact on her life. In making that observation, she also wonders how the losses impacted her current students. This was the beginning of her observations about the cycle of repeated exposure to violence and death and how it impacts the psychological functioning of individuals. That set of observations and curiosity led Foster to do more reading on the well-documented syndrome of post-traumatic stress disorder (PTSD). In researching PTSD as a possible consequence of continual exposure to violence and death, Foster noted that the absolute use of the psychiatric information associated with the disorder is beyond her level of professional expertise. However, despite that limitation, Foster noted that the PTSD syndrome, as described in the *Diagnostic and Statistical Manual of Mental Disorders* (DSM-IV-R), closely matched behavioral presentations she observed among her students. To test whether there was something she could do to be more helpful to students who were probably suffering from PTSD, Foster developed an assessment approach that could be utilized in the classroom.

The consideration of a mental health explanation for behaviors that occur in the classroom is not a revolutionary or new idea. However, the way in which Foster proceeded to try to understand the pattern of symptoms and their relevance for what she would offer in the classroom in terms of pedagogical style is revolutionary. Foster's approach to having more than a cursory understanding of mental health syndromes and how that knowledge can inform and make more sensitive the teaching process represents a significant departure from the ways in which many have suggested that teachers should proceed. Indeed, Foster's approach to understanding the mental health struggles of her delinquent adolescents enrolled in an alternative school is a forward step to creating a holistic learning environment, where all facets of the student's life are considered simultaneously. There has been much verbalization concerning such an approach, but the evidence supporting such integrated thinking is somewhat limited. Let me explain.

Frequently teachers are encouraged to think about the life experiences and contexts in which students function. In so doing, they are encouraged to try to identify how negative social experiences and living situations can adversely impact the lives of students. There is a voluminous literature concerning teachers and their attempts to be sensitive, especially to children who grew up in poverty and lives that are punctuated with a high level of familial instability. What is missing from much of that literature, it seems, is some evidence that in considering these factors, the teachers also plan classroom activities consistent with what Foster and others have termed "an ethic of caring." In the work described in this volume, Foster talks about structuring classroom activities in such a way that builds on the use of community activities as a catalyst for emotional and educational growth. She notes that open discussion of otherwise negative community activities is a highly desirable activity. It appears that such an approach does help young people understand that all facets of their lives are integrated in an ongoing way. It becomes terribly artificial, if not disruptive, to attempt to compartmentalize their lives in such a way that excludes from their ongoing social consciousness negative experiences outside of the school setting.

The observations made by Foster are considered valuable in that she deals exclusively with delinquent adolescents. It has been a very common pattern among educators and others working with delinquent adolescents to believe that they are beyond the point of serious rehabilitation. Indeed, this has been a very pronounced position in much of the gang literature evidenced in part by the overwhelming emphasis on law enforcement corrections and punitive measures as opposed to discussing creative ways to salvage lives that have otherwise become severely disheveled. Foster cautions that she does not see her work as replacing that of the mental health personnel in the school. Rather, she notes that her more-than-casual knowledge of PTSD places her in a prime position to identify things that might be most appropriately worked with by the identified mental health personnel. Again, this represents a progressive step in the direction of caring. Foster recognizes the limits of her training to deal with the issues in a major substantive way but does not use this as an excuse for not acknowledging the mental health needs and presentations of her students.

The approach used by Foster in working with the gang adolescents is a radical departure from what has been noted in other writings concerning working with such individuals. Specifically, there is an unchallenged belief that most gang members do not attend any type of educational setting. Instead, the commonly held belief is that once a young person joins a gang, they are likely to drop out of school and therefore not be in the pipeline of individuals needing services or special attention from school personnel. The assumption that gang members do not attend school has been challenged by the small body of literature noting the presence of gang members of various levels of gang involvement in schools, both secondary and at the elementary level (Monti, 1994).

The Foster chapter creates an image of a parallel process that exists between teacher and students. She starts by pointing out her own reactions to the loss of several students and raises the question of whether a similar pattern of loss and grief was being experienced by her students but was not finding overt expression. In taking such an approach, Foster has reminded us that the experiences that adults have relative to students and others may also be experienced by students but not directly expressed. Among adjudicated delinquent adolescents, this is a particularly interesting observation. First, many delinquent adolescents are not thought of as being emotionally responsive to violence and other acts that many of us assume are a part of their daily experiences. Foster has suggested that such may not be the case and that perhaps we are unrealistically expecting delinquent adolescents to be anesthetized to experiences that may continuously serve as a source of emotional stress for them. Second, Forster points out that the frequent experiences, even of antisocial acts among gang members, should be considered for their use as catalysts for creating an atmosphere of caring and sharing. She notes that this unconditional regard and expression of empathy toward many gang and other delinquent adolescents may be a novel experience and, as a result, precipitate reactions among the young people that distance them from sharing their true feelings. Despite the difficult of creating a sharing environment, Foster believes the ultimate result is not readily measurable in the historic ways in which educators and behavioral scientists have attempted to assess when students are progressing.

The writings of Foster suggest that schools can play a vital role in the lives of gang adolescents. She notes in this volume and in other places that it is the sustained relationship with the teacher or school administrator that forms the basis of one of the first stable relationships that many children and adolescents from troubled families experience. The centrality of the school and its statement of community power is further evidenced in Norman Randolph's chapter on energizing and organizing the community.

Randolph offers a model of how communities can be organized to offset the disruptive impact of gangs. He draws very heavily on sociological literature and his experience as a school administrator in the Commonwealth of Pennsylvania. Randolph's chapter is especially important because it makes a very profound effort to counteract many of the prevailing problems that have often prevented gang intervention efforts from succeeding. The most pervasive of those problems is the absence of a cohesive and coherent presentation on the part of the community. Randolph notes that this lack of cohesiveness is often the result of "turf battles" among community agencies and individuals having personal agendas that supersede the collective will of the community.

In his chapter, Randolph rather systematically outlines steps that he believes need to be taken to create a united community front. The first step, an informal beginning, he notes, should be taken by a government leader, perhaps the mayor of a city, to organize individuals in ways that may go beyond their own ability. It appears that it is very important to identify leadership structure, but the investment of leadership in that person is not so extensive that the efforts come to be identified as belonging to that person. The problem with overinvestment of power is that success then is all attributed to that individual's effort. On the other hand, failures, when they occur, are also often attributed to the identified leader. The result, then, is no one is seen as having ownership of the efforts over and beyond the "identified leader." Of the several steps that Randolph provides, his step for a community forum is a vital step to assure that multiple perspectives are represented and multiple players are involved in eliminating the disruptive effects of gangs in communities.

It should be noted that implicit in Randolph's presentation is the idea that the school should serve as a major player in helping to galvanize the efforts of the community. He proposes the school for several reasons, including its historic legacy of being a source of legitimized influence in communities populated by people of color. In addition, Randolph seems to suggest that because every community has at least one school and that there are facilities available through the school system, this seems to be a viable route to follow in trying to create a sense of a central place from which the community is working on its collective goal. Steps five and six of the Randolph plan are concerned with action groups and the maintenance of a community coalition. It appears that these are also vital steps in concretizing the efforts to make the community an effective vehicle for overcoming its own gang problems. The impact of empowering others to be part of "action groups" and functioning coalitions cannot be disregarded.

In many community efforts to overcome gangs, it seems that one factor that works against the ongoing effort is the lack of small goals that are time limited. In situations in which the interventions have failed miserably, a feature that is very common is that individuals are expected to make commitments of an open-ended nature. The result is that individuals become burned out or a sense of hopelessness and despair or both overtakes the group before it can experience any measure of success at even a small approximation of its larger goal of eliminating gangs from its presence.

The Randolph plan is articulated in such a way that it can be adjusted to the specific needs of a community and assessed at various stages of its evolution. This clear statement of a linear sequence is likely to be useful to individuals who are not accustomed to large-scale, long-range planning of social action programs. It also makes it easy for individuals to enter into the process at any point in the evolution of the community action plan.

The Randolph plan, as articulated here, is precisely that: a plan. It is not offered as an empirically tested approach, but he does provide some qualitative data to justify the inclusion of the steps that he has offered. This absence of extensive empirical data does not devalue the merit of the plan. Instead, it seems to create a design for an intervention that can be readily tested in a variety of settings. This returns us to the question of research and what is to be considered acceptable evidence in substantiating the effectiveness of interventions. In its current form, the Randolph plan has the potential benefit of allowing local communities to deviate from it slightly by adding additional necessary steps that might be required, based on their unique situation.

The role of the school in helping to draw the many dimensions of the community into a community action plan is readily apparent in the Randolph plan. It is also clear that with multiple agencies and organizations participating in the community effort there is likely to be a variety of reactions among community residents based on their prior experiences with those agencies. This, it seems, is a positive. For example, if individuals in a community have had mixed reactions to the police department or even the public school system, having a variety of other agencies involved in a community-wide effort will, to some degree, offset the negative impact of that checkered history. In planning and intervention, it should not be assumed that positive or negative relationships with an agency will transfer to the larger project at hand. Because that assumption is unfounded, it is strongly recommended that some level of discussion of the credibility of the agencies participating in a community-wide effort should be discussed. One point of discussion should be the type of relationships the agency also has experienced with gang adolescent families and members of the community in general. For example, it is not being proposed that the positive or negative relationships are one-sided. Rather, it is being suggested that agencies also may have a track record of poor quality relationships with community leaders and families in need of the services provided by the agency. One example where this is frequently true concerns the youth services agencies or the local department of social services or both. Because of the nature of their work, they are often perceived by community residents as being troublemakers and individuals who are serving as an extension of the punitive arm of the larger system, especially as it relates to people of color. To offset these kinds of complex relationships, some level of open discussion of consumer agency dynamics and how they might find inadvertent expression in efforts to create community-wide intervention programs should occur.

☐ References

Branch, C. (1997). *Clinical interventions with gang adolescents and their families*. Boulder, CO: Westview Press.

Branch, C., & Rennick, M. (1996). *The gang goes to school*. Unpublished manuscript.

Monti, D. (1994). *Wannabe: Gangs in suburbs and schools*. Cambridge, MA: Blackwell.

CHAPTER 4

Karim Abdullah
Curtis Branch

Denver County Court Probation Intervention with Gang-Affiliated Youth

The Denver County Municipal Court was established in 1988 as a system to intervene with youth who were coming into contact with law enforcement agencies.

Its initial design was to process city ordinance violations. Early beliefs were that the court would initially serve about one thousand cases per year. This was truly a gross underestimation of the severity of the gang problems that existed in Denver, Colorado.

The gang problem in Denver today is basically no different than any other city that has experienced the gang phenomenon. Denver, however, is unique in the fact that the majority of its gangs originated from the outside. There are several ways suggested as to how the problem initially developed in Denver.

One idea traces the origin of gang influence back to the early seventies when local law enforcement began to notice some young Hispanic youth dressed in what they labeled "Chollo" attire. After further investigation, it was determined that these youth had originated from East Los Angeles. They were living in Denver reportedly as a result of their families moving or they were sent to live with relatives to escape the gang influences of East Los Angeles. By 1982, Denver had an estimated 14 Hispanic gangs. Some of the earlier names that arose from these influences were The Warlords, The Clan, the V.U.C. or Varrio Unido Chicano, and the 44th Street Conquistadors, just to name a few. Of course, with this development came the claim for neighborhoods along with increases in violent acts and criminal behavior.

According to local authorities, by 1984, the problem in the Hispanic community began to subside. A lot of this was a result of community pressures, school, judicial, and police efforts. By no means did the problem dissipate. Those neighborhoods affected by these elements only saw a short-lived lull.

The African American gang problem, during these years, was centered in the east section of Denver. The African American gangs were pretty much limited to two major groups. They were identified as the "Boyz" and a group called the "Greeks" and a few other lesser known groups. Like the Hispanic gangs, the African American gangs went into a short-lived lull.

According to local authorities, it was reportedly in the fall of 1984 that the first "Crip" gang graffiti was noticed on the walls in Lower East Denver. It reportedly was referring to a sect known as the "Rolling 30 Crips Gangsters."

According to a local story, an officer investigated a family for some suspected criminal activity. It was noted at this time that this particular family had originated from East Los Angeles and, further, they were tied to the Crips gang in Los Angeles. The story goes on to suggest that the young members of this family were able to "roll over" the local gang known as the Greeks. Roll over is a term loosely used to mean convert the other group to their group.

By the spring of 1985, another form of graffiti was noticed in another section of East Denver. This graffiti also indicated that it originated from East Los Angeles. This graffiti was associated with a gang known as the "Bloods." They too originated from East Los Angeles. Not only did they bring the new graffiti and gang association, but they also brought with them a feud that could be traced as far back as the sixties in Los Angeles.

Today, in Denver, these two gangs alone comprise an estimated number of over 8000 gang members. The Bloods have an estimated 17 different sects with such colorful names as Crenshaw Mafia Gangsters (C.M.G.), Bounty Hunter Bloods, Lincoln Park Pyru, and Dog Posse Bloods.

The Crips, on the other hand, have an estimated 20 different sects, with some colorful names also, such as Rolling 30s, Rolling 60s, Anybody Killer (A.K.), Dog City Crips, just to name a few.

The gang phenomenon caused an unexpected rise in the utilization of juvenile detention facility space. Early projections had suggested that in the first year of its operation, the court would have about 1000 adjudicated cases. However, case facts show that during the first year, approximately 8000 cases were filed with the Denver Municipal Court. Table 4.1 presents a summary of filings with the court since its inception.

The latest figure predictions for 1997 anticipate that 15,000 cases will be filed. Such a dramatic increase in filings has seriously strained the resources

TABLE 4.1. Referrals to Denver Municipal Court by Year

Year	Number of Summons to the Court
1988	1575
1989	3028
1990	3865
1991	6089
1992	8211
1993	10,165
1994	9850
1995	9413
1996	9053
1997	Not available

of the court. In an attempt to expedite hearings and to provide services that are fair and of a high quality, the court has struggled to find new ways of proceeding. It has become apparent that simply hearing cases faster does not offer a long term relief of the problem. More filings are being made, suggesting that the problem of juveniles in need of judicial interventions is expanding. The increased demands for the court's time can also be interpreted to mean that there is a broadening of the parameters as to what constitutes a case to be filed with the courts. In either event, the courts are taxed. Something new and different must happen. Old methods of proceeding have been shown to be ineffective.

One of the most significant changes to occur was the court's view of itself. The judges of the court reasoned that simply hearing cases and rendering fair and stiff penalties for infractions were not causing changes in the behavior of young people in the community. It was also felt, by the court, that responding to young people only *after* they had committed offenses seemed to be counterproductive to reducing problems. After much agonizing, the court decided to embark on two programs designed to provide remediational services to adjudicated adolescents *and* their families. The inclusion of family members was a radical departure for the court from its traditional approach of seeing juveniles and their parents. Now younger siblings, and in some cases, significant extended family members (i.e., grandparents, aunts, uncles), were also served by the court. Including younger siblings was believed to be a preventative intervention, because most of them had not yet committed offenses that warranted court involvements.

☐ Intervention Programs

The court was ambivalent about undertaking programs that extended beyond its traditional role of hearing cases. One judge described the new role as one that could cause the court "to be seen as some type of social worker." Despite that misgiving, he actively supported the idea of something qualitatively different needing to be done if the court was to have a chance of handling its rapidly escalating case load. Two types of programs were created, one focusing exclusively on the adjudicated adolescent, and the other, a mental-health-focused program that was directed at the adolescent and the family. The programs were sponsored by the court but were implemented by the probation department and a corp of community volunteers.

☐ Work Fair

One of the early programs created by the probation department was to have immediate impact on the youth, especially the gang-affiliated youth. It came to be known as Work Fair. Being involved in the world of work was the primary objective of this program. Under the auspices of the probation department, youth were taken directly from the courtroom, on the day of their sentencing, to a work crew or project somewhere in the metropolitan area. Conceptually, this was a very popular idea, especially with parents. Since its inception in 1989, Work Fair has evolved into a program that is an important part of the court's repertoire of resources available to help youngsters. There are several requirements of the program that are believed to facilitate growth. Table 4.2 provides a summary of developmental requirements associated with successful participation in Work Fair and how the program provides opportunities for clients to develop them. Perhaps the greatest strength of the program is that it stimulates growth and development on the part of clients. Minimal emphasis is placed on "punishment." Rather, the focus is one of learning new skills and attitudes that may transfer positively to other situations.

The idea of being gainfully employed in a legal occupation, of course, is not a new idea. It is firmly rooted in the work ethic that suggests that working hard and evidencing some level of mastery over one's life space will translate to positive feelings about oneself and an internal locus of control (see Gonzalez, this volume). Obtaining and maintaining a regular job is a novel experience for many of the youngsters. Their lives frequently have been characterized by educational and social disengagement (see Quamina, this volume), which has rendered them to a status of invis-

TABLE 4.2. Developmental Requirements for Participation in Work Fair

Affective

Participants in the Work Fair Program are required to show evidence that they are emotionally mature enough to take critical feedback from supervisory personnel. Concrete evidence of maturity may be extracted from previous work history. This approach, however, is problematic for adolescents who have never held a job. In seeking to establish a candidate, range of affective responses to potential problem situations are also elicited. This includes asking the candidate how he might handle a conflict at work, for example, dealing with a coworker who appears not to be doing his share of assigned work. It is important to keep in mind that nonverbal messages and the level of intensity of verbal responses often tell as much about a person as his actual response.

Behavior

This is an area that is assessed directly by asking the client to comment on problems he has experienced in school and work settings. The idea is to note what types of conflicts are reported. It is sometimes helpful to start this evaluation point by saying, "most people have some type of difficulty in situations in which they have to relate to other people. What have been problem areas for you?" Special attention should be focused on the types of problems identified (i.e., interpersonal conflicts, relating to supervisors, tardiness, etc.). After the client confesses to having had difficulties it is often illuminating to ask him what his role was in fostering the problem. What could he have done differently about the problem? What prevented him from doing the same?

Cognitive

It is vitally important to understand how an adolescent thinks about the world and others around him. To gain a sampling of their thinking in abstract terms it is generally instructive to ask adolescents to describe themselves to me in the same way they would present themselves to another adult who is new in their world. Some adolescents are reluctant to do this task at first, but with a little prompting they usually comply. Special attention should be given to their responses. Younger and less mature adolescents tend to describe themselves exclusively in terms of physical traits (i.e., I have brown eyes) to the exclusion of psychological traits (i.e., I'm a considerate person). A special check should be made to determine if the adolescent has the capacity to take a perspective beyond that of his own.

ible beings. Working also disrupts the youngster's longstanding pattern of being idle during the day. In many ways, working places social demands on many of the youngsters that they would prefer not to have. Taking orders from others and being in continuous contact with others are two of the features of working identified by some youngsters as being especially negative to them. Recognizing these patterns becomes the first step for many adjudicated youngsters toward making a decision whether to become more socially connected to their community. Either they can persist in their pattern of disengagement, no, estrangement, from the community, or they can figure out how to develop the skills necessary for economic and social sufficiency.

A by-product of Work Fair is often that youngsters make discoveries about the loss of inner self. Specifically, many youngsters suddenly realize that they *don't* like physically challenging work. On the other hand, some youngsters have a brief moment of introspection in that they reconnect with dormant academic skills that have gone unused for months. The latter commonly occurs with youngsters who report that they had forgotten that they were once good in math, science, or computers. Being placed at a work assignment that they can't negotiate has helped them find, if only on a transient basis, the self they once knew.

Of course, none of this occurs overtly. The youngsters assigned to Work Fair often complain bitterly and loudly to their probation officers. The complaints are usually vague and poorly articulated (i.e., "I don't have time to be goin' to no job. . . . I got stuff to do"; "It's so boring"; "I don't like it 'cause that guy is always tellin' me what to do"). Deeply seated underlying issues are uncovered only when the probation officer probes beneath the superficial verbalizations. For many youngsters, working is a choice that is considered better than "sitting in juvenile hall all day."

Work Fair is a daily program in which the participants are transported to a work site. The duration of sentencing to the program varies, depending on the offense that brought them to the attention of the court. An evaluation of the success of the participation in the program is a very individualized and subjective matter. For some youngsters, the goals may be associated with providing structure and consistency in their lives. Others may be assigned to Work Fair as a holding pattern until much needed vocational and psychological evaluations can be completed. It is difficult to say categorically what constitutes success. One measure of outcome that is unquestioned, however, is that the participant was able to meet the orders of the court and that a significant amount of work was done, gratuitously, for the City and County of Denver. Some have argued that the "free work" for the municipality should be considered a civic contribution, partial payment for the infractions of the municipal code that got them into the court system.

The second intervention program offered by the courts, Family Intervention Program (FIP), represents a more radical departure from the conventional wisdom of Work Fair. In its original format, the FIP represents a collaboration between the probation department of the juvenile court and the local community of psychologists. The following section provides a brief overview of the program and its underlying assumptions. Readers interested in a more detailed description and analysis, including a procedure manual for it, are encouraged to consult Branch (1997).

☐ FIP

The FIP is an intensive psychoeducational program designed to help families at risk for fragmentation reconstitute themselves and to become more functional in their daily operations. It focuses on teaching families new methods of communicating their needs and expectations to each other. By examining the relationship between values and behaviors, the FIP highlights for families how and where they make faulty assumptions that lead to ruptures in the attachments within the family unit. We believe that these ruptured attachments are the origin of acting-out behaviors among early and middle adolescents and of family conflicts. Frequently, adolescents seek to find relief from family conflicts, real and imaginary, through peers who are engaged in antisocial behaviors.

Structurally, the FIP consists of two components: an eight-hour intensive prescriptive evaluation and three months of follow-up guided family development work (i.e., psychological counseling, vocational counseling, academic remediation, etc.). To address the two components of the program, clear conceptualizations of family functioning and family development are needed.

Rationale

Families of adjudicated juvenile offenders are often described as being dysfunctional. Conceptually, that is a bit of an overstatement. A more balanced and objective view of those families, we think, might be to conceptualize them as being in need of empowerment so that they can respond to the developmental needs of all of the family needs. Helping the family members examine their style of relating to each other about problematic and nonproblematic behaviors is one way of changing the family dynamics. Circular communication (i.e., giving mixed messages, etc.) is often at the root of many families losing control of their adolescents. The FIP is designed to address this and related issues in a culturally driven approach that highlights the families' strengths rather than their weaknesses. More specifically, the FIP is designed to address the question of what are the issues and dynamics that cause family members to seek primary attachments and validations outside of the family. Additionally, the FIP is based on a clinical approach for teaching families new ways of being that can reduce stress, alienation, and the need to bond with destructive extrafamilial forces.

Target Population

All families who have a member with an active case in the Denver Municipal Court are eligible to participate in the FIP. Given the racial and ethnic makeup of the court's caseload (e.g., people of color are overrepresented), a special emphasis is placed on Latino and African American families. Families having difficulty with issues of separation and individuation is a universal pattern. It exists in all cultures. However, we believe that this process is intensified among families of color in which the adolescents fit the profile for being at risk for antisocial acting-out behavior.

Goals and Objectives

The FIP is committed to helping families increase their level of psychological and social functioning. To accomplish this global good, the following specific objectives are pursued:

(1) To teach families to be observant of their own strengths and weaknesses, noting behavioral and verbal communication changes that may be used as cues for self-correction.
(2) To provide families with new methods of communicating.
(3) To engage families in a self-evaluation process focusing on the relationship between values and behaviors, from a culture specific perspective.
(4) To teach families strategies for disengaging in destructive behaviors that weaken the family as the members primary reference group.

The Work

Remember that the FIP has two program components: an eight-hour intensive and a three-month follow-up phase. The first part is clearly articulated and is the same for all participants. Table 4.3 gives the schedule for the first phase of the FIP.

It should be kept in mind that the FIP is conducted by licensed mental health professionals who take full responsibility for the participant's behavior during and after the shared experimental activities. Impressions about the psychological resources of each family are developed during the course of the day by the professionals conducting the exercises. Table 4.4 summarizes the exercises used and the type of information that they contribute to the overall assessment of the families' strengths and weaknesses. All families are evaluated on affective, behavioral, and cognitive function-

TABLE 4.3. Activities of the Family Intervention Project

8:30–9:00	Registration and informal interactions with facilitators
9:00–10:00	Welcome and Orientation
	"Why are we here?"
10:00–10:15	Coffee/Smoke Break
10:15–10:45	Black Delinquent Gang Exercise (Individual performance)
10:45–11:30	Black Delinquent Gang Exercise (Group performance)
11:30–12:00	Debrief Black Delinquent Gang Exercise
12:00–1:15	Lunch
1:15–1:30	Review of the morning activities
1:30–2:00	Threats to good communication
2:00–2:30	Teach rules of good communication
	Discussion
2:30–2:45	Break
2:45–3:15	Practice sessions: Good communication
3:15–4:00	Family worksessions
4:00–4:30	Debrief afternoon activities
	Planning the next steps

Reprinted by permission of Westview Press.

ing. Again, the reader who wants an in-depth discussion of the assessment process is encouraged to read *Clinical Interventions with Gang Adolescents and their Families* (Branch, 1997).

There are a few features of this program that make it revolutionary. First, it is an active collaboration between mental health professionals and an arm of the court. The work that is accomplished in the FIP is used for the purpose of understanding an adjudicated adolescent plus other family members, most of whom are not clients of the court. The inclusion of other family members in this work creates opportunities for prevention and family inoculation against recidivism of the patterns of antisocial behaviors already exhibited by the identified client. Like most mental health interventions, the FIP has a real life laboratory where family members can work collectively or individually on issues that get identified during the FIP. This is the three-month follow-up phase. Because of the idiosyncratic nature of individual family follow-up plans, there is no general way in which the three-month post-hoc development plan can be rated. Every family is working on something different and specific to its needs.

In the initial work session, there are communities that extend across all families. Every family who participates in the FIP will be involved in working on real life problems during the duration of their involvement. Role

TABLE 4.4. Summary of Family Intervention Project Exercises

Activity	Summary
Why are we here?	This is an introductory exercise which is designed to assess the client's ability to accurately verbalize the stated reasons for participation in the FIP.
	It is conducted in a communal setting with each person being given a chance to verbalize the reasons for his or her attendance. Distortions of facts and private agendas of participants are noted by the facilitators.
Black delinquent gang	A structure exercise in group decisionmaking, this activity provides an opportunity for the facilitators to observe who has the capacity to work in a group and who doesn't. Perhaps more important, it is a projective procedure in which participants make attributions to Black delinquent gang members. The distinction between values and behaviors is taught.
Threats to good communication	Factors which interfere with effective communication are identified during this group activity. Participants are encouraged to give examples and to note their role in fostering poor quality communication in various settings.
Rules of good communication	Five basic rules of effective communication are taught to the group. Each person is asked to write the rules down for use later in the day.
Practice sessions: Good communication	Simulated family units are created and participants are given an opportunity to use the rules of good communication learned earlier. The facilitators provide feedback.
Family work sessions	Authentic family work on a real problem under the supervision of a facilitator. Sessions last approximately 75 minutes. The first task is for the family to decide, by consensus, which problem they are going to work through.

playing and simulations are not employed as teaching strategies. Rather, the focus is on real issues and real behaviors. Passive observers and "visitors" are not permitted to attend the FIP. Everyone in attendance is expected to participate, as a family member or as a facilitator.

Another program innovation of the court is probation department intensive supervision and close monitoring. This program is significantly more intensive and limiting, for the client, than the usual supervision assigned by the court.

☐ Intensive Supervision

Designed to minimize the likelihood a youngster on probation will commit additional municipal code violations, intensive supervision requires weekly face-to-face contact between client and probation officer. In some special circumstances, more frequent meetings (i.e., semiweekly) may be required. The rationale of close supervision is that the probation officer can make a visual inspection of the client to aid their assessment as to whether other forms of probation are being met.

One of the problems probation officers frequently encounter in relationships with clients is the absence of a sense of trust. The origin of the mistrust could be traced to one of several sources. Many probation clients often have a long history of not trusting anyone perceived as having authority over them. Therefore, it would not be unusual or especially significant if they did not trust the probation officer. For the client, mistrusting the probation officer can be partially attributed to the client's disdain for the legal system. Probation officers are viewed, by many, as an extension of "the system." Still other clients find it difficult to trust their probation officer because of their own pervasive inability to trust *anyone*. This psychological handicap simply resurfaces when the client is assigned to a probation officer. Whatever the reason(s), a client who can't muster the capacity to be trusting of his or her probation officer negatively impacts their working together. Work relationships that are characterized by a pathological and unprovoked sense of mistrust are stormy and short in duration. Intensive supervision has the potential of undoing some of these dynamics. The frequent contacts between client and probation officer that occur during intensive supervision have the potential of helping clients work through their issues of trust. Let us explain.

Intensive supervision is predicated on a belief that adjudicated adolescents often need close and frequent supervision. For many youngsters it is the absence of these features in their early developmental history that has accounted for them being in the justice system. Close monitoring could potentially be a new experience for youthful offenders. Not knowing what to expect from the experience, many of them react with dread, fear, and even anger. Acting-out behaviors such as lack of cooperation during sessions, missed appointments, and even open defiance of the other conditions of probation are likely responses. The job of the probation officer is to attempt to engage the client in a way that he or she has not been engaged by the "system" and family and friends as a way of demonstrating what "could be," as far as their relationship is concerned. Contrary to popular belief, intensive supervision is not designed to be an intense surveillance program. Conceptually it was created to minimize the rates of recidivism among clients of the court and to provide a forum whereby probation officers can obtain information about clients on a "need to know basis," not in a post-hoc manner as happens in most court proceedings.

Rationale

The quality of the relationships that adolescents have had with authority figures in the past has implications for what their relationships will be like in the present. This is especially true of young people who are involved in the court system or some other involuntary situation. One way of altering negatively skewed relationships is to provide new and frequent opportunities for participants to learn new ways of relating to others. In the probation system this means new ways for clients to relate to authority figures. Initially there is likely to be resistance to this change. There may even be overtly negative responses to having to talk with someone who is seen as an extension of "the system." Most people learn new behaviors as a result of exposure to the new behaviors and being reinforced for emitting those behaviors. Put another way, we learn by doing and getting rewards for trying. The same can be said of adolescents. Because of that, it is critical to understand that adjudicated adolescents should be reinforced for even small approximations of prosocial behaviors. Intensive supervision provides opportunities for rewarding attempts at prosocial behavior (i.e., keeping appointments, meeting conditions of probation, acknowledging that others may have perspectives different from one's own, etc.).

Frequent contacts between probation officer and client are envisioned as a way to facilitate change in the direction of a troubled work relationship. It is assumed that if a probation officer sees a client often there will be multiple opportunities for shaping a positive work relationship. Situations that are characterized by negative affect can be reframed by the probation officer. Significant learning can be fostered by probation officers who meet the adolescent's negativity and erratic behavior with positive affect and consistency.

Finally, the intensive supervision experience can, if managed well, sample good and bad days of the client. This can be accomplished by the probation officer who may vary the frequency and time of day of scheduled visits. Meetings with extremely short advance notice are particularly effective in this regard. Remember, the program is designed to respond to adjudicated adolescents who are high risks for recidivism, have histories of not completing tasks, and demonstrate a minimal level of motivation to cooperate with the courts.

Target Populations

Intensive supervision was created with the aforementioned types of clients in mind. When properly executed intensive supervision can be helpful to each type, for different reasons.

High Risk for Recidivism

This category includes adolescents who have a history with the department. Occasionally more structured programs (i.e., residential mental health programs, vocational training in a residential setting, etc.) are not immediately available for high-risk clients because of waiting lists and other situations. Intensive supervision can be a holding pattern of intervention until the more appropriate referral and program enrollment can happen. A cycle of repeated failures is often a part of these youngster's history. The noted high recidivism risk may be a function of the absence of any sense of structure (i.e., parental supervision) or a high density of crime in the client's neighborhood. In response to the reality of the latter, the client often gives in to the temptations of the street and finds himself back in court again, even before the first set of charges can be resolved.

History of not Completing Tasks

The intensive supervision program is especially helpful for youngsters who seem to have a problem completing tasks. Not being able to complete tasks generally is the result of several factors interacting. Probation officers can assist these types of clients by giving them small and frequent assignments. The expectation is that the skill at focusing on what needs to be done and time management will have positive transferral to other domains of the young person's life. Having frequent contacts throughout the intensive supervision program can also be helpful to noncompleters of tasks because the expectation that they will follow through on assignments will not simply "go away" nor will the expectation of compliance from them be dropped.

Low Level of Motivation to Cooperate with the Court

This type of problem behavior is often observed among many juvenile offenders. Reasons for such behavior vary by cases but often include a negative attitude about the court held by parents and other family members. The consistency of expectations and not taking "no" for an answer attitude of the intensive supervision program is likely to create a state of dissonance among poorly motivated clients. Angry outbursts and verbalizations of "I don't give a damn" or "Fuck the judge" are likely to occur as the frustration of the demanding nature of the supervision program becomes apparent. Rather than meet anger with retaliatory action or more anger, the probation officer can use these occasions to try to introduce some introspection (i.e., "It sounds like you're really pissed off that you have to come in to see me so often," "It sounds like you don't want to do this any more," "I'd guess that you're pretty ticked off at the judge.... Tell me about another time when you got this angry. What happened?").

Intensive supervision has the potential of helping these types of youngsters because it disrupts their usual modes of functioning. This is one of the few instances where disruptions have a positive valence. In addition to altering the youngster's routine, intensive supervision provides the probation officer with multiple occasions, sometimes on consecutive days, to interact with the client who is at risk of failing again. Coming in to see the probation officer more than once every couple of weeks may be perceived as an inconvenience. It is very likely that the probation officer will "hear it from the client," behaviorally (i.e., habitual lateness for appointments, feigning physical illness, etc.) and verbally (i.e., "I got stuff to do," "I be sleepy in the morning"). Of course the probation officer uses all of these messages as part of his or her ongoing assessment of the client's level of compliance and their level of motivation.

Goal and Objectives

Intensive supervision is designed to closely monitor clients who are at risk for failure at their probation program. Unlike conventional probation approaches to clients, intensive supervision is also interested in teaching clients new skills that might be transferred to subsequent interactions with the criminal justice system and other settings.

Two specific objectives are addressed in all variations of intensive supervision, namely, (1) to teach clients new, more positive ways of relating to the authority figures with whom they must interact, and (2) minimize the risk that clients will commit offenses similar to those that have brought them to the attention of the court.

The Work

The exact mechanics of the intensive supervision program are idiosyncratic to the case being supervised. Probation officers are encouraged to use a variable schedule of appointments as a way to sample the client's behavior and mental status at various times of the day and under different circumstances. As described earlier it is entirely possible that a probation officer may choose to see a client on a daily basis, at different hours each day. This is an extreme example, but it could happen, especially if the client is not enrolled in an educational program and is not working. Clients who claim to be enrolled in school are required to submit regularly verification of attendance.

Individual sessions are the usual procedure for working with clients assigned to intensive supervision, but under unusual circumstances a client may be asked to attend and participate in a group activity. For example, seminars to help young people learn how to present themselves for job interviews are occasionally held in the community. It is conceivable that a probation officer participating in such a program may deem it appropriate to invite an intensive supervision client to attend. The client's participation will give the probation officer an opportunity to observe his behavior in a group setting.

The program is not exclusively about observing the client for infractions but is also an opportunity to give positive reinforcement for prosocial behavior. Remember, the purpose of the program is to teach the acquisition of new behaviors as well as the elimination of counterproductive antisocial behaviors. Any approximation of a larger positive behavior is acknowledged and rewarded, verbally if not tangibly, by the probation officer.

Because so many youngsters assigned to the intensive supervision program are reticent and reluctant to engage with the probation officer in the beginning phases of their working together, probation officers are required to be creative in finding ways to be connected to their clients. Verbal interactions are also difficult for some beginners, because they are fixated at anger about being in the program but are unable to verbalize the same. Instead, they internalize their feelings and act out in hostile manners with the program officer, despite the fact that the officer partially holds their fate in his or her hands.

☐ Evaluating Outcomes

The task of evaluating the effectiveness of these and other interventions of the court is a difficult and arduous job. We believe that simple outcome criteria such as rates of recidivism are inappropriate with the juvenile population for several reasons. First, we think recidivism rates simply point out the cases of repeat offenders who have been apprehended by the police. Recidivism rates do not fully capture the total population of young people who continue to engage in illegal activities. The offenders who have been smart enough to learn from their earlier encounter with the juvenile justice system and cover their tracks, so to speak, are not included in recidivism rates. Second, conventional methods of evaluating programs do not reflect the by-products of youngsters who are assigned to probation. In some cases younger siblings and even parents are helped in ways that are not reflected in the court's statistics. Common examples of these types of secondary improvements have included mothers who find some empowerment in the process of "dealing with the courts." This often takes the form of mothers who insist that they have learned new things about setting limits and about allowing their adolescents to be responsible for the acts that they commit, especially illegal and antisocial acts.

In an ongoing effort to assess the effectiveness of our work we compare our outcome findings with those reported in the professional literature. This has proven to be a difficult task, because our service delivery system and related data are protected under state law. Information gathered on adolescents for purposes of court-related services are to be used for those purposes only. To date program evaluation has not been included in that definition. Despite these problems we are able to assess the impact of our attempts at creative programming on an ad-hoc basis.

Probation officers frequently report that having access to clients in a variety of settings and more often than once weekly or biweekly makes their job less complicated. Frequent contacts with clients expand the knowledge that probation officers have of their clients. It also increases the likelihood that they and their clients have greater opportunities to work on the quality of their work relationship, reducing tensions where they exist. The multifaceted programs introduced, on an experimental basis, by the Denver Municipal Court are similar to those reported by Minor and Preston (1990). They investigated the effectiveness of expanded juvenile court services (job preparation, outdoor experiential, and family skills building components) versus traditional supervision in reducing probationary offense activities of adolescent offenders. Forty-five subjects were included in the study. Minor and Preston reported that the experimental intervention failed to yield the desired results, although experimental subjects with extensive crime backgrounds displayed fewer offenses during followup than comparable control subjects.

Clients were chosen to participate in the intensive supervision program based on their extensive criminal background. Additional support for creative programming is found in the research of Fashimpar (1991).

In a study that lasted over two years, Fashimpar compared the effectiveness of two traditional approaches to rehabilitating delinquents (probation and probation and recreation) with an innovative approach (a mini-bike club based on ecological and behavioral systems models of treatment). The three approaches were compared with a control group of delinquents on the variables criminal offenses, status offenses, grade point average, school attendance, and self-esteem. Surprisingly the mini-bike club offered the greatest potential for rehabilitating delinquents. Fashmipar concludes that social group approaches to rehabilitation appear to be more effective than probation casework or the deterrent effect of arrest. Support for nontraditional approaches is also found in the works of Nichols (1994) and Stumphauzer (1985). Nichols employed an approach that combined sports and counseling, based on principles of social learning. His 12-week program introduces each participant to a structured program of sports and leisure activities that provide positive experiences and achievements, and his program works with participants to the point that they can pursue such activities independently. The independent pursuit of activities is much like the transfer of learning we attempt to achieve in the intensive supervision program. Stumphauzer shows that social learning theory and probation service delivery are compatible also. He reports that the natural mediators found in the adolescent's natural environment are effective deterrents to future problems when they are combined with stress interventions (i.e., supervision by probation officers). These are only a small sample of the larger number of intervention programs that have suggested that creative programming outside of the conventional probation department strategies can be effective with adolescent offenders (Waldman, 1994).

The work conducted by the probation officers is often done without clinical consultations or input from other professionals. Consults can be obtained as they are deemed necessary, usually after the youngster has appeared in court. Such an after-the-fact arrangement is problematic and often results in psychiatrically fragile clients not being so identified until an inappropriate probation plan has been approved. Branch (1997) argues that mental health consultations should be a required part of evaluations that comes before sentencing. He thinks many adolescents who are involved in criminal activities have ongoing and pervasive psychiatric conditions that are treatable. Foster agrees and points to her experiences in a public school setting as supporting evidence for her position. In the next chapter she discussed her experiences with a group of inner-city adolescents among whom PTSD appeared to be very pervasive.

☐ Conclusion

The developmental needs of adolescents who are involved with gangs are varied. It is commonly assumed that because of their gang affiliation they have no interest in prosocial activities nor do they have the skills for such behaviors. Experiences of the Work Fair and family intervention programs produce evidence to the contrary. Specifically, many adolescents who have been actively involved in the Work Fair program have been observed to make substantial progress in the area of social engagement and relating to authority figures in a positive manner. It is not always clear if such improvements are novelty effects or if they are sustained over an extended period of time. Dispositions by the court or relocation to another community are reasons that often make follow-up comparisons impossible. The FIP has repeatedly demonstrated that families of adjudicated delinquents are dynamically like most other families, with the additional burden of dealing with a juvenile member who is in trouble with the courts.

The frequently observed struggles for validation observed among the FIP participants raise questions about the need for approval as being a universal. If that is true, the documented seeking of approval interpretation applied to adolescent gang members is even more powerful.

Work Fair and the FIP have provided rare opportunities to see delinquents and their family members at work in therapeutic settings. The information garnered by observing them is invaluable in making clinical decisions about who has what strengths and who is "ready" to work on their problems. The benefit of both programs is that the observations are direct and not secondary reports from an outside consultant who saw the clients in an artificial setting, not the naturalistic environs of a work situation or a multiple family therapeutic setting.

Thinking about families and their delinquent juveniles dictates that multiple approaches be utilized if we are to arrive at a full understanding of the complex behaviors and situations confronting many of our probation clients. Work Fair and the FIP are two pilot steps in the direction of revolutionary programming. We think they both have tremendous potential.

☐ References

Branch, C. (1997). *Clinical interventions with gang adolescents and their families*. Boulder, CO: Westview Press.

Fashimpar, G. (1991). From *probation* to mini-bikes: A comparison of traditional and innovative programs for community treatment of delinquent adolescents. *Social-Work-with-Groups, 14*(2), 105–108.

Minor, K., & Preston, E. (1990). The effects of a multi-faceted intervention on the offense activities of juvenile practitioners. *Journal of Offender Counseling, Services & Rehabilitation, 15*(2), 87–108.

Nichols, G. (1994). An evaluation of West Yorkshire sports counseling project: Workshop report. In Adventure-based interventions with young people in trouble and at risk. *Proceedings of Adventure-Based Intervention*. Ambleside, England.

Stumphauzer, J. (1985). Probation programs: Contracting to stay out of trouble. *Child and Youth Services, 8*(1–2), 125–136.

Waldman, K. (1994). Probation sports counselling scheme. In Adventure-based interventions with young people in trouble and at risk. *Proceedings of Adventure-Based Interventions*. Ambleside, England.

CHAPTER 5

Lorita A. Purnell

Youth Violence and Post-Traumatic Stress Disorder: Assessment, Implications, and Promising School-Based Strategies

During the 1990–1991 school year, three of my students lost their lives as the result of gang violence, all within a three-week span. In 1993, a former student and neighborhood resident was gunned down across the street from my home. In 1994, a former student was killed less than an hour after I had seen her smiling and joking with friends on the school playground. In each case, I grieved deeply, not only because of their deaths, but also because the events triggered my own memories of the deaths of two friends who were victims of gang violence almost 30 years ago. I knew that if it affected me, the students were certainly suffering, so I paid close attention to my students' behavior and academic performance, and in the case of the neighborhood resident, I kept contact with several youths who were friends of the victim.

There were increases in the number of school absences and number of times tardy, an increase in complaints of tiredness, having headaches and other ailments, and withdrawn behavior—as if the students were somewhere else. Not only did the quality of work decline, but the actual number of assignments completely dropped. In my neighborhood, the response was similar. When former students from the neighborhood were asked how they were doing academically, the response almost always indicated that their interest level and performance level had dropped.

It was obvious the youth were experiencing some trauma from the violence: when you live, as I do, in a neighborhood where gunfights at 3 a.m. are common, and your bedroom has windows, you do not need a textbook for explanations. The rationale for investigating the trauma was derived from personal experience. However, I was aware of a cluster of symptoms that war veterans experienced as a result of combat duty, and figured it was natural that persons living in urban battle zones might have similar reactions. I decided to research post-traumatic stress disorder (PTSD) and develop a simple assessment to use in the classroom.

The essential features of PTSD as listed in the *Diagnostic and Statistical Manual of Mental Disorders* (DSM-IV-R), (American Psychiatric Association, 1994, pp. 427–429) include the following:

A. The person has been exposed to a traumatic event in which both of the following were present:
    (1) the person experienced, witnessed, or was confronted with an event or events that involved actual or threatened death or serious injury, or a threat to the physical integrity of self or others.
    (2) the person's response involved intense fear, helplessness, or horror.
        Note: In children, this may be expressed instead by disorganized or agitated behavior.
B. The traumatic event is persistently reexperienced in one (or more) of the following ways:
    (1) recurrent and intrusive distressing recollections of the event, including images, thoughts, or perceptions.
        Note: In young children, repetitive play may occur in which themes or aspects of the trauma are expressed.
    (2) recurrent and distressing dreams of the event.
        Note: In children, there may be frightening dreams without recognizable content.
    (3) acting or feeling as if the traumatic event were recurring (includes a sense of reliving the experience, illusions, hallucinations, and dissociative flashback episodes, including those that occur on awakening or when intoxicated).
        Note: In young children, trauma-specific reenactment may occur.
    (4) intense psychological distress at exposure to internal or external cues that symbolize or resemble an aspect of the traumatic event.
    (5) physiological reactivity on exposure to internal or external cues that symbolize or resemble an aspect of the traumatic event.
C. Persistent avoidance of stimuli associated with the trauma and numbing of general responsiveness (not present before the trauma), as indicated by three (or more) of the following:

(1) efforts to avoid thoughts, feelings, or conversations associated with the trauma.
(2) efforts to avoid activities, places, or people that arouse recollections of the trauma.
(3) inability to recall an important aspect of the trauma.
(4) markedly diminished interest or participation in significant activities.
(5) feelings of detachment or estrangement from others.
(6) restricted range of affect (e.g., unable to have loving feelings).
(7) sense of foreshortened future (e.g., does not expect to have a career, marriage, children, or a normal life span).
D. Persistent symptoms of increased arousal (not present before the trauma), as indicated by two (or more) of the following:
(1) difficulty falling or staying asleep.
(2) irritability or outbursts of anger.
(3) hypervigilance.
(4) exaggerated startle response.
E. Duration of the disturbance (symptoms in Criteria B, C, and D) is more than one month.
F. The disturbance causes clinically significant distress or impairment in social, occupational, or other important areas of functioning.

The symptoms in the DSM-IV-R were strikingly similar to what was observed in the students' behavior. I developed a simple assessment based on the diagnostic criteria that would give a "snapshot" of the possible incidence of PTSD in the students. The assessment is self-administered and contains 15 questions to indicate incidence of symptoms and frequency. In addition to administering the assessment to the students, Afriye Quamina, an educational consultant in the Oakland, California, region, graciously agreed to "test the test" with several classes at an Oakland middle school.

The results for both groups pointed to a definite existence of PTSD symptoms among a substantial number of students who had either witnessed, or been victims of, gang violence. Of particular interest were the responses dealing with observable behaviors in the classroom. In both groups, the students who reported that they experienced a cluster of PTSD symptoms (i.e., hypervigilance, difficulty concentrating, problems with memory, emotional distancing, loss of interest in activities once deemed pleasurable, and difficulty meeting goals) were the same students who reported a high incidence of witnessing or being victims of gang violence. The few variances existing between the two sets of numbers could be due to several factors, including regional differences in gang environments or differences in the availability of intervention for the youth or both.

☐ PTSD and Pedagogy

Several implications arose from this assessment. Teachers constantly test students on their academic performance but do not possess nearly enough information on the consequences of students' exposure to gang violence, particularly the ways in which exposure may affect day-to-day performance and behavior. During a four-month span, I worked with teachers throughout the school, observing their classrooms, and team teaching with several teachers whose students needed special intervention and remediation. The arrangement provided a rare opportunity to observe what happens in classrooms unencumbered by the daily responsibilities of classroom management.

Mrs. Stewart's class is about to begin workbook exercises designed to give students practice in taking standardized tests. The class is visibly anxious. "Is this the real Iowa Test?" one student asks. Mrs. Stewart tells the class that the booklet contains practice exercises, and that practicing now will help the class perform better on the real test when it is given next spring. A few students appear skeptical. "Do we fail if we don't pass the Iowa Test?" another student asks, and the entire class is again riveted to attention. The students are concerned about failure and the possibility of being retained— a consequence of low test scores. The teacher is also concerned about failure, introducing the practice exercises eight months in advance of the test. The teacher does not want to be perceived by the administrator or school board as negligent—a consequence of low test scores. The mood prevails until one student announced, "It's almost one o'clock! It's time for gym!"

During the next several days, variations of this scene are repeated in classrooms throughout the school as teachers and students begin the annual ritual of test preparation. This ritual, according to Eisner (1985) has roots in "the aspiration to develop a scientifically based technology of educational practice" (p. 8), and was espoused by Edward L. Thorndike near the turn of the century. Thorndike believed that tested standards and procedures for directing the student's learning were necessary and that teachers could rely "not on intuition, chance, artistry or talent" (p. 8) since the use of these would not allow for control of the research or results. But almost 100 years later, what has this line of thinking produced in the way that students and teachers relate to each other, especially when students have been traumatized by gang violence?

When a teacher and class spend eight out of ten months focusing on testing, dialogue disappears, intervention is impeded, and education becomes subservient to test proficiency. The development of critical thinking is stymied, and the students become unwittingly involved in having to play catch-up. Some never make it, drop out, and become gang violence statistics. Conditions are needed that stimulate exploration, imagination, and cultivation in the classroom. Education occurs when an environment exists that encourages the growth and development of the teacher–student relationship. The environment is not only physical: it is social, experiential, and active. When the environment is not consciously shaped or is impacted by dictums externally prescribed in a one-size-fits-all manner, education is thwarted.

Dewey (1966) speaks strongly to this point:

> Too rarely is the individual teacher so free from the dictation of authoritative supervisor, textbook on methods, prescribed course of study, etc., that he can let his mind come to close quarters with the pupil's mind and the subject matter. This distrust of the teacher's experience is then reflected in lack of confidence in the responses of pupils. The latter receive their aims through a double or treble external imposition, and are constantly confused by the conflict between the aims which are natural to their own experience at the time and those in which they are taught to acquiesce. (p. 109)

What kind of relationship do teachers and students craft when their relatedness is reduced to a mechanistic production, and PTSD and performance anxiety are the common denominators? What occurs is born of crisis, and the joint aim is to survive rather than thrive. Teachers and students may bond, based on fear, but fear denotes lack of power. The student who reminded the class of what they were supposed to do now made an attempt at autonomy. He realized not only that it was time for gym but also that the students needed a break—now—and that everything does not depend on a test zone. Everyone else in the room felt pressured. Lack of agency is an environmental poison for teachers and students. Successful intervention and education are contingent upon being able to ask questions, interpret experiences, see alternatives, and make informed decisions. Greene (1978) notes that the challenge for teachers is to help students begin the journey:

> The problem, most will agree, is not to tell them what to do—but to help them attain some kind of clarity about how to choose, how to decide what to do. And this involves teachers directly, immediately—teachers as persons able to present themselves as critical thinkers willing to disclose their own principles and their own reasons as well as authentic persons living in the world, persons who are concerned—who care. (p. 48)

If a teacher can determine via assessment that a sizable number of students are possibly impacted by PTSD, then adjustments to instructional content and delivery can and should be made. The teacher assessment should not be used as conclusive evidence of PTSD but rather as an alerting indicator: follow-up referrals to the school counselor or school psychologist are the appropriate next step. There is also a glaring need for more research on gang violence and PTSD. In one of the definitive texts of PTSD (Peterson, Prout, & Schwarz, 1991), an entire chapter is devoted to its incidence in children. The experiences of youth ravaged by warfare in Central America and Cambodia are recounted, but no mention is made of youth in urban, inner-city environments in the United States.

There was a need to send some definite signals to my students, to make them aware that I more clearly understood what they were experiencing. Through our dialogues, the students realized that I knew they felt psychologically, emotionally, and academically overwhelmed, and that I would help them learn in spite of the trauma. This was communicated in several ways: most academic posters and charts were removed from the classroom and replaced with charts that specifically dealt with overcoming the odds, having self-confidence, and working toward peaceful conflict resolution. The only academic materials that remained were those pertaining to whatever subject we were working on at the time—the emphasis had to be on the students' feelings and perceptions. The charts were used as daily instructional and motivational aids. I increased my chats with small groups of students, often as they were working on assignments. I increased my chats with visits to the students' homes, and made weekend visits and phone calls, to be more available to working parents.

Dillon (1989) cites the necessity for teacher–student relationship building in order to create an open, risk-free environment in the classroom: the teacher must work to bridge the students' home culture with school culture and thus becomes a translator and intercultural broker. The students began to seek me out in increasing numbers. Some of them provided their home phone numbers—which I already had—but they did this because they wanted to talk about their lives and knew they had a teacher who would listen. Students often followed me to my car to talk, and when I would see a student after school or on weekends while running errands, we would stand and talk on the spot for 10 to 20 minutes. The students shared their frustrations, pains, and aspirations without hesitation, often providing private details.

☐ A Promising Approach: Small Schools, Détente, Virtues, and Caring

Although the student–teacher relationship is impacted as never before by circumstances that threaten it, teachers and students persist in their efforts to make sense of the world. The virtue of constancy resides in the practice of teaching. Constancy enables students and teachers to continue to seek understanding across differences and over time—to strive toward the acquisition of other virtues, especially those that are communicative. Small schools encourage the cultivation of communicative virtues and provide an arena for effectively addressing the needs of students who have been participants in, or victims of, gang violence.

Meier (1996) cites several benefits of small schools:

1. Governance—A small faculty has the ability to meet and resolve situations on the spot, and has the flexibility to quickly implement changes when a particular strategy does not work.
2. Respect—A climate of respect requires that students and teachers know each other well. Small schools make this possible.
3. Simplicity—When the organizational structure of a school is simple, the students become the prime focus.
4. Safety—In a small school, strangers are easier to spot, and teachers are more likely to notice students whose behavior might be troubling.
5. Belonging—Each student in a small school is known by the entire faculty—no one gets lost in the shuffle. The students' academic performance and behavior are assessed by the entire staff, and this makes curricular adjustments more effective (pp. 12–13).

Rice and Burbules (1992) suggest that the competitive and impersonal nature of formal education works against the cultivation of communicative values, including patience, tolerance for alternative points of view, respect for differences, sincerity, and honesty. They encourage educators to examine how schools might be made more conducive to the communicative virtues.

Such an examination was undertaken in the creation of an alternative public high school on Chicago's Near North Side, in the shadow of the Cabrini-Green public housing development. Facilitating the acquisition of communicative virtues is of particular importance when the majority of a school's students are gang-involved or live in environments rife with gang activity. Establishing détente was crucial to the opening and operation of the school. Not only did the school have to be perceived as neutral territory but also as a place where students from rival gangs could realistically coexist.

The creation of the school involved bringing together disparate groups, including the Chicago Public Schools (CPS), DePaul University, the Chicago Housing Authority (CHA), and representatives of several community organizations. Each entity brought an element to the school: CPS provided the site and teaching staff; DePaul provided the administrator, curricular and technical support; the community organizations recruited the students and encouraged active parental/community support; and CHA provided security. The meetings and process were the enactment of dialoguing across differences, and there were substantial differences and motivations for each group. The fact that the school opened and still functions despite those differences provided a sense of real hope that the school could have a positive impact. I was the school's first teacher, and the experience offered concrete evidence that school-based interventions can succeed, if planned with care.

The alternative "second-chance" school, which opened in September 1996, has 103 students and 16 staff members. The school is in a wing of an existing high school and operates from 3 p.m. to 9 p.m. This means students are in class during the hours when street conflicts often occur. Students who have children love the schedule because they can make arrangements for child care with relatives who have returned home from work or school. Negotiations to provide an in-house child care service were successful, and the school now offers on-site child care. Some students bring their children to class. The teachers and students have learned to deal with the toddlers' presence and still get their work done. Even more remarkable, the children have a positive and nurturing effect on all involved. It is not unusual to see teachers or even so-called hard-core gang members gently rocking a baby who is crying.

The climate exists due to the deliberate and sustained efforts by the staff and community to make the school a nurturing place, a place where students and teachers talk about and enact possibilities despite traumatic experiences and circumstances. Staff members were selected based on input from various community organizations across the city. Priority was placed on identifying and selecting teachers who were known for their caring demeanor. This did not exclude consideration of how well teachers knew their subject matter. Teachers presented proposals and sample lesson plans to the school's board. The selected staff members and principal held planning sessions over a six-week period prior to the school's opening. When teacher inservice sessions are held, the discussions are about the students—their challenges and conversations are the focus. Moreover, the staff discuss and share readings that encourage praxis—critical reflection and action upon the situations in which the students exist, as opposed to readings regarding curricular mastery and proficiency.

The participation of community organizations in the development of the school is illustrative of how schools can be organized with ease. The organizations selected a member from each of their groups, and these persons became the school's recruiters. Flyers were distributed, phone calls were made, notices were sent to the local media, and registration was conducted at various sites throughout the neighborhood. Since the school was created for youth who were dropouts or gang involved or both, the involvement of the community was crucial in identifying prospective students. However, the students were not hand picked. Many students heard about the school, and because they believed in the integrity of the community workers involved with the school, they decided to enroll.

There are four major gangs in the neighborhood, and the school enrolled youth who were known to be active from each gang. The community representatives also talked with gang regents (neighborhood gang leaders who act as midlevel "management"). The purpose of the talks was not to acquiesce the school's power to the gangs but to create détente, where the school is viewed as neutral territory. At Cabrini-Green (and elsewhere), this is especially important since students will not cross gang boundaries unless they believe it is safe to do so. This is one area that has not been given the consideration it deserves by school administrators since it impacts directly on student attendance. With détente, the school's safety is enhanced. The addition of security by the housing authority is also beneficial. The housing authority police selected were familiar with the neighborhood youth and could provide security without being perceived as insensitive or brutal.

Students know what is expected in terms of attendance, study, and responsibility. Students are not rewarded for merely showing up, nor do teachers engage in power-tripping antics to coerce students to learn. At first, the students expected coercion and everything else that goes along with traditional authoritarian high schools. What they received instead—respect and caring—has made all the difference.

When the alternative school opened, the students came ready for battle. They were prepared to be treated with indifference and disdain, so they arrived in full gear. Males and females wore outfits associated with gangs: baggy pants, plaid shirts, caps tilted to the left or right (depending on affiliation), and gym shoes tied with laces in the gang's colors. No students smiled when photographed for their school I.D.s.

When the students began to realize that this school was different, their clothing changed, and the staff immediately took notice. The females stopped wearing caps and baggy pants, started sporting full-blown couture-quality hairstyles, makeup, and wore either skirts or pants that had shape. The males, not to be outdone, traded in their gear for designer-inspired sportswear and jackets, but did keep their Nike Air Jordan shoes. With the difference in look came a pronounced and positive change in behavior. The males and females began to pay more attention to each other, and less attention to their respective cliques. Smiles, laughter, and pranks generally associated with adolescent silliness abounded. Attendance went up and stabilized. Teachers began receiving more completed assignments from more students, and when students returned from being absent, they asked for the work they missed—and completed it!

The students repeatedly tell teachers that they know the teachers care about them, and the care is consistently demonstrated. Several staff members have made court appearances on behalf of students and have gone to the police station when students have been arrested. The teachers usually eat lunch with students and talk with them. The conversations are so lively that the students do not think about acting up—they are too engaged in discussion.

Paulo Freire (1996) points out that an educator "must be up to an understanding of the world the people have" (p. 26). Students are more inclined to listen and learn in the classroom because they respect their teachers as individuals who also listen to and learn from them. A major factor in the success of the school is staff demeanor, and Noddings (1988) clearly expresses the importance of this perception:

> Moral education, from the perspective of an ethic of caring, involves modeling, dialogue, practice, and confirmation. . . . Teachers are, of course, concerned with their students' academic achievement, but, more importantly, they are interested in the development of fully moral persons. This is not a zero-sum game. There is no reason why excellent mathematics teaching (for example) cannot enhance ethical life as well. . . . The teacher models not only admirable patterns of intellectual activity but also desirable ways of interacting with people. Such teachers treat students with respect and consideration and encourage them to treat each other in a similar fashion. They use teaching moments as caring occasions. (p. 26)

The students are changing. Not all have relinquished their gang ties, but many have, and the ones who remain gang involved are interrogating their lives and the world. The following essay excerpt was written by a 17-year-old female former gang member (Brumfield, 1997) about the racially motivated beating of Lenard Clark in Chicago in 1997:

> Friday, the Chicago Black United Community Organization marched in Bridgeport while Lenard lay helpless in the hospital. I was there along with the history teacher and assistant principal. Despite the rain, the whole community knew we had a cause. We marched to De La Salle Academy, and then to the 11th District police station. . . . People watched as we so proudly walked through their so-called peaceful and kind community. Some were shouting racist slurs, others waved, and some just closed their doors so that they couldn't hear the truth. There was only one white person in the march, a senior citizen. This man was trying so hard to stay on the front line. I felt so good knowing I was a part of a movement to preserve and uplift our people. I was so proud to see our young brothers and sisters marching. There were small children and older people too. It was a wonderful experience.

The student author was so moved by participating in the protest that she began to seek other forums where she could voice her concerns.

She became a columnist for the school newspaper, providing reportage on community meetings and commentaries on issues impacting the school and neighborhood. She and 39 other students participated in a 10-day East

Coast college tour, and she now plans to attend college to pursue a career as a journalist.

The stories and successes of classrooms and schools such as this one have not been told or publicized nearly enough. There is a tendency to downplay the human/humane factor in gang research and to reduce those involved to mere statistics. These students defy the stereotype and have become more vocal, political, and active: they are a part of a growing constituency that can no longer be regarded as merely violent or dismissed as ineffectual.

One possible reason for their exclusion from public notice is that the research conducted on gang-involved youth is often not informed by those who have an indigenous perspective. The stories of teachers who work in urban classrooms and live in similar neighborhoods must be told. There are subtle nuances missing from the research—nuances that can only be observed and articulated by persons who live and work in the communities affected. They are the ones who can provide the evidence necessary to encourage a massive paradigm shift in our intervention and pedagogical strategies.

☐ Conclusion

There are as many reasons for violent behavior among young people as there as people engaging in such behavior. School settings have recently become a very popular site for violent acts involving youth. The seriousness of the youth violence problem demands that in schools teachers be equipped to recognize warning signs of violence about to erupt. In order to accomplish that goal it may be necessary to help teachers by expanding their understanding of the dynamics of the cycle of violence and how young people may be at risk based on their exposure to family violence in the home. Researchers have consistently pointed out that children and adolescents who are exposed to family violence are at greater risk for engaging in violent behavior than youngsters who are not.

It has been proposed in this chapter that many of the young people who have serious violence as part of their out-of-school experiences may be suffering from PTSD. If that is true, school personnel should be made aware of the dynamics associated with the disorder and how they manifest themselves in the classroom.

Poor academic performance in the classroom in the absence of an objectively verifiable learning difficulty may be a signal of underlying emotional problems. Rather than dismissing poor achievers as being unmotivated, teachers and other school personnel should consider the possibility that the poor performance is the result of emotional interference, maybe even PTSD.

☐ Appendix

Gang Violence Post-Traumatic Stress Disorder Questionnaire

Age _____

Grade Level _____

Sex: M _____ F _____

Directions: If an item below affected you in the past five years, circle "Y" (for yes); then circle the time period that indicates how long ago the behavior occurred.

1. Witnessed gang violence   Y   N
    less than one month   1–5 months   6 months–1 year   1–3 years   3–5 years

2. Victim of gang violence   Y   N
    less than one month   1–5 months   6 months–1 year   1–3 years   3–5 years

3. Have dreams about the experience   Y   N
    less than one month   1–5 months   6 months–1 year   1–3 years   3–5 years

4. Have recurrent memories of the experience   Y   N
    less than one month   1–5 months   6 months–1 year   1–3 years   3–5 years

5. Have feelings that the experience is happening again   Y   N
    less than one month   1–5 months   6 months–1 year   1–3 years   3–5 years

6. Have extra alertness/reaction to unexpected noises   Y   N
    less than one month   1–5 months   6 months–1 year   1–3 years   3–5 years

7. Have feelings of guilt about the experience   Y   N
    less than one month   1–5 months   6 months–1 year   1–3 years   3–5 years

8. Avoid activities that remind you of the event   Y   N
    less than one month   1–5 months   6 months–1 year   1–3 years   3–5 years

9. Have difficulty feeling/expressing emotions   Y   N
    less than one month   1–5 months   6 months–1 year   1–3 years   3–5 years

10. Have difficulty concentrating in school   Y   N
    less than one month   1–5 months   6 months–1 year   1–3 years   3–5 years

11. Have problems with memory   Y   N
    less than one month   1–5 months   6 months–1 year   1–3 years   3–5 years

12. Have difficulties with other family members   Y   N
    less than one month   1–5 months   6 months–1 year   1–3 years   3–5 years

13. Have boredom with school   Y   N
    less than one month   1–5 months   6 months–1 year   1–3 years   3–5 years

14. Have difficulty falling asleep   Y   N
    less than one month   1–5 months   6 months–1 year   1–3 years   3–5 years

15. Have difficulty meeting school goals   Y   N
    less than one month   1–5 months   6 months–1 year   1–3 years   3–5 years

☐ References

American Psychiatric Association. (1994). *Diagnostic and statistical manual of mental disorders* (4th rev. ed.). Washington, DC: Author.

Brumfield, T. (1997). *The beating of Lenard Clark.* Unpublished essay.

Dewey, J. (1966). *Democracy and education.* New York: The Free Press. (Original work published 1916)

Dillon, D. (1989). Showing them that I want them to learn and that I care about who they are: A microethnography of the social organization of a secondary low-track English-reading classroom. *American Educational Research Journal, 26,* 227–259.

Eisner, E. W. (1985). *The educational imagination on the design and evaluation of school programs* (2nd ed.). New York: Macmillan.

Freire, P. (1996). *Pedagogy of hope: Reliving pedagogy of the oppressed.* New York: Continuum.

Greene, M. (1978). *Landscapes of learning.* New York: Teachers College Press.

Meier, D. W. (1996). The big benefits of smallness. *Educational Leadership, 54,* 12–15.

Noddings, N. (1988). An ethic of caring and its implications for instructional arrangements. *American Journal of Education, 96,* 215–230.

Peterson, K. C., Prout, M. F., & Schwarz, R. A. (1991). *Post-traumatic stress disorder: A clinician's guide.* New York: Plenum.

Rice, S., & Burbules, N. C. (1992). Communicative virtues and educational relations. In Philosophy of education (on-line). Available: htpp://www.ed.uiuc.edu/COE/EPS/PES-Yearbook/92_docs/rice_burbules.HTM

6

Norman Randolph

Energizing and Organizing the Community

Thinking about what needs to be done about youth violence and gangs, one cannot help but feel a bit overwhelmed—especially in a time of economic retrenchment and cynicism about what public education, private enterprise, and government can do at any level. Yet there are positive forces at work. For one, the idea of reform is in the air. People of all political, economic, and religious persuasions realize that there are many areas where changes in our institutions are needed. The issues today are less over whether changes in the delivery of human services are necessary, than over what shape these changes will take, including who will carry any tax burdens of change.

One situation that has been developing is that gangs are becoming so dominant in many localities that (in spite of large expenditures on law enforcement and gang task forces) some will be forced to do something other than what has been tried. Perhaps communities are analogous to alcoholics who "hit bottom" before they seek major changes in lifestyle. Perhaps in some communities the situation must become much worse before there is sufficient leadership for change.

There are, of course, those who will work to maintain the status quo. They may, however, lose some of their ability to maintain conditions as they are, especially if wide collaboration in the community can be energized. Surely, if the community is to be successful in attacking the gang problem, it must create much more motion for change in every neighborhood than has been the case so far.

129

Working for changes in neighborhoods through neighborhood leaders and collaborators, however, will not relieve anyone from feeling a bit overwhelmed. And overwhelmed everyone will be, unless there is a useful plan and criteria by which to proceed. Each neighborhood needs to create guidelines that will keep its eyes on three questions:

- How can it help young people at risk who have not as yet joined a gang to stay out of gangs?
- How can it effectively encourage gang members to leave their gangs; or if they don't leave, how can it rechannel the gang's activities into legitimate pursuits?
- How should it respond to young people who are disruptive, criminal, or violent, and not within its power to change?

In order to successfully answer these questions, the community needs to attack the critical, personal, and social conditions that undergird each problem. For example, the research literature and the testimonies of gang members, street workers, and others who have direct experience, show common agreement that many who join gangs suffer from alienation. Depending on the individual, the alienation may be from work ethics or compassion for others. They may feel no meaningful connection to the social process valued by most citizens. Their alienation is usually toward the critical political, educational, law enforcement, and economic institutions.

In the gang-infested neighborhoods of my county, far too many people have learned to be estranged from education and our other public institutions. This must be reversed. By reducing resentment toward our institutions among youth and adults, we have vehicles for reducing the vulnerability of young people to gangs. We also increase our opportunities for channeling some gangs into socially valuable pursuits. To do this, however, we need to change those conditions that cause people to be alienated from our culture (see Gonzalez, this volume).

Among the characteristics needed to avoid being estranged from education, for example, is a belief in one's own ability to learn what education has to offer. When we teach youngsters to believe that they are dumb and cannot learn an academic subject, we teach them to be alienated from the process of learning and schooling—and eventually from society at large. Educators and parents teach incompetence by expecting little and teaching little. We then blame the recipients of our biases for lacking the competencies that they have never been taught. Next, we often fail to provide opportunities to legitimately earn a reasonable living because they are "uneducated." It is little wonder so many of these alienated youth feel justified in striking out against a society that has branded them as losers.

We know, of course, that in a direct sense, parents play an especially critical role in how their children evaluate their competencies (Brookover,

Erickson, & McEvoy, 1996). However, we also know that many parents take their cues for how they evaluate their children by what they believe teachers think about their children, and what teachers thought about them (the parents) as children. Thus, teachers play both direct and indirect roles in the development of student conceptions of their competencies to learn.

The difficulty we face is twofold: (1) enacting changes that inoculate young people from becoming alienated, and (2) reducing the alienation of those already estranged from desirable values and institutions. Yet these and other fundamental achievements are not beyond a community's grasp if it takes into account what is required to achieve the following objectives.

☐ Community Objectives

A. Restated, the major accomplishments in helping high-risk youngsters who have not yet joined a gang will be in
   1. reducing the likelihood that youth in gang-prone areas will become alienated from desirable social values and the preferable economic, family, educational, and political institutions;
   2. creating in gang-prone areas an environment that is safe from personal violence; and
   3. providing a variety of means to move from school to work that are seen as viable alternatives by youth.
B. The primary achievements in helping gang members to leave their gangs will be through
   1. reducing gang-generated violence;
   2. modifying attitudes of social alienation among gang members and others in their neighborhoods; and
   3. creating opportunities for members, who have the desire, to safely leave their gangs.
C. The major accomplishments when dealing with young people who seriously disrupt schools or engage in violence or other crime in their communities will occur through
   1. assessing the character and extent of their psychological, social, or educational impairments;
   2. determining the character of treatment and services that should be provided to socially impaired young people in schools, in alternative schools, in their communities, or in residential settings; and
   3. making changes in schools and other institutions that contribute to a reduction in the social impairments of youth, regardless of how they were created.

Obviously, the attainment of any one objective affects the attainment of the other objectives. For example, it will be easier for members to leave their gangs if gang-generated violence is minimal. Minimal violence will also decrease the likelihood of young people joining gangs, and it will make it easier for care providers to respond to delinquency.

Keeping one's mind on achieving these objectives, it becomes necessary to have a plan. And to be most effective, citizens within the community should create the plan and take full responsibility for assisting in its implementation. What can be pointed out for citizens to consider in making a plan are ideas based on the triumphs and failures of others about a process of community collaboration that maximizes the chances of success.

☐ How Shall We Proceed?

It would be easy to proceed with a discussion of a variety of community collaboration efforts that probably would be worthwhile. These programs, in my experience, usually involve a task force established by a government leader like a governor, mayor, or police chief, and include mostly professionals administering various law enforcement and social agency organizations— along with a smattering of lay persons of prominence and a few residents from the neighborhoods of focus. Usually these collaborations are subsidized by a national, state, or local governmental agency, or a foundation. The Office of Juvenile Justice and Delinquency Prevention, U.S. Department of Justice, has published several reports describing a number of these kinds of community collaborations (Cronin, 1964; see also References and Selected Resources at the end of the chapter).

If there is such collaborative effort in your community, it should be supported. If there are no effects then perhaps steps should be taken to institute such a task force to unite various governmental and community organizations to share services and coordinate efforts. On the other hand, I believe that one reason that these programs often are not more effective than they are is because various groups and individuals are not included. A second reason is that the focus of their work is often too restricted. In addition to intervention programs, five areas of related prevention work must be addressed in detail. These include the following: (1) creating safe streets, (2) educating all students to have essential academic skills and knowledge, (3) preparing all youth for transition to work, (4) involving all youth in team activities that stress interdependence and social values, and (5) requiring wide participation by both youth and adults in community economic and social "uplifting" activities. It is proposed that consideration be given to energizing and mobilizing the total community in a populist movement that builds on the sentiments of the public. This organization of populist involvement should not exclude professionals and others already committed to intervening with gang members but would include them and provide support and resources for their work as well.

Guided by these added objectives, the following recommendations are offered for reducing the relevance of youth gangs. They focus on the process of organizing a community from the "grassroots," a community-wide forum for individual and action groups. Organized discussions and the development of community consensus through a community forum receive first priority in this model. After consideration of the process of developing a community forum, suggestions will turn to the recruitment of citizens and energizing activities. For only after there has been considerable and coherent community discourse, democratically arrived-at decisions, and extensive involvement can any program to reduce gangs be adopted that is likely to meet with community-wide success.

The forum also should recognize that to achieve a policy is not the same as being effective in implementing that policy. Many good and needed policies are enacted, yet not implemented. Often the reason for failure is that those who are needed to implement the policy have been left out of the policymaking process. A community that creates and has responsibility for implementing a change in itself can do much to bring about that change. The pressures for change that a community can bring to bear on its institutions and individuals is considerable when it is organized to function collaboratively.

The next big chore for a community forum is to assure organization at the "grassroots" level of the neighborhoods. One concern may be how to organize and solicit input from the residents in various poverty neighborhoods. The neighbors, if properly organized, will make a big difference in the success of the program. Another task will be to get the community agencies working together in the neighborhood and in harmony with neighborhood organizations. How is this all to be done?

One should not expect to have a positive impact in only one or a few neighborhoods and expect the solution to last. Experience in ridding drug sales and crack houses from neighborhoods shows that the overall problem is not reduced. The crack houses merely move, and move back in again when enthusiasm lessens. In other words, the wider the community impact, the better. But the effort must start somewhere.

The overall approach that offers the most hope is one that has a large number of persons in various positions participating at every level: from the neighborhoods up through the county, state, and federal levels. It can start, however, with only a few concerned citizens who learn not everything but quite a bit as a group about gangs. They should learn some of what communities must do to help keep youngsters out of gangs, what is known about how to get gang members to quit their gangs, and how to treat those who do not live by the rules for a sane society. This ad-hoc group need not depend on experts to tell them what to think—although it should seek their input.

Step 1: An Informal Beginning

Usually the approach that is taken is for a government organization or leader, like a mayor, to appoint a gang task force. Where such an appointed task force is present, they should be soon involved. However, it is recommended here that a group of volunteers should first take a somewhat different approach to organizing a community-wide force of citizens.

A first step is for a few concerned citizens in each general area of the county or city to form ad-hoc groups—to come together and work at becoming well informed on the topic of gangs. The members should feel that they have a personal stake in reducing gang activity. The size of a group initially should be small. They also need to make a strong commitment to "hang together" until their job is done. They must accept the responsibility to do what they can as a group to "uplift" their community. Hopefully, several members should be from areas of high gang activity. These groups also may include religious, school, and other leaders in the community, and former gang members. Effort must be made, however, to assure that the group is one of equal peers looking for answers.

For their long-term effectiveness, the memberships of ad-hoc groups need to hold in abeyance, as much as possible, their political, economic, social or religion-based opinions. They must work individually and collectively to find out as much *factual* information about gangs as possible. The members should also agree to await the collection and analysis of information before they make their collective conclusions on what must be done.

The small ad-hoc groups then need to merge into one community-wide ad-hoc group. This larger ad-hoc group will then need to set an agenda for eliciting the involvement of the larger community. Then the community-wide ad-hoc group should prepare to bring about a major community response through a community *forum*.

Restated, before any effort is directed toward the formal involvement of the total community at large, it is suggested that a citizens group become well informed about the nature of various types of gangs, their extent, trends, impact, and treatment. They also should become aware of various programs that currently intervene with gangs in their area or other parts of the country. One member with a computer and access to the Internet can produce considerable information to be studied. Another member who is familiar with library resources can add more.

It also will be important for the group to consider ways of organizing their neighborhoods that have a chance of bringing about change. Many a community program has failed simply because the community was not appropriately organized. In this regard, they should know that persons who feel they have a personal stake in doing something about reducing the relevance of gangs will keep the group functioning when others tire. For this reason alone, the group should include persons who feel they have something to lose if gangs cannot be contained in their community.

While emphasizing the importance of ad-hoc citizens groups, this does not mean that the leadership resources in a community should be ignored—particularly those that have histories of concern for community development. A leader may come from La Raza, NAACP, a church, a temple, a mosque, Aspira, or any other organization, but the ad-hoc groups should be representative citizens groups.

Leadership is important because the objective of collaboration requires leadership for motivation and order. Leaders should be drawn from or developed in every area—particularly in and from poverty-plagued neighborhoods where gangs are active. Local organizations that have among their purposes improving life in the area are usually excellent resources for leadership. However, care should be taken. Some leaders may have a different agenda than what is needed.

When an ad-hoc group is developing information, there are several recent books and articles on the topic of gangs that should be read for preparation. There also are a number of materials that, while not directly on the topic of gangs, are pertinent to conditions that make gangs attractive to youngsters. For example, there are ample research articles and books on how tracking in schools creates alienation from school and from society, resulting in poor academic skills and thus contributing to gang membership (see Quamina, this volume). There also are books on working with gangs at school as well as in community centers.

Obviously, each member of the group will not have the time to read all that he or she needs to know. Hence, the members should divide up their reading and provide summaries to the others. In addition, former gang members and persons with expertise and direct experience with gangs should be invited to share their views and recommend further reading. In this regard, the United States Department of Justice, Office of Juvenile Justice and Delinquency Prevention, has a clearinghouse that provides a wealth of information that is free or inexpensive on the topics of youth gangs and violence.

The group should next be prepared to meet regularly and share what they have learned in an organized and summarized manner. In addition to charts, listings, and descriptions, a resource library should be put together of books, videos, and articles. There also should be listings of resources such as researchers in nearby universities who study juvenile crime and violence, local police officers on gang task forces, information centers on the Internet, government agencies that will provide assistance, and so forth.

If the group takes its task seriously and the members have acquired a reasonable grasp of what others have found or concluded about youth gangs, it is time to take the next major step of branching further out into the community at large. In so doing it is recommended that the group obtain the assistance of a sponsoring organization.

Step 2: A Sponsoring Organization

The sponsor should not be an organization that has responsibility for the implementation of anticrime or antiviolence programs, such as the schools or the police department or other long-standing organizations that, while needed to be involved, would elicit turf competition or carry too much "baggage." It should be a relatively impartial organization, such as the League of Women Voters or the major newspaper in the area. The dominant newspaper in the area, if its publisher and senior editorial staff can be persuaded to accept the responsibility, has many resources that can be used—both to its own advantage and to the advantage of reducing the gang problem.*

Two local newspapers serving as sponsors of two different community improvement programs in two Southern cities are detailed for consideration (*Bradenton Herald*, Bradenton, Florida, and the *Charlotte Observer*, Charlotte, North Carolina). The *Bradenton Herald*'s concern was with what the citizens knew and could do to reduce childhood sexual abuse in their county—a task that to many people seemed formidable. With the input of a small group of local "experts" and their reporters, the newspaper began by running articles every several days that educated and sensitized the community to the problem of child abuse in their area. They did this without compromising the ethics of journalism to report accurately and critically.

Then the *Bradenton Herald* called for and sponsored a public forum of meetings to be held over several weeks to come up with useful suggestions for what the various institutions in the county and state could and should do to lessen the problem of child abuse and to help survivors.

Several hundred citizens from the community showed up for these meetings. The newspaper's executive editor acted as the facilitator for discussion.

---

*The Pew Center and the Poynter Institute for Media Studies (St. Petersburg, Florida) have commissioned studies of eight public journalism projects around the country describing, How did it happen? What impact did they have on both the community and the newsroom? and What lessons were learned?

The editor began the first forum with a brief overview of the problem. The editor next had two local persons briefly present their information on child abuse in their county. Then the editor facilitated from the floor the expression of a wide set of feelings and beliefs. During the subsequent week's forum, the facilitator invited the audience to divide up into action groups. The groups were asked to report back their findings and recommendations. During this forum, reporters from the paper and other media were there to report objectively on what was happening.

As a sponsor of the community-wide forum, the newspaper had several advantages. It granted credibility to citizens that a community-wide problem existed and that it was time for the community to act—that the problem was more than just a task for social agencies and the police. Another big advantage was that the newspaper was in a position to create public saliency and concern. It is still keeping people's attention on what needs to be done without compromising its integrity. A big advantage of the newspaper was in bringing about the involvement of leaders in the community, region, and state, with much wider support than would have occurred otherwise.

Another illustration of civic journalism is the recent work of the *Charlotte Observer* in North Carolina. The focus of their project was on crime and its solutions in some of Charlotte's most violent neighborhoods. The *Observer's* role is to get people in the neighborhoods to reach out and meet the needs of their community. The *Observer*, in order to protect its journalistic integrity, assigned a person who would have absolutely no role in reporting on events. That person acted as a resource person and helped to develop leadership skills at the neighborhood level. Four journalists from the *Observer* kept their professional distance to cover the stories that emerged.

It is important that a newspaper's ethical journalistic integrity remain intact. The newspaper must not become an advocate for any position other than community dialogue, planning, and action. The newspaper must be free to report on and critique any community event. It must not be beholden to any group or program to be expected to advocate a particular ideology.

If the sponsoring organization of a forum on youth gangs is the local newspaper, a major step in the right direction will have been taken, if it also assures the newspaper's independence to report on events. And along with the sponsor, it will be time for step three—the creation of a community group of citizens and a steering committee.

Step 3: The Community Group

The process of selecting the community group should begin with an invitation to all critical departments of local government and private social service; business, labor, and fraternal organizations; community foundations and associations; and churches, temples, and mosques. Special care should be taken to respect protocol, beginning with the top elected or administrative officials and then, with their blessing, the top personnel in each organization.

In addition to those organizations with direct involvement with gangs, such as the courts, law enforcement, youth centers, and school-based gang intervention programs, every effort should be made to involve all organizations that will be important for prevention planning. Included are child care departments, children and youth services, disaster preparedness agencies, economic development offices, emergency medical services, fire and health departments, housing agencies, libraries, parks and recreation, planning and zoning, labor, public transportation, public works, and social services agencies. All the religious institutions should be invited as well as all of the civil rights organizations. The National League of Cities produced a report—Rethinking Public Policy (1994)—that describes the importance of each of these areas and of mobilizing all segments of the local community.

The first purpose of the community group is to select a steering committee and begin the fostering of a community network committed to collaboratively addressing the gang problem. The remainder of the community group (i.e., those not on the steering committee) should then plan on joining the forum described in Step 4. The steering committee, with its subcommittees, will plan and facilitate the community forum and take charge of assembling information for the forum to consider. Following the receipt of suggestions from forum action groups, it will prepare the draft of position papers to which the forum will respond.

On the steering committee, there must be leaders from neighborhood ad-hoc groups where the gangs are most active. These leaders will have a crucial role as the process evolves. And no organization that has a program for gang intervention or high-risk adolescents should be left out of the invitations. Thus, it may be necessary to have subcommittees to accommodate all the organizations to be involved.

The term "neighborhood improvement" association is used because that is a common phenomenon and term used in middle- and upper-class neighborhoods. More crime-oriented phrases that also may be appropriate are "Take Back the Neighborhood Association" and "Neighborhood Watch." However, I favor a more uplifting term, and a term that will emphasize another role—that of facilitating prevention through socializing programs.

Middle- and upper-class persons have learned the power that associations can have on local events. If there is no such association in an area, seek help in developing one by approaching clergy, street workers, or other leaders to assist with the process. In any event, there needs to be the involvement of neighborhood associations dedicated to reducing gang activity before a public forum is called.

The steering committee will probably need to expand on the information provided by the ad-hoc groups. This resource may require some small amount of funding. Skilled social research specialists may need to be available to the forum, its action groups, the community group, and the sponsor.

Before this is done, however, the community group and steering committee members should be cautioned with the same advice the initial ad-hoc group members gave to themselves: the members should make every attempt to not be glib or quick to arrive at solutions. Conjectural solutions at this point should be ignored in favor of learning as much factual information as possible—even if conjectural solutions are offered by experts. The charge to each new member should be to be as open minded as possible and to consider all of the relevant information that can be acquired before making up his or her mind.

To facilitate such open mindedness and willingness to learn, it will be extremely important to have persons with excellent group processing and motivational skills to facilitate the first citizen's ad-hoc groups, the community group, the steering committee, the forum, and the action groups that are to be planned. Some will want to dominate the process and this should be resisted. Thus, effective leadership will be required.

Step 4: A Community Forum

With a steering committee in place, the sponsoring organization should call for a public forum to study and make recommendations. There should be considerable advertising of the event. The setting for the forum should be large enough to accommodate a large number of people. Some will argue that this should be done by the steering committee. Unfortunately, there have been hundreds of steering committees—usually referred to as joint task forces—set up to deal with gangs. Most of these task forces failed, I surmise, because representative citizens from the involved communities were left out.

At the first meeting of a public forum on gangs, there should be a summary presentation of information known about gangs in the area that has been prepared by members of the community group. The areas of needed attention also should be reported for consideration by the forum and its future action committees. These include (1) how to help at-risk youngsters to avoid gang membership in the first place; (2) how to help young gang members to leave their gangs; and (3) how the community should respond to youngsters who engage in disruptive behavior in school or who commit crimes.

The forum should be helped to recognize that the conditions for successfully addressing one problem are likely to be quite different from the other two. It is something like, "What do you do after the barn door has been left open and the horse has run away?" "What do you do to keep the horse in the barn?" and "What do you do when someone is lighting fires in the barn?" It also should be pointed out that while the approaches to solving each of these problems are different, the success of each solution depends on solving the other two problems.

The forum must then be helped to understand that while the gang problem must be attacked on all three fronts, the solutions that are presented must be viable and possible within the resources that are available, and within the values that are generally shared in the community. For example, under current economic conditions, there is not going to be much extra money allocated for schools. If certain changes in education are to be sought, they should be capable of implementation within or close to the current budget, or a case must be made for shifting resources. This will make the forum's charge complex and difficult, but it should not be avoided.

By the end of the first two forum meetings, the audience should be invited to join special interest action study groups that are to be formed to address the specific concerns that are expressed in the forum (e.g., what should be done to improve juvenile detention, the schools, organization of neighbors, law enforcement, community agencies, legislation, and so forth). At this time, by prior arrangement, members of the core group should join these action groups. Subsequent chapters list a number of issues that the forum may wish to address.

Step 5: Action Groups

The overall task of each action group is to clarify its particular role and then, after a thorough study and discussion of its topic of focus, to make recommendations for suggested action to the community forum. Again, priority in the action groups should be given to making recommendations that are based (as much as possible) on solid research rather than opinions or anecdotal testimonials. Discussions involving ideology or political rhetoric should be avoided. This will be difficult, but if there are skilled group facilitators and social research specialists available for helping to gather information, the relevance of biased opinions will be lowered. Research specialists will be of critical importance to the research action groups. Most universities of any size have social research specialists who may be enticed to help the action groups in acquiring the hard data they will need.

Hard data is almost the only way to bridge the gaps that exist in our highly diverse population of competing religious, economic, political, and cultural perspectives. This is why the facilitators in each action group must focus on the commitment to seek as much hard information as possible about the nature, causes, and consequence of gangs in their community.

The facilitators should foster group cohesion by emphasizing the one shared value that unites them—the desire to reduce gang activity. And, of course, all sorts of socializing activities can help in creating this needed cohesion.

During this time, the newspaper should strive to make the findings of the action groups salient to the forum and the community. People should be informed about the information that is available on databases.

Toward the end of the action group meetings, fundamental questions and suggested answers should be developed. Examples of questions that the action groups might report answers to the forum include the following:

(1) What is the extent of gang development in our area? In our schools? What types of gangs are they? What are they like?
(2) What factors best explain why some youngsters join a gang? How relevant to gang participation are such factors as the lack of work skills or opportunities, alienation from school, attitudes toward the police, or living in dysfunctional homes? What other factors should be studied for possible relevance? (See Doucette-Gates, this volume.)
(3) What conditions in our public institutions (e.g., schools, housing projects, police departments, courts, detention centers) need to be changed because they foster gang membership or activity in our community?
(4) How should the forum go about eliciting such changes?

Again, useful answers to these questions depend on the acquisition and analysis of information that should be collected in a way that reduces the likelihood of dispute. If this task is done well, it will lead to more questions and answers. More important, the quest for answers by the entire community may lead to action—action that may bring about a healthier community.

Step 6: A Community Coalition

At this point, the forum should focus on producing a "reality platform" with as much community-wide consensus as possible on what needs to be done. Once a platform is arrived at by the forum, it is time to change the focus of the study groups into the community coalition of action groups to aggressively press for the changes that have been recommended.

Many of the organizations in the community, if their representatives have participated in the action groups and forum, will welcome the assistance of a community coalition of action groups in pressing their agenda. Often personnel in the schools, police departments, and other community agencies desire certain changes in their organizations, but they feel there is nothing they can do because they do not have the support of the community or their superiors. With the aid of a strong community coalition, these personnel may attempt to make needed changes in their organizations. Many also will act to facilitate their associates in other organizations.

The process of democratic community-wide discussion and organization, of course, will not appeal to some. They may want quick and simple authoritative solutions, or they may offer simple solutions based on a glib political, law enforcement, psychological, or religious argument. More difficult, however, will be the resistance of those who benefit from the status quo. These may be otherwise good people who put their jobs or pride ahead of what is best for the community. Selfishness is not easily overcome.

Social planners are often frustrated when the people they seek to help resist their efforts. The suggestions offered here are intended to get around this hurdle by suggesting a process of involving citizens who are not only targeted to be helped but are critical for the success of any program aimed at stemming the growth of organized youth crime.

No desirable solution to youth gangs, not even an otherwise valid suggestion, will work unless there is wide and aggressive support at the neighborhood level. Thus, there is the need for neighborhood mobilization to effect desired changes. Gangs in the Pittsburgh area create major social problems, as they do in other areas of North America. Every neighborhood in the community may have its own complex set of circumstances that only it can take into account.

It is beyond the capability of one chapter to suggest all of the specifics of what a community forum should consider regarding youth gangs. In a general sense, the forum will need to address three areas: (1) reducing violence, (2) dealing with gangs, and (3) prevention (i.e., reducing the number of youth who are at risk of becoming gang members). The process that will have the most success will be the one that figures out how to get a large portion of the adults and adolescents in the targeted neighborhoods to join and gain valued self-identities from being members of neighborhood "socially uplifting" organizations. For the young, communities must figure out how to get a large proportion of its youth into rewarding organizations, including those organizations that help make life in the neighborhoods better. Each youngster must be given a way to achieve pride in a group activity that is not a gang.

It is this last area that will cause a problem with acceptance. This is because effective prevention requires modification of economic and social conditions with the costs incurred now and the pay-off received later. Thus, many self-serving politicians will be hesitant to give leadership to primary prevention activities. A community must avoid the tendency to ignore primary prevention and mistakenly focus only on intervention to control gangs. Without reducing the number of youth who join gangs in the first place, a community will have little hope of holding back the growth of violence and crime among both youth and adults.

There is a second caveat about forum discussion. It is not to become enmeshed in topics over which little or nothing can be done. For example, some will want to spend time blaming various groups or events in the past. No one can undo the past. Hence, forum and group discussion leaders will need to constantly redirect concern to what needs to be done within the power of the forum to accomplish. This means that the resources available to the forum must be taken into account.

☐ Changing Organizations

Collaboration among organizations usually means that some changes in the organizations involved are required. When it comes to making changes in an organization, however, expect resistance. Any organization will, at times, seek to go its own way; often serving the needs of its administrators, staff, or a small vested group at the expense of the larger society. This should be anticipated for all private and public institutions. All human service organizations, while there to serve their sponsoring community, tend to act in their own self-interest, even if it is at the expense of the community that it is supposed to be serving. There may be rhetoric about serving the common good, but when a community's interests come in conflict with those of an organization within it, often it is the community's interests that need protection.

The same can be said for units within an organization. Scholars studying organizations have documented this problem. It is almost "natural." A critical task of any leader, whether the President of the United States, a principal of a school, or the organizers of a citizen's group, is how to get the units and individuals of the system to function together for the larger good.

Many people, it seems, tend to forget also that units within an organization, as they grasp for more resources and power, seek to operate more and more independently from the organization (see Branch, this volume). School people, for example, tend to not want community agency personnel, the police, or politicians, to impose themselves on school policy, any more than people in other institutions want "outsiders" telling their organization how to function.

Going further down the organizational ladder, it should also be noted that the members of an organization often put their personal interests ahead of the missions of their units. Teachers and administrators, similar to others, may give priority to their own working conditions and salaries over and against what may be needed by their school or community. One of the most important working conditions that is jealously guarded is that expressed as the curriculum—the experiences the staff is to provide students.

If you ask educators to change the way their schools are run and they see this as a threat to their well-being, you can expect many of them to resist. Even if a school is clearly failing in its mission to teach its students, there is likely to be resistance from the school staff for change. The "comfort zone" for some will be the status quo, even if the status quo is failing to meet the need of students. This is especially true if the staff members view the change as a threat to how they wish to work or what they will get paid.

Most people seem to be unaware that when significant changes in an organization are sought, change is also being sought in how the staff lives. As a result, the staff may do its best to resist unless there are adequate incentives. Teachers, for example, will be quick to recognize that with major changes in a curriculum some may be laid off, some may be reassigned, and, most assuredly, many will have to be retrained. It should, therefore, come as no surprise that proposed changes in a school's curriculum or the operation of any community or governmental organization will be resisted. Thus, maintaining the status quo is easier than changing an organization.

One consequence is that as a society's needs change for how its youth need to be educated, how law enforcement should be delivered, what welfare services should be offered, and so forth, there is still an investment in the status quo. This presents a big problem when there are quick and significant changes in the society. For example, with the massive economic and technological changes of the last few years, many schools are way out of step, as demonstrated by the large number of students who are not taught what they need to know.

One implication is clear. If a community action group seeks to make changes in the character of what teachers or the staff members of other organizations do, they will be most effective if they can reduce any perceived threats to them and provide incentives for change. The way to do this is to involve them in a way that they will see that it is in their best interest to facilitate desired changes. These changes should be feasible within their capacities and interests. There are some who do not believe, unfortunately, that poor inner-city students can be effectively taught. These teachers feel inadequate to such a task. And this mistaken belief is reinforced by school practices such as ability grouping, which function to maintain mistaken self-fulfilling prophecies about student learning abilities. This is a problem, but it can be overcome with appropriate inservice and reinforcement.

Another problem is that for too many years we have placed too much of a burden on school superintendents, principals, and administrators of programs, expecting them to be able to deliver on their own positive results. An effective school, for example, means educating nearly all students to have a mastery of core skills and knowledge to be able to successfully go on to college, go to a technical school, or enter the world of work. While this is a reasonable and an appropriate goal for administrators, more than authority is required for this to occur. Leadership for school change must involve the cooperative support of the school staff—particularly the teachers who in the end must carry out any changes. Thus, leadership must be shared, and the voice of the teachers must be heard if schools are to become effective institutions.

This same prescription applies to every other organization. For example, the police on the beat need to have input, and so forth, from organization to organization. The idea that leadership in an organization should be shared among those who must implement change must be recognized by community-wide action groups. To repeat, no outside force can expect to elicit cooperation and skill on the part of workers by edict alone. Yet the community has not only the right but the obligation to intrude into every community function, including its schools and other institutions. The question is, "How is this intrusion to be accomplished so as to effect cooperation from the staff in each organization?"

It seems that the old ways of schools, community organizations, and local government agencies cooperating, particularly in urban poverty areas, are not always desirable. Too often such cooperation is largely limited to the leaders. For this reason, it is particularly important to have in the community forum as many implementing staff as possible from each of the organizations to be affected. Just getting the leaders together seldom proves effective.

A community forum should also avoid the common tendency of creating the illusion of change with no meaningful change in outcome. It is deadly to the process of change if leaders appropriate the energies, hopes, and good will of the rank and file workers, issue reports and other rhetoric, yet do little to ensure that program changes are implemented. It is little wonder that organizational staff are often cynical about proposed task forces that are supposed to point to new directions. If task forces are to foster real change, then the means of implementing the recommendations affecting all levels of an organization must be considered.

Most staff workers, however, are not granted the time under present arrangements to participate in community development activities. They are far too busy in their typically overloaded programs, and few systems have sufficient capital to provide the released time that is necessary. However, because the objectives are so socially and economically important to the community at large, some way should be found to help defer part of the cost. These costs include helping teachers to leave their classrooms, police officers to leave their posts, and social workers to limit their case appointments. Another cost will be the time spent on inservice for making the needed changes.

There is really no point in planning for changes in schools or other organizations unless the necessary funds are available. However, such costs will be far, far less than what will be spent on prisons and damages to local economies if the needed changes are not made in how schools and other organizations function—particularly in high-crime areas. If a community should try to make changes "on the cheap," it is likely to get a program that is enacted in name alone, and not really implemented. This may be because the persons who are to implement the program never had the time or resources, and therefore the inclination, to learn what it is they should be doing.

No community, however, is likely to receive as much financial assistance from outside governmental sources as it has in the past. Rather, the monies will be decreasing. Whether a decrease in outside support is desirable is being debated. Whatever the case, each community must look more to itself for solving its problems. As a community, it must do nearly all the critical work. This is true regardless of outside support or the fact that youth gangs now cross state and national boundaries. Youth gangs are still fundamentally a "grassroots" problem. It is a grassroots responsibility.

☐ Conclusion

The salvation of the residents of communities resides within the community and in its most precious commodity, the residents. It has been suggested in the foregoing chapter that if communities are to be effective in combating problems of gangs and other disruptive forces, the community must be an active agent in helping to inoculate itself from toxic invaders. The process of activating a community can be a challenging and invigorating experience. Perhaps the greatest benefit to be derived from energizing a community is the fact that the subsequent demands for community action will be a less daunting task after the first experience. Everyone in a community has something constructive to offer its struggle against disruptive forces. Identifying the resources of a community before a crisis is one simple step that can be completed often, even when there is no "problem." Doing so also serves the purpose of building a sense of community cohesiveness.

Schools play a vital role in the lives of most communities. Because of their strategic and historic position of power, they can be instrumental in energizing communities. In order for schools to accomplish this task they will need to invite other community leaders not associated with the education of the communities' children to share in the very important work of making communities safe from outside forces, gangs included.

☐ Appendix

Selected Resources

Two adjacent neighborhoods.
The Neighborhood Network Center, 735 East Michigan Avenue, Lansing, MI 48912

Six public housing and four residential neighborhoods.
PACE, Norfolk Virginia, 302 City Hall Building, Norfolk, VA 23501

Public housing complex.
Neighborhood Resource Team, 27325 South Dixie Highway, Miami, FL 33032

Newspapers as sponsors.
Charlotte Observer, Charlotte, NC; *Bradenton Herald*, Bradenton, FL

☐ References

Brookover, W. B., Erickson, F. J., & McEvoy, A. (1996). *Creating effective schools*. Holmes Beach, FL: Learning Publications.
Cronin, R. C. (1964). *Innovative community partnerships: Working together for change*. Washington, DC: Office of Juvenile Justice and Delinquency Prevention.
Rethinking public policy. Washington, DC: National League of Cities, 1994.

MENTAL HEALTH
INTERVENTIONS

The chapters in this section of the book are concerned with the issues involved in providing mental health services to gang-affiliated adolescents and their families. The focuses taken by the different authors all seem to converge on the point that mental health and some level of self-regulation are essential to successful interventions with gang adolescents. This approach is somewhat different from the more prevalent law enforcement suppression attitude, readily apparent in the intervention literature, that purports to be concerned with helping gang adolescents and the communities in which they live.

The first chapter in this section by Vargas and DiPilato recognizes that the primary issue of adolescents is identity crystallization. They suggest that in the process of attempting to resolve the "who am I" question, adolescents of color also have the additional issue of negotiating potentially several cultural worlds as points of psychological reference. Vargas and DiPilato suggest that ethnic culture is a very important feature in the process of identity development. Despite its centrality to the identity development process, ethnic culture has been suspiciously absent from the writings of many developmentalists, including Erickson. He specifically does not stress the importance of ethnicity or race, but rather negates these factors and, at one point, suggested that race was simply a matter about which "neurotic" Black boys spent a fair amount of time being concerned and focused.

The utility of ethnic culture in the identity development process, suggests Vargas and DiPilato, means that it can serve as a protective factor in aiding young people in their quest for self-identity, or it can, at the other extreme, be considered a bit of a liability. They outlined briefly the pluses and minuses that ethnic culture can occupy in the great matrix of factors assisting adolescents in resolving the identity questions.

Self-esteem and ethnic identity are offered by Vargas and DiPilato as being two inextricably intertwined concepts. The authors note that many gang members feel negatively about themselves and their ethnic group membership. The result of such negativity is that the young person internalizes these views of their reference group and uses them as a blueprint for making decisions about themselves personally. The gang then offers adolescents who are negative in their self-appraisals an opportunity to overcome feelings of social alienation and rejection. Within the gang, these "outsiders" become valued and experience unconditional acceptance by a group of peers. For many such young people, the gang then comes to be the psychological representation of a "group."

Vargas and DiPilato suggest that since affiliation and belonging are important to gang members, perhaps group is the modality of best practice for working with troubled adolescents. According to them, groups have several advantages over individual one-on-one psychotherapeutic interventions, including opportunities to learn by observing others, being the psychodynamic approximation of the family of origin, and therefore providing yet another forum for an adolescent to work through developmental issues that are traceable to family of origin, and a safe space in which new skills can be practiced and receive positive reinforcement from others deemed to be important by the adolescent.

Culture-focused group therapy is offered by Vargas and DiPilato as a preventive strategy. They suggest that the cognitive–behavioral–theoretical orientation that underlies the group is ideally suited for work with troubled adolescents. The authors do not offer an explicit definition of cognitive–behavioral interventions, but their description of it very much resonates to the definition offered by Carylon and Jones in the next chapter; that is, cognitive–behavioral interventions are by definition strategies that are very much dependent on teaching the clients self-control through delay of gratification procedures.

Vargas and DiPilato offer some details about their culture-focused group therapy as an approach to help gang members and other troubled adolescents reconnect to a sometimes lost part of their developmental history. Throughout the work, the focus is on self-discovery, not gang membership. In focusing on self-discovery, the adolescents are experiencing new levels of self-control, acquiring vital skills in the area of decisionmaking, and through capitalizing on cultural legacies, drawing on their rich developmental past, which they may not have perceived as being particularly important. Another feature that the authors seem to be suggesting is that the shared cultural experiences of many of the adolescents have the therapeutic impact of creating connections between individuals in the group in situations where there might not have been any sense of perceived similarity among the group members.

The model articulated by Vargas and DiPilato is important for several reasons. It makes use of traditional mental health models and adds to it a contemporary and culturally relevant flavor. This, from the perspective of many, is a creative way of blending two views of what is necessary to help troubled adolescents, the first view being that the medical model which is the basis of most traditional mental health programs has some value, even in working with troubled and socially marginalized individuals. The second view is that ethnic culture of origin has the potential of helping troubled adolescents reconnect to that part of themselves that has been discarded in anticipation of acculturation into the larger society. The second point that Vargas and DiPilato have articulated in their work is the idea that structured, varied, behaviorally oriented approaches have been shown to be far superior in working with troubled adolescents rather than the less concrete and less specific approaches of psychodynamically oriented psychotherapy. In this situation, referring to the therapies as concrete is not at all suggesting that it minimizes the intellectual capacity or the ability to be engaged in the therapeutic process that the clients bring to the situation. Rather, it is offered here as a statement of there being very clearly identifiable parameters and procedures for the therapeutic work. It is apparent that this approach helps the therapist and the consumer by eliminating the margin of error in the direction of ambiguity and lack of definition. The problems of lack of clarity about the goals being worked on and nonspecificity of anticipated outcomes are two very common impediments to success with antisocial adolescents, most notably, gang members. The approach identified by Vargas and DiPilato represents a move in the direction of overcoming these difficulties. The culture-focused group therapy, as they have outlined it, represents use of concrete and tangible shared history as a catalyst for dealing with very specific things in the here and now. The model also is a good way of helping individuals who are not particularly motivated to work to look at their past and try to understand how it has directly given rise to their behavior in the here and now. It seems that this is a particularly powerful message that can be conveyed to troubled adolescents very clearly and directly when several members of a culture-focused group share in a common ethnic heritage, as is the case with the groups conducted by Vargas and DiPilato. The absence of a high level of congruence in ethnic identity among group members is not necessarily an interference to culture-focused group therapy being an effective tool to working with troubled adolescents. Rather, when there is a mixed cultural representation in the group, the differences that the individuals have may be used for therapeutic purposes, talking about differences and how those differences sometimes can be used as a way to reflect on one's own cultural legacy and its contribution to their functioning in the here and now.

The second chapter in this section by Carylon and Jones is concerned with cognitive–behavioral interventions in schools and how they can be facilitative of systemic changes. The authors began their chapter by providing a brief but cogent categorization of theories of gang affiliation. This is a task that has been accomplished by others in other settings, but the Carylon and Jones presentation here is crisp and void of theoretical bias. The absence of any implicit valuing of one orientation over the other makes it very easy for the consumer to read and digest the information without giving greater credence to one theory's attempts to explain gang behavior over another. The classification provided by the authors is important because it challenges the older position that gangs are bred exclusively in communities besieged with economic poverty. The authors also show that gangs are not the repository for social misfits and losers. Rather, gangs are collections of people by self-selection who are actively engaged in trying to find a place for themselves other than the place in which they currently rest psychologically. The last important feature of the Carylon and Jones classification of gangs is that they note explicitly that gangs are not settings for free-floating psychopathological behavior that gets emitted without sanctions by the reference groups.

In commenting on the different theoretical positions about gangs, the authors note that different theories have focused on different dimensions of the developmental process and in so doing have made obvious that they have not given acknowledgment to other developmental features that are absent from their theory. This singularity of focus, according to Carylon and Jones, has led to distorted attempts at intervention and remediation. They believe that youth gang affiliation may fill needs that are often unidentified or even unknown to researchers. Specifically these needs are "mechanisms to allay the typical adolescent fears of abandonment, independence/dependence striving, affiliation and rejection issues, as well as fears of closeness and intimacy." This level of analysis represents a movement beyond the superficialities of being concerned exclusively with overt gang behaviors.

Carylon and Jones conclude that gangs may provide support and closeness not previously experienced by its members. "As many families of origin continue to experience rapid and often terminal deterioration, young gang affiliation becomes a more attractive option for many youth." Despite the apparent belief that gangs represent substitute families, the authors caution that this positive surrogate family stance must be questioned as "gangs become increasingly violent."

The school-based gang intervention procedures offered in the Carylon and Jones chapter is seen as an intervention of choice for several reasons. It is clear that every community, no matter how poor or dysfunctional, has in its presence at least one public school. The continuous presence of schools, suggests Carylon and Jones, is a statement that perhaps schools and what they represent can become the conduit for effective community and mental health interventions targeting gang-affiliated youth and their families. In addition to the presence of schools in every community, there is also a variety of personnel inherent in the school faculty and administration who can be utilized to contribute to the intervention efforts. The authors note that support service personnel, i.e., janitorial staff, educational aides, transportation personnel, etc., should be considered as valuable resources in reaching many adolescents who might be involved in gang activity. One other feature of schools as a social institution of choice in responding to gangs is the fact that most public schools do not have the marginalized economic status and serious budgetary constraints that often characterize community organizations. Carylon and Jones suggest that program planning and implementation in a very methodical way are central steps if a program is going to be successful. The school psychologist is identified as an individual who has some level of understanding of behavior and who also, because of his or her role in the school, can be utilized effectively as an organizational consultant.

Theoretical and empirical support for cognitive–behavioral interventions in schools strongly justifies the use of such an approach. The current psychological literature notes that cognitive–behavioral interventions are particularly useful in dealing with individuals who have questionable prior socialization because of the potential for transfer of knowledge and skills across settings. That is to say that lessons about self-control, understanding the impact of one's behavior on others, and similar self-observational lessons can be utilized in the classroom, in community settings, and even in interpersonal relationships. This makes the skills and growth produced by the interventions highly generalizable and not situation specific.

The best practices section of the Carylon and Jones chapter critically evaluates what has been done in other settings that have used cognitive–behavioral interventions in schools. The value of this section of the chapter is that it saves the psychologist from repeating the errors of his or her colleagues. Carylon and Jones end their chapter by offering a strategic planning showing very concretely "how to do it." This is a unique contribution of this chapter to the field of intervention with gang adolescents. Other resources for working with gang adolescents have identified issues and have taught perhaps in a much more detailed way than Carylon and Jones, but none have been more behaviorally specific. The value of the Carylon and Jones chapter also is tremendously enhanced by their looking at systemic problems within organizations as a real threat to mental health interventions being effective with gang adolescents. This is a new approach, which moves beyond demonizing gang adolescents and blaming them for the failure or ineffectiveness of intervention programs. The Carylon and Jones approach of looking at systemic changes seems to suggest that problems in implementing programs may be traceable to philosophical problems within organizations. They note that unless an 80% agreement rate among personnel in the school can be achieved, intervention work should not be attempted. It appears then that they are suggesting that the buy-in of all parties involved in the intervention is perhaps as important as the voluntary acceptance of the interventions by the identified clients. This movement away from simply blaming the consumer to seriously critiquing the attitudes and united presentation of the service providers represents a new approach in that it reminds us that both provider and consumer need to be evaluated throughout the process of an intervention.

Chapter 9 is an essay by the author. It is focused on the large question of what is being done by researchers and interventionists concerning gang-affiliated adolescents and their psychological needs. Branch has titled the essay "Pathologizing Normality or Normalizing Pathology?" His basic premise is that the critiquing of gang membership as well as the interventions that are directed toward gang members should be subjected to frequent and strenuous review. In the early stages of the essay, Branch draws parallels between the normal developmental task of adolescents and the psychological dynamics of the behaviors exhibited by youngsters who choose to join gangs. He raises the question whether or not joining the gang is an attempt at individuation and separation from parents, even at the expense of personal safety and one's own continued well-being. Branch notes that it is very rare that the act of joining the gang is ever evaluated other than from an assumed position of pathology. He raises the question whether or not researchers can set aside the behaviors engaged in by gangs and individual gang members as an issue separate and apart from what psychological dynamics are associated with the act of joining the gang. He notes also that in choosing to join a gang, most adolescents appear to be making multiple statements about themselves, including two very powerful psychological needs statements. The first need is they have a need to be attached and affiliated with others. The affiliation and attachment that is assumed to come with gang membership often runs counter to the values and behaviors acceptable to parents. The result is that many gang adolescents feel a need to supplant the family of origin with the gang family. Whether or not this happens in reality or is just a verbalized act remains open to debate and is in need of strenuous psychological research. The second statement that joining a gang makes about an adolescent is that they think of themselves as having the capacity to tolerate the psychological demands of gang membership. Again, Branch notes that many gang members report that they want to join gangs as a way to meet a need. Unspoken, unfortunately, is their limited capacity for tolerating all of the complexities that are associated with membership in the gang and any other organization. The unfortunate outcome to many gang affiliations is that the members suddenly discover that the act of belonging to the group often requires that their personal goals are made secondary to the superordinate goals of the group.

In further thinking about whether or not joining the gang is a "normal" attempt at individuation and separation, Branch raises the question of how researchers can look at the dynamics of a behavior without being contaminated by the outcomes of the relationship that ensues subsequent to joining the gang. Put another way, that means how can researchers understand what compelled young people to join the gang without being unduly influenced by their ongoing biases against the gang? The contexts in which many young people find themselves functioning are often judged against adult standards and norms. It is rare that the adolescent context is critiqued from the perspective of the adolescents affiliated with the organization or activity. This inside versus outside perspective is another example of the emic–etic distinction that has been talked about extensively in the cross-cultural psychology literature.

The other side of the dichotomy of normality and pathology in understanding or thinking about adolescents and gangs has to do with whether or not some researchers have unwittingly attempted to normalize pathology in an attempt to show that they are "sensitive" to the plights of marginalized and other outgroup adolescents. Such behavior would represent an extreme case of not calling pathology pathology when in fact it really is pathology. For example, this type of normalizing of pathology has recently found expression in the form of psychiatric jargon being utilized by members of the legal profession to defend otherwise unacceptable behavior. Specifically, there has been a great deal of recent litigation in which adolescents accused of murder and other violent acts have been defended under the guise that they are suffering "urban psychosis" and therefore should not be held accountable or responsible for their behavior. This urban psychosis designation is implicitly offered as an explanation for otherwise unacceptable behavior. The rationale undergirding such a diagnostic label is because a young person has suffered economic poverty and deprivation for such a sustained period of time, he or she should not be held responsible for their attempts to move themselves out of that domain, even if they choose to take the life of another. This, from my perspective, is a clear example of normalizing pathology. The pathology in question is acting aggressively without provocation against another. The problem with this urban psychosis defense also can be found in the fact that many other youngsters have experienced the equivalent or more severe economic and emotional poverty but have somehow managed to exercise a level of self-control that has prevented them from acting spontaneously and maliciously in an antisocial way.

The normalizing pathology versus pathologizing normality is a distinction that researchers and interventionists need to think about very intensively before undertaking intervention work with gang adolescents. From my perspective, it is more than merely an academic question. It is a question of the assumptions that are being made of what are the limits of acceptable behavior within the context of individuals who have lived marginalized lives, as well as how much can society forgive of an individual's antisocial behavior because of earlier deprivations that have been visited upon them by the larger social systems.

7

CHAPTER

Alice M. Vargas
Marina DiPilato

Culture-Focused Group Therapy: Identity Issues in Gang-Involved Youth

☐ Identity

Erickson states that the shaping of self-identity starts with early life experiences, when a person's racial background and parental influences, more than forces external to the family, begin to make impressions (Erickson, 1963). He and others also state that the most important task of adolescence is the formation of an independent adult identity, which involves the development of peer relationships, a sense of sexual identity, and reduced dependence on parents. In addition, the adolescent must obtain a feeling of security from his developing mastery over himself and his environment (Slaff, 1979).

According to Wallace and Fogelson (1965), identity can be thought of in terms of four basic parts of the self: the ideal self (what a person would like to be); feared self (what the person would not like to be); claimed self (what a person would like others to think he is); and real self (what a person believes he is). The development of self-identity comes about largely through interpersonal interaction, and Whiting (1980) has observed that "patterns of interpersonal behavior are developed in the settings that one frequents and that the most important characteristics of a setting are the cast of characters who occupy these, in particular, the age and sex of these characters" (p. 103).

If the setting and the cast of characters are so important to the formation of identity, it makes sense that a person's culture is basic to identity and identity formation. Ethnic minorities must negotiate several cultural worlds. Some ethnic minorities must operate in three cultural worlds: the realm of the indigenous ethnic culture, which includes the cultural values of the original homeland; the minority realm, which includes the elements of minority ethnic status; and the mainstream culture.

The interrelations among these realms are complex, and they often come into conflict. For example, competencies that are highly valued among a cultural group may be dismissed or even punished in the mainstream culture. For those whose native language is not English, language problems compound the cultural conflicts.

However, there may be benefits to operating in multiple cultures. Ethnic minority youth faced with hostile or devaluing messages from the mainstream culture may be able to buffer those messages because they receive messages from their own cultures that help them develop a positive identity and a sense of worth and value (Buriel, Calzada, & Vasquez, 1982).

Culture can also serve to mediate between social forces and behavior. For youth, culture can buffer the negative effects or risk factors in the social environment. It can serve as a protective mechanism by supporting positive ethnic identity formation, by providing a set of values and a pattern for living, by building a sense of group cohesion, and by giving youth appropriate guidance as they face the challenges and transitions of growing up.

Culture may fail to protect, however, in a number of circumstances: for example, when social risk factors in the mainstream become overwhelming; when there is substantial conflict between mainstream culture and ethnic culture; or when ethnic culture is denigrated in the mainstream or dismissed as nonexistent. Culture also may fail to protect when, in an effort to adapt to the inequities of the mainstream, ethnic cultures adopt maladaptive behavior patterns to attempt to meet basic needs for power or for a sense of personal efficacy. This failure may also occur when ethnic minority youth have not been socialized to function effectively in the multiple cultural realms with which they must deal (Topper, 1992; Vigil, 1983).

Among the specific components that have been suggested as key elements of ethnic identity are self-identification and attitudes about oneself as a group member. In addition, attitudes and evaluations relative to one's group, the extent of ethnic knowledge and commitment, and ethnic behaviors and practices also appear to be important elements of ethnic identity.

In reviewing the literature, Phinney (1991) finds that the components of ethnic identity vary independently. Someone may identify with a group and have generally positive feelings about it but exhibit few specific ethnic behaviors associated with it. On the other hand, someone may be very involved in the language and culture of the group but have negative feelings about the group or about being a member of the group. If the components of ethnic identity vary independently, then to understand the relationship of ethnic identity to self-esteem, it is necessary to examine each component (e.g., language, values) in relationship to self-esteem.

The studies on self-esteem and ethnic identity suggest that stereotypes and negative evaluation of one's group may be related to low self-esteem, although others do not agree (Brigham, 1973; Crocker & Major, 1989; Grossman, Wirt, & Davids, 1985). Having some negative views of one's group does not necessarily mean lower self-esteem. Those individuals who distance themselves from the negative aspects and relate to the positive characteristics of the group may have high self-esteem. Likewise, those who dismiss negative experiences as being based on stereotypes may not be personally affected. A study by Phinney and Alipuria (1990) suggests that self-esteem, at least for members of some disadvantaged groups, may be enhanced by actively learning about one's culture. This would seem particularly the case if the information learned is positive or if the learner also gains a positive view of the information.

The literature suggests that in a setting in which there is no ethnic diversity one's identity as a group member is likely to go unnoticed. It appears that awareness of a person's ethnic identity may result in large part from contact with other ethnic groups (Phinney, 1991). The literature further suggests that good adjustment among minority group members is likely to be related to one's relationship with both the ethnic culture and with the mainstream culture.

There are some data that suggest that a positive mainstream orientation coupled with high ethnic identity is correlated positively to high self-esteem. However, self-esteem issues may be problematic for a person with high ethnic identity without at least some adaptation to the dominant culture (Phinney, 1991). A low ethnic identity may be particularly damaging to the self-esteem of the marginal or isolated individual (Stonequist, 1961). For the assimilated person, the low salience of ethnicity may mean that self-esteem is unrelated to ethnic identity.

Finally, the literature discusses a sense of commitment to one's group as, perhaps, a central component of ethnic identity. The concept of commitment derives from Erickson's (1968) discussion of ego identity formation. According to Erickson, adolescents face the critical task of integrating childhood identifications, together with personal inclinations and societal pressures, to make a commitment to who they are and what they will become. As with other components that have been discussed, the findings are conflicting regarding the relationship between self-esteem and ethnic identity commitment or a more global conception of ethnic identity.

The discussion of cultural identity is an important issue in exploring the gang involvement of young people. It can be argued that youth with a limited or negative sense of ethnic identity, coupled with few successful mainstream adaptations, will be most vulnerable to external forces, including gangs, that seem to offer some solutions to young people in hopeless or failing circumstances.

☐ The Attraction of the Gang

Conflict in self-identity emerges most strongly during adolescence. Role diffusion and ambiguity in particular are important in this phase of development, especially in terms of age and sexual identity. Many of the gang members come from mother-centered households, where male influences are limited (Adler, Ovando, & Hocevar, 1984; Morales, 1992; Vigil, 1988a, 1988b). So, as Erickson (1963) points out, "the danger of the stage is role confusion where this is based on strong previous doubt as to one's sexual identity." Vigil (1988a, 1988b) agrees generally with Erickson's statement and says that the identity crisis experienced by male Chicano adolescents who are drawn to gangs involves their confusion about their masculine identity.

For many male gang members raised in female-centered households, where adult male role models are absent or transient, real (female-raised) and feared (weak) identities come into conflict with the ideal male (strong) identity that the street gangs represent.

According to Freud (1923), a person's self-identification is facilitated by involvement in the primary group. The preadolescent barrio youth more and more models himself after others in the immediate spatial and social environment. Once a person joins a group, he identifies with the norms and standards of the group and makes the group the ideal for himself. Being a part of the group appears to also correspond with the strong sense of familialism among Latinos—a tendency in certain cultures to value group and extended family ties (Colman, 1975).

Self-identity usually begins under parental influences, and for gang members these are often very stressful. Vigil and other researchers (Adler et al., 1984; Morales, 1992; Vigil, 1988a, 1988b) state that most of the regular gang members with whom they have interacted came from troubled families. For example, they came from larger than average families living in smaller than average homes, usually in the poorer barrios, many "female-centered" families where there was inadequate parenting or supervision of children, domestic violence, family members with histories of alcoholism and drug addiction, and pressures of acculturation and discrimination. Parents often were only periodically employed, and one or both might be absent. Many of these youth were raised by grandparents, by their mothers in their fathers' absence, or by other relatives (Adler et al., 1984; Morales, 1992; Vigil, 1988a, 1988b).

Belitz and Valdez (1994) point out that a violent male father figure often has greatly affected the young person's emotional development as well as the family's history. The father figure is seen by the young man as the most powerful person in the family group. This person gets his needs met through the use of intimidation or aggression or both. A large number of the youths have experienced physical abuse by the parental male in their lives. In addition, they have also seen their mothers, brothers, and sisters abused by this male.

The boys have intense feelings of abandonment and powerlessness that they have built up in the environment described. Belitz and Valdez (1994) state that to prevent these feelings and to "mobilize their rage," these young men identify with the father figure whose abuse they have experienced and witnessed. The lesson that they have learned is that they can gain power and control by being aggressive themselves. In addition, by developing their own aggressiveness, they can prevent victimization in the future. The boys look more and more like their offensive role models as they approach adolescence. They continuously attempt to impose their wishes on their family and try to get their needs met at the expense of their other family members.

All the problems in family life outlined previously generally lead to regular and prolonged exposure to street activities that affect the development of self-identification. Lack of parental supervision, often accompanied by feelings of rejection by one's family, operate together with the readiness of older street youths to recruit and socialize other young men to their way of life (see Abdullah and Branch, this volume).

In fact, the socialization for these largely unsupervised and unprotected youths comes to depend primarily on the influence of street supervisors and protectors, including peers and older role models (Rogoff, 1981). Self-identity formation, then, becomes street based. Older gang members, "veteranos," serve as role models for the latency and preadolescent youths. So, the behaviors, attitudes, and values of known gang members are adopted and internalized by these youths. This occurs at the same time when the youth is identifying with the aggressor at home and when he is having a more and more conflict-ridden relationship with his mother.

Morales (1992) states that the street gang acts like a "surrogate family." The concept of the family (or "la familia") is an important value that the child has learned and that has been supported in his environment all his life. If, as described previously, the young man has not experienced his own family to be the supportive environment he has been taught to expect, he will look outside his natural family. His surrogate family (the gang) provides sustenance for the members' emotional needs. Morales states that, "the gang member receives affection, understanding, recognition, loyalty, and emotional and physical protection." According to Erickson (1968), a family is usually expected to provide for basic kinds of human needs. In addition to providing for the boy's emotional needs, the barrio group provides norms and patterns for emotional stability, social interaction and friendship, protection, and street survival (a tough "male" identity).

Aggressive made behavior is a valuable aid to survival in the street life of the barrio. Male young people undergoing this role dilemma turn toward attitudes and behavior that overemphasize these "male" survival qualities. As part of working through their self-identity, each negotiates the feared self (insecure) with the ideal self (tough male role model) and strives to reshape the real self into the ideal. However, in actuality, these youths have little opportunity to attain a balance among the real, ideal, feared, and claimed aspects of identity. Vigil (1988b) argues that individual concerns about the ego ideal become suspended as the gang dominates self-identification. Thus, the individual ego ideal is relinquished to the group ego ideal in the service of group solidarity.

Vigil (1988b) further states that membership in a gang provides these young men with a sense of competency and purpose. These youths have failed to gain competency in the tasks typically assigned to children. They have previously felt like failures and have experienced intense feelings of isolation and marginality within their families, culture, and other systems in which they participated, i.e., school, community, church.

Another attraction to the gang is the opportunity it affords the youth to put aside his personal fears over forming a self-identity, since the group roles, as exhibited by the groups' heroes (real, legendary, and imagined), provide a more or less clear framework for thinking and acting along age and sex lines. So, the young person has a simpler, narrower range of roles from which to select. Even more attractive for the young man is the fact that the gang offers a wide variety of identities to be claimed or established. A youth can be respected and feared by nongang youth. He can claim or show he has courage, integrity, loyalty, and coolness in gang situations. In other words, the gang provides opportunities in the form of identity-generating situations so that the youth can be a "somebody" (Sanders, 1994).

A social identity thus helps shape one's personal identity. The individual needs the group for identity formation, and the group provides the individual with implicit and explicit role expectations to demonstrate group allegiance, which when played out, shows the merging of individual into the group ideal of thinking and behaving. In other words, in the process of playing out the role the gang has prescribed, one can, in turn, demonstrate allegiance to the group in an observable, public performance while also clarifying one's self-identity in a personal private way.

☐ Culture-Focused Group Therapy

In light of the perceived benefits of gang membership, it can be argued that the most effective mental health intervention is a group format that addresses the psychological needs being met by gang affiliation (see Abdullah and Branch, this volume). Group therapies have long been described as the ideal match for adolescent psychotherapeutic needs (e.g., Berkovitz, 1972; Sugar, 1986; Yalom, 1985). In particular, the group provides an opportunity for work on identity issues. The adolescent is provided the chance to define himself apart from the family context via interpersonal learning that occurs in the context of his relationships with the group members and leaders. It can be argued that this opportunity for protective factors results from the development of positive ethnic identity. The group also provides the opportunity for corrective child–adult experiences (Berkovitz, 1972; Sugar, 1986), also described as a corrective recapitulation of the primary family group (Yalom, 1985). This is particularly the case when group leaders provide an appropriate level of directiveness (Brackelmanns & Berkovitz, 1972) and protection (Berkovitz, 1972; Sugar, 1986), which Belitz and Valdez (1994) argue has been missing from the typical family experience of the adolescent male gang member.

The literature suggests that traditional group psychotherapeutic techniques require some revision in treating multiproblem youths (e.g., Corder, 1983). Specifically, groups have been designed that provide more structure and a more clearly defined psychoeducational focus. Goldstein and Huff's (1993) comprehensive handbook outlines specific approaches to build skills (e.g., anger management, social skills, stress management) in gang-involved youth.

The consistent and systematic addition of cultural variables into group psychotherapies has been a difficult objective. It has been argued that a large proportion of gangs and gang members are ethnic minorities and thus cultural sensitivity on the part of the therapist is strongly indicated (Goldstein, Harootunian, & Conoley, 1994). It is impossible for each therapist to have knowledge about the nuances of a number of different cultures, particularly because culture is not static. However, it is possible for therapists to develop awareness that cultural variables are present in all therapeutic interactions, even when the therapist and client are from the same ethnic background. Thus, therapists can be sensitized to the inclusion of cultural context as a variable in therapeutic change (Koss-Chioino & Vargas, 1992).

The group outlined here was developed for early adolescent psychiatric inpatients in a University-affiliated hospital that serves patients from a geographically large state. It includes patients from multiple ethnic groups from both rural and urban communities. All male and female patients in the units containing the oldest patients, aged 12 to 15 years, are included in the group for purposes of prevention and intervention. The most common patient problems included a mixture of aggressive behavior, sequelae of physical and sexual trauma, and learning delays. Although some patients had no gang involvement at all, most had been exposed to gang-involved peers and some claimed gang membership.

The theoretical guidance for designing the group was based on (a) addressing those psychological factors, including ethnic identity issues, leading to gang involvement identified in the literature, and (b) psychoeducational and cognitive–behavioral strategies allowing for short-term and focused intervention. The group therapy format that is described here attempts to weave cultural and other identity issues into more traditional and commonly used group interventions.

The group framework includes one session outlining the relationship between thoughts, feelings, and behavior; two sessions to address sequelae of trauma; three sessions to teach anger management and assertiveness; and, finally, six sessions focused on identity and self-esteem. Recognition of cultural factors is important throughout the group process and is most salient during the sessions on identity.

The session on thoughts, feelings, and behavior provides a common language and frame of reference for the group. The conceptualization presents the idea that thoughts, feelings, and behavior are each different and separate from each other but that each strongly affects the others and that they are related to each other. This framework allows members to observe and differentiate their own patterns of thinking, feeling, and behaving in different contexts. An illustration is presented in which the words "thoughts," "feelings," and "behaviors" are placed in a circular formation with arrows connecting them. The terms are defined by examples: feelings words (e.g., anger, sadness), self-talk or thoughts (e.g., "Why am I always so stupid?"), actions or behaviors (e.g., throwing something). The crucial points communicated in this session are (1) that there doesn't have to be an invariable link between certain feelings and certain actions or between certain thoughts and certain actions, and (2) that change can occur in any one of the three factors and this would affect the other two factors. Concrete illustrative examples are given: If one thinks differently, or draws a different conclusion, about someone who is teasing you, your subsequent feelings and behaviors are likely to be different than if you think the teasing is powerful and has merit.

Belitz and Valdez (1994), as well as others (Vigil, 1988c; Quicker, 1983), suggest that many gang involved youth have experienced different kinds of trauma and stress. As was previously discussed, these include an aggressive male authority figure in the home, inadequate supervision, and early unsupervised experience in the streets. Therefore, it is important to treat the traumatic sequelae that is thought to be driving at least a part of the aggressive behavior demonstrated by the young person. Again, his behavior serves a self-protective function for the young person. In addition, he may not have learned to express feelings (i.e., anger, frustration, etc.) in less violent ways. By discussing these issues, it is hoped that the youth will come to an understanding of the possible contributions to their aggressive behavior and use the awareness to make changes.

During the 12-session group format, two sessions are spent on trauma. Obviously, two sessions of group therapy is not adequate to deal with the experiences of trauma in a young man's life. It is important to note that the group format discussed here is not an isolated treatment. Each of the young people in the program also have individual psychotherapy several times a week. Therefore, these sessions on trauma are easily followed up with the individual work. In these sessions, in large part, a psychoeducational and cognitive–behavioral approach is used. The group therapists discuss common symptoms to help the young people begin to understand that their behavior could be related to their trauma experiences. The information is not presented as an excuse for violent or aggressive behavior. Rather, the idea is that if the person can cognitively understand how these behaviors developed, they may have a better chance to work with the emotions connected to the trauma and change their actions in the future. For example, the group therapists talk about possible symptoms such as physiological arousal, anxiety, and tension. They explain to the young people that this arousal can be discharged inward. However, more commonly (especially in males), it seems to be released outward. In further discussion, the group learns that the young person is typically anxious to discharge this emotion because if he doesn't, then he's at risk to experience feelings such as sadness, loss, or abandonment. He prefers to experience rage and aggression, which he can direct outward. The group members learn why it is important to have a positive resolution to their trauma experience. The youth are told that if they don't, they will continue to live with the negative feelings they experienced with the traumatic event(s).

Although this part of the group is only for two weeks, the members can be encouraged to share experiences that they have during that time (or have had prior to beginning the group) that demonstrate some of the "symptoms" of abuse they learn about in the group. For example, a young man who was 13 years old had an experience in which he was playing football with some of the other boys in the hospital. One of them accidentally ran into his shoulder. The boy immediately turned to the other boy and hit him. In exploring this incident with the therapist in group, it was learned that he had experienced a flashback. The moment he was hit by the other boy, Carlos (not his real name) saw his stepfather hitting him and he immediately fought back (as he had promised himself he would do, if he was ever in that situation again). In these sessions, it is important to help the young people separate the trauma experiences from their understanding of what their culture includes. For example, their experiences of violence could be viewed by the young people as part of their tradition.

The sessions on anger management and assertiveness focus on teaching alternative responses and identifying circumstances that trigger anger and aggression. Accepted means of anger expression can be strongly influenced by culture. Thus, the primary focus is on finding acceptable alternatives for aggression.

Strategies from cognitive–behavioral models include helping members to identify the types of situations most likely to make them angry and then identifying and changing the thoughts and conclusions that mediate angry feelings or aggressive behavior (Carylon and Jones, this volume; Dodge, 1985). Group members are also encouraged to identify body sensations associated with anger and to identify ways to use these sensations as a cue to make different behavioral choices. The group format makes use of verbal and nonverbal means of expression such that members are encouraged to write, draw, talk about their thoughts and feelings, or perform all of these activities. Thus, each group follows a format in which the premise or idea is explained (e.g., "Sometimes we find there are similarities between the situations in which we get angry, and if we understand better what those situations are, we can take more control over our feelings and our behaviors"). Time is then allowed for members and group leaders, as role models, to write and draw about these situations. Finally, the remaining group time is used for members to share their work and receive feedback from peers.

Using drawings to augment verbal communications is helpful because (1) it provides an additional avenue of expression for learning and academically delayed patients, (2) it draws on artistic talents, and (3) it provides a physical image that can be viewed with psychological distance, allowing for increased objectivity as well as the possible recognition of important patterns of thinking, feeling, and behaving. One member drew himself completely in blue with stiff icicles coming from his arms and legs in communicating how his body feels when he is angry. He stated that his whole body went cold and stiff. He indicated that this frozen feeling kept him from handling situations the way he would like to once he feels angry. The combination of his words and his drawing created a very vivid image for the group and for him. Thus, because his experience was communicated so clearly, the group was able to show considerable empathy and support for him and, ultimately, help him generate ideas about how he would like to handle situations differently when he is angry.

The purpose of the last half of the group (identity/self-esteem) is to iden-tify and expand the positive, protective elements of culture in several differ-ent spheres that encompass every aspect of daily living. Following a similar format, ideas and premises about culture and tradition are presented about which members can write or draw or both and often present within the group. The idea of culture is expressed very simply to the group as being the things passed on from generation to generation that can relate to any aspect of daily living. For example, a particular meal, stories, and special events, even the smells associated with daily living. However, it is stressed that these experiences are those that the member finds particularly comforting or provides continuity or stability and pride.

In groups with members from very diverse backgrounds, this section of the group can be initiated with a modified bingo game (Pasternak, 1979) in which group members indicate information about themselves in a category (e.g., foods, beliefs, experiences). Group leaders collect the answers, which are then represented on cards in a bingo format. The cards are distributed to members who mark their cards when answers shown on their cards are called out (e.g., favorite food: hamburger; favorite food: green chili stew). This allows members to get to know each other, introduces the notion that aspects of daily living can be quite different for each group member, and initiates the process of attending to these aspects of daily living.

The group format is particularly helpful in identifying and expanding elements of culture because as each member shares memories of supportive family traditions, this helps other members to identify or reevaluate forgotten or lost experiences such as a holiday visit to grandmother, summer activities with siblings, or helping a parent to make a favorite food. Usually even the member from very chaotic, or even abusive, family circumstances can identify an aspect of tradition that was helpful or was experienced in a positive way. The drawings most often created by members included family gatherings, usually including extended members beyond the nuclear family, on a holiday with special foods present. Often seemingly minor things were remembered quite fondly, for example, that grandmother always made a certain pie or that everyone always watched television together.

Members receive encouragement to create culture and tradition and to write and draw about traditions they want to continue, modify, or invent. There is encouragement for the members to think of culture as something that can be changed or modified (Rogler, Malgady, Costantino, & Blumenthal, 1987). Therefore, the group member can create his own traditions. This is particularly suited to a group format where young people from similar, but somewhat different, backgrounds are sharing experiences and information that stimulate memories and serve as a catalyst for new ideas. An example is given of a tradition created by two friends who met at the state fair and subsequently, over a period of many years, went back to the fair together each year to celebrate their friendship and mark the passing of the year. This is a very simplistic example, but it introduces the notion that the patterns of daily living are not static. More complex aspects of living, including interpersonal roles, relationships to authority figures, and ways of interacting are also open to modification. This is particularly important for members who have been exposed to the least functional and most distorted aspects of their cultural group.

Over several sessions, group members get encouragement to look toward the future via creating collages with pictures from magazines. They are instructed to depict what they hope for themselves in the future. This exercise, particularly when magazines are used, can help members with values clarification regarding perceptions of "mainstream" values versus individual or family values. Although this is a very simple activity, it provides the most access to subtle aspects of culture and identity. For example, the collages can reflect beliefs and expectations regarding interpersonal relationships, the relative importance of material possessions, the nature of roles in the work force, relationships to the physical environment, and many other themes. Similar to a drawing, the collage brings the same strength of being a nonverbal form of expression that allows psychological distance. The collage also vividly conveys information about the member to the group.

One 12-year-old female group member created a collage completely filled with images of mothers and infants. Her collage provided an avenue for work within the group regarding her expectation that motherhood is the only role open to her. A 13-year-old boy created a collage with flashy cars, expensive houses, beach-front property, and seductive women. Most of the group members were initially very attracted to the images, but ultimately they stated that they could never have these things or any valued material things. This provided an avenue to address striking feelings of disenfranchisement and "marginalization," as discussed in the literature. The therapeutic goal is to instill a realistic sense of empowerment and hope.

Many authors have written about the factors that contribute to gang involvement and particularly to aggression in gang activity. Group interventions provide an ideal therapeutic format to address these contributions. In addition to providing skill building materials, these groups provide the opportunity to address the positive and buffering effects of cultural identification.

The use of traditional mental health models with gang-affiliated youth is an area that has not been explored very widely. Abdullah and Branch (this volume) note that multiple family therapy models have some utility for assessing gang-affiliated families. In the foregoing chapter we have articulated our experiences with group psychotherapy as a modality for working with troubled adolescents, including gang members. The problems of appropriateness of traditional approaches (i.e., client has an investment in being cooperative; the chosen method has been shown to be effective with the consumer group) are enormous. Despite the complexity and severity of adapting procedures for use with delinquent adolescents, we think it is an area that should be explored more extensively. We have also shown that issues of cultural variation should be included in attempts to make interventions more relevant. Adapting traditional procedures should consider the individual consumer (i.e., individual client) and organizations (i.e., schools, communities). The following chapter by Carylon and Jones provides a detailed discussion of how organizational interventions can be culturally relevant (i.e., sensitive to the life circumstances of the client) and at the same time rooted in traditional theoretical concepts. They make a strong case for using cognitive–behavioral interventions to bring about systemic changes that directly improve the quality of life for gang-affiliated adolescents and their families.

☐ Conclusion

Culture-focused group therapy has been shown to be an effective way to engage young people who may be reluctant to share personal information in a therapeutic setting. One of the assumptions of the technique, that everyone has something valuable to share when they are ready, bodes well for involving the shy and introverted adolescent. Because the cultural focus draws on what young people already harbor as part of the life experiences it does not require them to learn anything new or to take risks that may not have positive outcomes for them.

As we have practiced culture-focused group therapy it has been beneficial as an adjunct to more traditional mental health approaches whose utility with minority adolescents is questionable at times. Culture-focused therapy creates opportunities for adolescents to connect with others by sharing a personal dimension of themselves that they may not have previously considered to be unique or special. If others in the group share in cultural beliefs or practices, then bonds of similarity are created. If differences exist among the members, then "learning about others" occurs. In either situation the group member is helped to understand that his or her world may become a catalyst for psychological connection to others. This is a valuable lesson in the area of social facilitation and a maturational milestone that may open the door for exploration in private mental health work and in relationships outside of the therapeutic community.

☐ References

Adler, P., Ovando, C., & Hocevar, D. (1984). Familiar correlates of gang membership: An exploratory study of Mexican-American youth. *Hispanic Journal of Behavioral Sciences, 6,* 65–76.

Belitz, J., & Valdez, D. (1994). Clinical issues in the treatment of Chicano male gang youth. *Hispanic Journal of Behavioral Sciences, 16,* 57–74.

Berkovitz, I. H. (1972). *Adolescents grow in groups: Experiences in adolescent group psychotherapy.* New York: Brunner/Mazel.

Brackelmanns, W. E., & Berkovitz, I. H. (1972). Younger adolescents in group therapy: A reparative superego experience. In I. H. Berkovitz (Ed.), *Adolescents grow in groups: Experiences in adolescent group psychotherapy.* New York: Brunner/Mazel.

Brigham, J. (1973). Ethnic stereotypes and attitudes: A different mode of analysis. *Journal of Personality, 41,* 206–223.

Buriel, R., Calzada, S., & Vasquez, R. (1982). The relationship of traditional Mexican-American culture to adjustment and delinquency among three generations of Mexican-American adolescents. *Hispanic Journal of Behavioral Sciences, 4,* 41–55.

Colman, A. (1975). Group consciousness as a developmental phase. In A. D. Colman & H. Bexton (Eds.), *Group relations reader.* Sausalito, CA: GREX.

Corder, B. F. (1983). A structured group for undersocialized, acting-out adolescents. In M. Rosenbaum (Ed.), *Handbook of short-term therapy groups.* New York: McGraw–Hill.

Crocker, J., & Major, B. (1989). Social stigma and self-esteem: The self-protective properties of stigma. *Psychological Review, 96,* 608–630.

Dodge, K. A. (1985). A social information processing model of social competence in children. In M. Perlmutter (Ed.), *Minnesota Symposium Child Psychology,* Vol. 18. Hillsdale, NJ: Erlbaum.

Erickson, E. H. (1963). *Childhood and society.* New York: Norton.

Erickson, E. H. (1968). *Identity: Youth and crisis.* New York: Norton.

Freud, S. (1923). *Group psychology and the analysis of the ego.* New York: Norton.

Goldstein, A. P., & Huff, C. R. (1993). *The gang intervention handbook.* Champaign, IL: Research Press.

Goldstein, A. P., Harootunian, B., & Conoley, J. C. (1994). *Student aggression: Prevention, management, and replacement training.* New York: Guilford.

Grossman, B., Wirt, R., & Davids, A. (1985). Self-esteem, ethnic identity, and behavioral adjustment among Anglo and Chicano adolescents in West Texas. *Journal of Adolescence, 8,* 57–68.

Koss-Chioino, J. D., & Vargas, L. A. (1992). Through the cultural looking glass: A model for understanding culturally responsive psychotherapies. In L. A. Vargas & J. D. Koss-Chioino (Eds.) *Working with culture: Psychotherapeutic interventions with ethnic minority children and adolescents.* San Francisco: Jossey-Bass.

Morales, A. T. (1992). Latino youth gangs: Causes and clinical intervention. In L. A. Vargas & J. Koss-Chioino (Eds.), *Working with culture: Psychotherapeutic intervention with ethnic minority children and adolescents.* San Francisco: Jossey-Bass.

Pasternak, M. G. (1979). *Helping kids learn multicultural concepts: A handbook of strategies.* Champaign, IL: Research Press.

Phinney, J. (1991). Ethnic identity and self-esteem: A review and integration. *Hispanic Journal of Behavioral Sciences, 13,* 193–208.

Phinney, J., & Alipuria, L. (1990). Ethnic identity in college students from four ethnic groups. *Journal of Adolescence, 13,* 171–183.

Quicker, J. C. (1983). *Homegirls: Characterizing Chicana gangs.* San Pedro, CA: International Universities Press.

Rogler, L. H., Malgady, R. G., Costantino, G., & Blumenthal, R. (1987). What do culturally sensitive mental health services mean? *American Psychologist, 42,* 565–570.

Rogoff, B. (1981). Adults and peers as agents of socialization: A highland Guatemalan profile. *Ethos, 9,* 18–36.

Sanders, W. B. (1994). *Gangbangs and drive-bys: Grounded culture and juvenile gang violence.* New York: Aldine De Gruyter.

Slaff, B. (1979). Adolescents. In J. Noshpitz (Ed.), *Basic handbook of child psychiatry. Vol. III* (pp. 504–518). New York: Basic Books.

Stonequist, E. V. (1961). *The marginal man: A study in personality and culture conflict*. New York: Russell and Russell.

Sugar, M. (1986). *The adolescent in group and family therapy*. Chicago: University of Chicago Press.

Topper, M. D. (1992). Multidimensional therapy: A case study of a Navajo adolescent with multiple problems. In L. A. Vargas & J. Koss-Chioino (Eds.), *Working with culture: Psychotherapeutic interventions with ethnic minority children and adolescents*. San Francisco: Jossey-Bass.

Vigil, J. D. (1983). Chicano gangs: One response to Mexican urban adaptation in the Los Angeles area. *Urban Anthropology, 12*, 45–75.

Vigil, J. D. (1988a). Street socialization, locura behavior, and violence among Chicano gang members. In J. F. Kraus, S. B. Sorenson, & P. D. Juarez (Eds.), *Research conference on violence and homicide in Hispanic communities*. Los Angeles: UCLA Publication Services.

Vigil, J. D. (1988b). Group processes and street identity: Adolescent Chicano gang members. *Ethos, 16*, 421–445.

Vigil, J. D. (1988c). *Barrio gangs: Street life and identity in Southern California*. Austin: University of Texas Press.

Wallace, A. F. C., & Fogelson, R. (1965). The identity struggle. In I. Boszomeniji-Nagy & J. L. Framo (Eds.), *Intensive family therapy: Theoretical and practical aspects*. New York: Harper and Row.

Whiting, B. B. (1980). Culture and social behavior: A model for the development of social behavior. *Ethos, 8*, 95–116.

Yalom, I. D. (1985). *The theory and practice of group psychotherapy* (3rd ed.). New York: Basic Books.

8

CHAPTER

William Carylon
Dion Jones

Youth Gangs, Cognitive–Behavioral Interventions in Schools, and System Change

Research related to the explanation, prediction, and control of behavior, especially aberrant behavior, has been paramount in the behavioral sciences. Although external manipulations of behavior have often been the focus of such investigations, management and ultimate control of behavior by the individual has received considerable attention. Explanations for individual behavioral choices have been offered by numerous theorists such as Bandura and Walters (1963), Goldfried and Merbaum (1973), Kanfer (1973), Skinner (1953), and Thorensen and Mahoney (1974).

Goldfried and Merbaum (1973) assert that behavioral choices are based on the individual's desire to achieve highly specific goals. Further, that these goals are predetermined by the individual, and through conscious deliberation, the individual arrives at a personal decision regarding their behavioral choice. Bandura and Walters (1963) explored the concept of self-control. They suggest that there are specific observable events from which the process of self-control is inferred. These include the ability to accept delay or denial of a desired reward, the ability to impose self-control over temptation or pressure to engage in deviant behaviors, and the establishment and maintenance of both self-imposed standards and self-rewards for achievement of the personal standards and goals.

Many of the behavioral control studies in the literature can be described as representing self-control through delays in gratification. In most studies, where the participant exhibits appropriate behavioral controls and choices, it is asserted that the individual is demonstrating the capacity to accept that a greater reward provided at a later date is more desirable than a lesser, although immediate, reward. Thus, they are demonstrating self-control. Can we reasonably expect adolescents, especially those from impoverished backgrounds, to exhibit the capacity for self-control based on these definitions? Is it a developmental deficiency or environmental experiences that predispose many adolescents to deviant behavioral choices, often done on impulse and based on immediate gratification?

For many youth, adolescence is a time filled with self-doubt, turmoil, conflict, and anxiety. Many youth experience tumultuous feelings about identity, affiliation, gender stereotypes, self-worth, and often sexual preference. In past years, it was believed that only a minority of youth experienced difficulty during the adolescent years, and that the majority or average adolescent experienced only the mildest of discomforts (Atwater, 1988). More recently, as is being evidenced by increasingly violent and delinquent acts perpetrated by adolescents, this average, well-adjusted youth is quickly becoming the minority. Current research suggests that the vast majority of our youth, especially those living in urban and inner cities, appear to be very troubled (Corsica, 1993; Spergel, 1990). The degree of maladjustment present in these youth is evidenced by actions including, but not limited to, sharp and rapid increases in sexual promiscuity, resulting in rising rates of teenage pregnancy and sexually transmitted diseases; drug and alcohol abuse; violent acts including aggravated assault and murder; property crimes; and vandalism (Berland, Homlish, & Blotcky, 1989; Furlong & Morrison, 1994; Greene, 1993; Rogers, 1993). These delinquent behaviors being committed by America's adolescents are impacting virtually every corner of our society.

Current classroom climates in both urban and rural areas are such that virtually every classroom will contain at least one aggressive student. This student will be perceived as posing a threat to not only fellow classmates but often to the teacher as well. Data currently being collected strongly suggest that the majority of these aggressive youth will be either peripherally involved with gangs or will be members of gangs. Mental health providers clearly need more information to more effectively intervene with the youth gang population.

As early as 1980, it was estimated that one-fifth of the adolescent boys in communities of 10,000 or more belonged to groups, or gangs, whose activities centered around delinquent behaviors (Berland et al., 1989). Further, Miller (1982) suggested that gangs comprised approximately 1.5 million members in the 2100 American cities and towns with populations of 10,000 or more. Current research estimates the figures to be approximately triple that of previous studies (Bernardio, 1994).

☐ Theory and Gang Affiliation

Much speculation exists about why violent aggression, delinquent behavior, and gang affiliation occur. The theories range from familial deficit causes to individual psychopathological explanations. Attempts to understand the etiology of adolescent violence and gang affiliation are not new, and are often viewed through the framework of a sociological perspective (Baittle & Kobrin, 1964; Campbell, Munce, & Galea, 1982; Malmquist, 1978; Thrasher, 1936). This perspective would suggest, according to Thrasher's definition, that adolescent dysfunction occurs most frequently in the geographical areas that are characterized by social, economic, and familial instabilities. Bernard (1990) supports this theory by suggesting that there is not enough economic opportunity available in the inner cities to meet the needs of the young people. Further, from a psychological perspective, it is generally believed that gang membership is influenced by developmental challenges of adolescence, when uncertainties about self-identity, trust, and future are most prevalent (Atwater, 1988).

Traditional theories of deviance suggest that gangs may form spontaneously as a defense or resistive maneuver with a deliberate purpose. This purpose may include the taking control of the environment, as demonstrated in "turf" issues, to reverse the balance of power and to render control strategies ineffective (Rinsley, 1980). Berland et al. (1989) suggested that gangs arise from instability and conflict within the environment. They then exacerbate the conflict and foreshadow any possible underlying individual dynamics or pathology.

Moral development theorists see gang formation and affiliation as a result of inadequate or underdeveloped capacities for moral judgment. Kohlberg (1969) suggested that moral decisions based on fear of punishment were inferior to those decisions based on shared goals and values, the common good, or social justice. Thus, growth or transition through different developmental stages is associated with forming different strategies for decision-making. The stage at which gang affiliation and participation would be most conducive would be Stage I reasoning. At this stage, most commonly with preadolescents, moral decisions are made based on the power of authorities, the threat of physical punishment, and the cost–benefit ratio between success and punishment if caught (Kohlberg, 1969).

As adolescence progresses, moral reasoning development requires that the adolescent increasingly consider shared rights in relationships, reputation, and a widening sense of social involvement and concern (Kohlberg, 1969). It is at this time that the adolescent's standing in a peer group, reputation, and increasing awareness of being affiliated with a widening social group begin to emerge as primary motives for behavior and moral dilemmas.

In a review of recent research, Clark (1992) suggested that alienation and rapid psychosocial and biological growth were significant contributors in the development of ineffective coping strategies in adolescence. These conclusions were based on his work with adolescent street gangs, Satanic cults, and neo-Nazi skinhead groups. He suggested that the choice to participate in deviant subcultures was directly influenced by an individual need for approval, belonging, and self-worth. Clark suggested that additional external influences such as "heavy metal" rock bands, occult books, album covers, movies, and videos may play an important role in the enticement of youth into these subcultures. With respect to violent street gangs, however, Clark suggested that specific individual personality characteristics were predictive of affiliation. These included a high proclivity for violence, alienation from parents, defiance of parents, truancy, substance abuse, failure to experience guilt, low self-esteem, and a lack of positive role models. Clark suggested that by preventing alienation from occurring in the family, at school, and with peers, and by paying close attention to those adolescents who have low self-esteem, ineffective coping strategies, and compromised development, negative group affiliation could be prevented for at-risk adolescents.

Theories about the causes and precursors of gang affiliation are many, although few theories are offered to account for the higher rate of violent crimes in gang members. Thornberry, Krohn, Lizotte, and Chard-Wierschem (1993) conducted a longitudinal study with juvenile gang members to examine this issue. They proposed a three-model theory that included the "selection model," the "social facilitation model," and the "enhancement model." The selection model suggests that gang members are chosen from pools of adolescents who are already delinquent or who display a high propensity for delinquent behavior. The social facilitation model suggests that gang members are intrinsically no different from nongang members. Specifically, it is the group process of the gang and the normative support it provides for delinquent behavior that generates an environment in which such delinquent behavior flourishes. The enhancement model, which combines the previous two explanations, asserts that the gang recruits members from adolescents who are already delinquent but then facilitates the enhancement of such behavior. Thornberry et al. (1993) findings support the facilitation model in that the highest frequencies of general delinquency occurred during membership, and, before and after active gang membership, the mean level of delinquent behavior was not significantly higher than boys who never belonged to a gang.

Kennedy and Baron (1993) examined youth violent offending and victimization in terms of "routine activities" and "subcultural" theories. The routine activities explanation suggests that street crime is a product of opportunity. The subcultural approach, however, suggests that through adherence to a set of norms that define violence as a necessary response to actions, individuals are more likely to perceive many situations as requiring a violent response. Further, those violent responses are backed up with social rewards and punishments that include admiration and respect by fellow subculture members as well as tangible rewards. Their results suggest that the routine activities theory, with a component of personal choice, and subcultural theory complemented each other in this study. Thus, youth behavior is sometimes guided by choice, at other times influenced by cultural norms and processes, and still at other times by routine activities. They further concluded that the member's choice to enter the subcultural group may actually promote certain conflict styles that are continually modeled and reinforced within the group.

Although gang affiliation is often viewed as a negative response to adolescent development, it may well serve an important positive function for many youth. Wright and Wright (1982) suggested that during the period of adolescence the gang may serve as a transitional family between one's family of origin and one's family of choice. To be more specific, the gang may indeed be seen as a vehicle to promote and provide an important social anchor that permits and eases the development of adult autonomy and independence in the youth.

Youth gang affiliation may fill other, often unidentified, needs. Specifically, these needs are for mechanisms to allay the typical adolescent fears of abandonment, independence/dependency striving, affiliation and rejection issues, as well as fears of closeness and intimacy. Generally, once the youth is accepted into the gang milieu they will receive unconditional support, experience strong affiliation, and have many attachment and familial needs met by members. This strong attachment may be evidenced by the gang members' reference to the gang as their "family," with individual members being brothers and sisters. Often youth, when fully subsumed into the gang family, will deny or dissolve any further ties with their family of origin. Moreover, gangs may provide support and closeness not previously experienced by its members. As many families of origin continue to experience rapid and often terminal deterioration, youth gang affiliation becomes a more attractive option for many youth. This positive surrogate family stance must be questioned, however, as the gangs become increasingly violent.

School-Based Gang Intervention

Introduction and Background.   The complexity of the etiology of gang involvement and propagation should clearly reflect the need for comprehensive, multimodal, multisetting, and prescriptive programs for prevention and intervention parallel in complexity to the problem. The history of gang intervention as recognized by Spergel (1992) consisted of a series of essentially unidimensional approaches. The human services and social strategies that predominated in the 1950s and 1960s focused, respectively, on removing youth to therapeutic settings to deal with "pathology" or sending "detached workers" into neighborhood settings to lead delinquent gang youth toward conventional adaptation.

Following rather disappointing evaluation results regarding the effectiveness of the detached worker programs in particular, social scientists in the late 1960s and 1970s called for strategies to address the educational isolation and economic oppression that they believed drove youth into street gangs. The resulting programs focused on opportunity provision, which included recreation, education, job skills training, and job placement creation strategies. With few exceptions (e.g., Klein, 1968; Thompson & Jason, 1988), opportunity provision strategies were not systematically evaluated. For the most part, there is insufficient information regarding the short-term (e.g., degree to which youth took advantage of opportunities) or long-term (e.g., degree to which youth left gangs) effects of opportunity provision programs (Goldstein, 1993).

At the end of the 1970s and into the 1980s, the heavy increase in gang involvement in drug trade and the subsequent burgeoning of violent crime among gang youth, which took place in the context of an increasingly conservative political climate, resulted in a focus on "get tough" law enforcement suppression strategies. Thus, social control replaced social improvement as the major focus of gang intervention. For the most part, surveillance, deterrence, arrest, diversion, probation, prosecution, incarceration, and parole still prevail as the overarching themes in current gang-related programs as indicated by Spergel and Curry's (1993) 1990 survey of 254 criminal justice and community agencies across 45 U.S. cities. Clearly, considering the serious trend toward escalating gang violence, law enforcement strategies must remain a part of gang intervention efforts but in the context of a more balanced and comprehensive approach. Suppression efforts alone are not likely to have much impact. Huff and McBride (1993) summarized what is known so far by saying that law enforcement "response must be part of a broader community-based strategy" (p. 401), and Goldstein, Glick, Carthan, and Blancero (1994) expressed a realistic view of the situation succinctly:

> Indeed, it is a primary responsibility of society's officialdom to protect its citizens; gang violence in its diverse and often intense forms must be controlled. But much more must be done. Gang youths are our youths. They are among us now and, even if periodically incarcerated, most will be among us in the future. We deserve protection from their predations, but they deserve the opportunity to lead contributory and satisfying lives without resorting to individual or group violence. Punishment may be needed, but punishment fails to teach new, alternative ways to reach desired goals. (p. 162)

The remainder of this chapter will present a short review of one group of strategies that relates most directly to school environments and that has potential for at least partially addressing Goldstein's (1993) call for facilitating youths' ability to find "alternative ways to reach desired goals." Specifically, cognitive–behavioral methods for students and parents are offered as interventions with strong potential. Emphasis is given to the preventive potential of these strategies. While it is recognized that schools' reactive responses to current gang involvement are essential (e.g., school safety issues, liaisons between schools and law enforcement, school climate responses to gangs in schools), the highest return for intervention effort within schools is likely to remain with early prevention and continued follow-up programming. It is our opinion that early intervention focused on social cognitive–behavioral skills is closely aligned with the established goals and capabilities of educational systems and therefore may offer a "path of least resistance" as a first-line preventive strategy that could be implemented effectively within schools.

This is not to discount many other school variables that are closely related to the potential for delinquency and gang activity, most notably academic failure (Dryfoos, 1990; Hirschi, 1969). More broadly, schools have the potential for playing a critical role in gang intervention efforts, not only for necessary academic remediation but also as collaborators in the provision of other social services, recreational programs, and antigang and psychosocial curriculum delivery. Although many gang members are dropouts who have been long alienated from the school environment, sizable percentages of gang members are still active school participants (Spergel, 1990). As such, gang-aware school staffs, supportive school environments, and vigorous school academic and social programs may be an essential component in intervention for many gang members and potential future gang members (Taylor, 1990). Because schools hold the greatest time and programmatic responsibility for school-age children and youth outside of the family, it could be argued the schools should serve as the coordinating hub of wraparound services for at-risk, delinquent, and gang-involved youth and their families and as a major center for preventive efforts as well (see Randolph, this volume). However, our goal here is to provide a sense of how complex the best practices planning, implementation, and appropriate evaluation of even a single strategy can be, and offer ideas for how the change process can be accomplished with the highest probability of success.

Most discussions of gang intervention heretofore have listed and described multiple strategies, decried the paucity of strategic planning and evaluation, but have failed to offer a description of how such processes may be carried out successfully. School psychologists in particular have the training to aid in efforts to plan, implement, and evaluate school-wide programs designed to increase the likelihood that children will have the social cognitive skills necessary to combat the lure of gang life. Therefore, program planning and implementation are described from the perspective of the school psychologist as organizational consultant. The example of how social cognitive–behavioral strategies could be integrated in intensive school-wide programs through a process of planned change, staff training, and consultation will provide a model of how any antigang preventive or reactive program (or comprehensive integration of programs) may be accomplished at the school or community level.

☐ Theoretical and Empirical Support for Cognitive–Behavioral Skills-Based Training in Schools

At-risk children and gang youth who remain in school spend six or more hours a day in a relatively safe microcosm of middle-American society. As such, schools have great potential for influencing the behavioral outcomes of these students. Extensive meta-analyses of treatments for delinquency are clear in suggesting the specific psychological interventions that have the best potential for positive influence on aggression, delinquency, criminal behavior, and, potentially, gang activity. In summarizing the results of quantitative reviews, Hollin (1993) suggests that structured, focused programs that feature behavioral, skill-oriented treatments may work better than unstructured treatments such as counseling and other nondirective, client-centered approaches. More specifically, interventions that include cognitive components that address the attitudes, values, and attributions that support antisocial behavior and include training in positive social–behavioral alternatives seem to be more effective than those that do not (e.g., Izo & Ross, 1990). Such cognitive–behavioral methods have thus been described as the current "dominant psychological model for the treatment of delinquency" (Clements, 1988, p. 292).

Cognitive–behavioral methods, although difficult to define, are based in social learning theory and cognitive developmental theory and generally seek to identify and correct maladaptive cognitions (i.e., social and interpersonal attributions, beliefs, self-statements, perceptions) and build positive coping skills (e.g., interpersonal problem-solving, prosocial skills, anger control) for dealing with challenging social situations. The assumption is made that faulty social cognitions and specific skills deficits result in gaps in delinquents' role-taking ability, impulse and anger management, moral reasoning, social perceptions, or social competence, or all of these (Hollin, 1993), and these skill gaps result in the use of antisocial alternatives. From the social learning perspective, use of negative social alternatives is further exacerbated by poor or absent adult and peer models of social behavior. Note that these processes fit closely with the description of the selection/social fa- cilitation models of gang affiliation offered by Thornberry et al. (1993), in which youth with poorly developed social skills align themselves with others with similar proclivities, thus creating a subculture where such tendencies are rationalized and supported.

The relationship between social–cognitive skill deficit models and delin- quent behavior generally has been supported by cognitive–behavioral in- tervention studies that have included post-treatment delinquency measures (e.g., subsequent police/court contact, number of new offenses, aggressive behavior, school suspensions, family interactions) and have addressed such specific skill areas as social perspective taking (e.g., Chalmers & Townsend, 1990), moral reasoning (e.g., Arbuthnot & Gordon, 1986), anger control (e.g., Feindler, Marriott, & Iwata, 1984), youth social skills (Gross, Brigham, Hopper, & Bologna, 1980), and youth/parent reciprocal social skills (Serna, Schumaker, Hazel, & Sheldon, 1986).

Multimodal treatment packages that include cognitive–behavioral, skill- building, and contingency management components may have the great- est potential for gang prevention and intervention. For example, Goldstein and Glick's (1987) Aggression Replacement Training (ART) includes train- ing in an array of specific aggression-related social skills (skillstreaming), anger control, and moral reasoning. A two-year research evaluation project reported by Goldstein, Glick, Carthan, and Blancero (1994) is one of the rare psychological treatment studies conducted with actual gang members (subjects and controls representing 10 gangs in Brooklyn, New York). Rea- sonable measures were taken to assure efficient program planning, a rel- atively rigorous research design, and treatment integrity. Results indicated significant gains among participants in the prosocial skills trained and on selected measures of community adjustment (e.g., employment status) but not on self-reported anger control. Most impressive was that only 5 of the 38 (13%) ART participants were rearrested during an eight-month tracking period in comparison with 14 of 27 (52%) of the control subjects. Goldstein et al.'s (1994) findings tentatively suggest that combinations of cognitive– behavioral and contingency management strategies provided in the context of overall school and community programming may have promise with ac- tual gang populations as well.

Cognitive–behavioral models of training may be especially effective in dealing with aggressive responses. Evidence suggests that aggressive chil- dren and youth often ascribe external causes to their social failures, which reduce the likelihood of acknowledging personal change as an avenue for improving relationships (Crick & Ladd, 1993). In addition, aggressive youth are more likely to show what has been termed "hostile intent bias" (Crick & Dodge, 1994), which results in the perception of malicious intent in am- biguous or neutral peer behavior. As a result, aggressive youth may often feel justified in using aggressive retaliation as a response, rather than even well-rehearsed adaptive alternatives. Guerra and Slaby (1990) were able to improve aggressive, adjudicated adolescents' social problem-solving skill and, subsequently, blind ratings of their social behavior with a cognitive–behavioral training model that included instruction and practice in reading and recognizing nonhostile social cues and gathering information before selecting a social response. Interventions in this area may have potential in reducing the retaliatory responses often seen with gangs following relatively innocuous provocations (e.g., "flashing" of gang signs, getting "looked at").

Antigang curricula more specifically designed to address gang activity prevention and suppression often include cognitive–behavioral techniques. Such curricula are designed to circumvent gang initiation by providing anti-gang information, bolstering self-esteem, and providing problem-solving and gang resistance skills to students beginning in the early elementary grades. An example of this type of programming in schools is Dr. Lila Lopez's Mission SOAR program in the Los Angeles Unified School District (reported in Stephens, 1993). This elementary level curriculum is taught by regular teachers and covers self-esteem building, goal development and planning, interpersonal problem-solving and conflict resolution, and information about negative aspects of gang affiliation. As with most programs of this type, no formal evaluation has been completed, but it includes cognitive–behavioral and skill-based techniques that have potential for success with the younger students for which it is targeted.

☐ Best Practices in Preventive School-Wide Social–Cognitive Skills Programs

Although the evidence presented above suggests cognitive–behavioral interventions' targeted utility regarding delinquent and gang-related populations, these treatment techniques may have wider efficacy in school-wide prevention efforts with younger at-risk children and youth. The link between early childhood experiences and later social behavior has been clearly established. If early deficits or excesses precluding social competence are not addressed at their origin, children are at risk for a host of more serious problems later, including the constellation of behaviors associated with delinquency and criminal gang activity (Fox & Savelle, 1987). Therefore, pervasive treatment of social–cognitive skills deficits beginning at the earliest grades is recommended.

Teachers' acceptance and successful implementation of cognitive–behavioral training in the context of general classroom activity is enhanced by the didactic instructional nature of the training methods (i.e., skill conceptualization, direct instruction, modeling, guided and distributed practice) that parallel the pedagogical techniques teachers use every day. Teachers generally relate to the similarities and need only be convinced that social–cognitive skills are as legitimate and crucial a content area as math or reading for all children, as has been suggested by mental health prevention experts (e.g., DeLeon, 1986). Because most of these intervention methods can be comfortably applied by teachers and other staff within schools if appropriate training and support are in place, school-wide programs that include social skills training, interpersonal problem solving, moral reasoning training, and so on, are possible, and models for school-wide training and reinforcement of interpersonal skills are appearing in the literature (Cartledge & Milburn, 1986; Jones, Sheridan, & Binns, 1993). These training packages are delivered formally in short sessions several days a week in regular classrooms. The training may occur separately or in the context of other subject areas.

Equal in importance to the issue of early prevention is the process of skill generalization (see Abdullah and Branch, this volume). While it has been demonstrated that children can readily learn these interpersonal skills in the context of structured groups, the ultimate goal of intervention is to facilitate the generalization of skill use to natural, day-to-day contexts (Stokes & Osnes, 1986). School-wide programming can be most effective in enhancing the generalized transfer of trained skills because the creation of a school "culture" is possible in which (1) all school personnel (including teachers, support staff, bus drivers, cafeteria staff, secretaries, administrators, etc.) take responsibility for "coaching" and reinforcing children's use of interpersonal skills "on the fly" as critical social challenges occur in the natural course of the school day (see Randolph, this volume); (2) a strong external incentive and infusion system is in place that may include token systems, bulletin boards, daily announcements, contests and friendly competitions, and integration of interpersonal skills into academic curricula; and (3) strong parent involvement is encouraged and actively programmed. Each of these components is elaborated below.

The "on the fly" training experiences described above are accomplished by training all school staff in the consistent delivery of social skills teaching interactions wherein they reinforce the spontaneous use of trained skills or prompt, cue, and reinforce children through brief minitraining experiences as actual negative social events occur. Boys Town has articulated and refined this teaching interaction process in their social skills training model and offers training materials and workshops to schools and professionals (Dowd & Tierney, 1992). These interactions are initiated whenever and wherever a social problem occurs within the school context. Note that the focus here remains educative rather than disciplinary. The major premise is to teach and enhance prosocial skills such that these will replace the negative alternatives rather than simply suppressing the negatives (see Abdullah and

Branch, this volume). These activities take time, especially in the beginning, and staff must be encouraged to give social skills teaching interactions priority equal to that of other content areas. In the long run, academic engaged time will increase as the social abilities of students make discipline less of an issue.

The individual teaching and prompting efforts of staff are enhanced to the extent that the school is an overall milieu for frequent reinforcement and focus on social interaction skills. Prosocial alternatives must be emitted with high enough frequencies in natural environments that the positive social responses of adults and peers will eventually "entrap" and maintain those behaviors after programmed intervention has been terminated (McConnell, 1987). Initially, this requires a restructuring of the social environment to increase the probability that prosocial alternatives will be reinforced. Token systems, in which staff and peers have opportunities to award spontaneous skill use, are helpful in this regard. For example, the first author facilitated the implementation of "Life Skills Lotto" in an alternative school for conduct-disordered adolescents. Students receive tickets for participating in social skills groups and for exhibiting the "skill of the week." Both staff and peers can award tickets. Weekly drawings are held in the cafeteria on a class-by-class basis. Prizes include free meal coupons and other goods donated by local businesses and parents. Also, activities and events that emphasize the use of social cognitive skills add to the overall prosocial culture of the school. Daily announcements about the skill of the week, art contests and student skits illustrating prosocial alternatives, provocative guest speakers who emphasize the need for prosocial skills in their work and life, and colorful bulletin boards dedicated to skill emphasis all give the message to students that social–cognitive development is an important aspect of their school and community lives.

To support student skill use outside of school, parent involvement is essential. Parent participation can range from information dissemination to direct parent training and support. Parents may offer home facilitation and generalization of interpersonal skills training if they receive a newsletter that describes skills that students are working on and offers suggestions for how parents can encourage their children's use of skills outside of school. Direct parent training may emphasize general parenting skills, stress management, child interpersonal skills facilitation, or monitoring and behavioral contracting or all of these activities with adolescents. Since parent involvement is clearly linked to academic and behavioral success (Christenson, Rounds, & Franklin, 1992), providing at-risk parents with "news they can use" in dealing with their children at home paves the way for greater trust in the school, increases collaboration between school and home on other issues, and enhances the potential for generalization of trained skills beyond the school environment. In dealing with at-risk parents, who often

have histories of school failure and mistrust themselves, school professionals may initially increase participation in parent training efforts by collab-
orating with other agencies to provide such services outside of the school
and after-school hours. Community centers situated in the neighborhoods
where at-risk families reside provide a viable location. Arranging for transportation and babysitting often are essential to successful participation with
at-risk families.

Whereas school-wide programs have the potential for teaching and "en-
trapping" prosocial behavior in greater numbers of at-risk children, they
offer a challenge in terms of the prescriptiveness with which cognitive–
behavioral interventions can be applied. Not all children who are at risk
for gang membership necessarily have difficulties within specific cognitive–
behavioral areas, and not all parents can be provided, or need, training.
Fortunately, interpersonal skills training has never been shown to have negative effects on any type of trainees, so reinforcement and overlearning of
known skills poses no particular risks for children who are already well
adjusted. Thus, procedurally, school-level programming may begin with delivery of an established social skills curriculum to all children (e.g., Dowd &
Tierney, 1992; McGinnis, Goldstein, Sprafkin, & Gershaw, 1984).

Prescriptiveness at this broad level of intervention would involve getting teacher, student, and parent input to prioritize the target skills for initial training. Jones et al. (1993) describe a multigating procedure whereby
screening data is utilized to identify initial skill targets as well as to identify
children that are at greater risk for social failure. Brief teacher and student
self-report screening instruments and sociometric measures are used for this
purpose. At-risk children enter a second gate of assessment to more prescriptively describe their specific deficits. This assessment may include more
comprehensive rating scales, observations, and functional analyses of their
social behavior. Particular attention is paid to intervening cognitive, emotional, and attitudinal variables that may prevent students from using newly
learned social skills (e.g., anxiety, anger management, impulsivity, hostile
attributional bias, tendency toward externalizing blame/responsibility for
social outcomes), and intensive small group training is provided by professional support staff to address specific cognitive–behavioral deficits. This
prescriptive training logically may be provided by a school psychologist, but
any other student services support staff (e.g., guidance counselors, school
nurse, behavioral specialist) with appropriate training may run these focused groups. Efforts can then be made to involve parents of these targeted
at-risk children with various levels of support, from consistent home–school
communication with the goal of parent facilitation of skill use, to active parent training.

It should be clear that (1) orienting entire schools to the need for social
and cognitive–behavioral skills training as an established part of the curricu-

lum; (2) convincing school administrators and personnel that they are the best group to deliver these interventions; (3) providing training and support such that they have the knowledge, skill, and confidence to implement the programs; and (4) appropriately evaluating the relevant outcomes of programs involves a daunting level of system change. The next section will describe the steps of strategic planning, training, and ongoing consultation as they apply to school-wide social–cognitive intervention programs. A description of how these steps are applied to a specific intervention should suggest how they could be applied more broadly to comprehensive gang intervention programming.

☐ Strategic Planning and Program Evaluation

Much can be learned from a historical analysis of delinquency and gang intervention. The overarching theme is that the failure of programs may be more a function of organization and implementation breakdown than necessarily a function of the relative merit of specific interventions. It is readily apparent that many of the shortcomings of previous attempts to prevent or rehabilitate criminal gang involvement could be overcome by integrating the approaches reviewed here and elsewhere in this book into prescriptively applied, well-implemented, well-monitored, and rigorously evaluated, comprehensive programs. The recommended multimodal/multilevel strategies will require considerable resources, detailed coordination, and high intervention integrity. Intervention integrity refers to the extent to which interventions are implemented as designed. The history of gang intervention programs is rife with examples of poor intervention integrity. Work with gang youths will continue to offer many unpredictable variables and situations, and intervention plans must have some built-in flexibility. However, systematic methods of planning, training, and evaluation must be in place that can create needs-specific programming and track its effects with outcome variables that are socially relevant and empirically verifiable.

Program conceptualization, operationalization, and evaluation must revolve around the basic principles of organizational change and staff development. Without true strategic planning, fully supported staff training, and ongoing consultation, schools will respond to mandates for reform in superficial ways that minimize actual change. In short, organizational change happens through and to people, and people are fragile. The anticipation of change and the need for new knowledge and skills can breed fear, and fear often leads to resistance or inaction. Without an understanding of the processes of guided organizational change, principals, school psychologists, and other change agents are unlikely to overcome these barriers. The basic steps in strategic project planning and staff development as they relate to school-wide cognitive–behavioral training programs are outlined below. These steps were adapted from a number of sources dealing with strategic management in education (Valentine, 1991), descriptions of actual successful school reform efforts that have applied the principles of organizational change (Knoff & Batsche, 1995; Kovaleski, Tucker, & Duffy, 1995), and the experience of the authors in school-wide projects.

Administrative Entry

Step one in the change process is to educate and enlist the support of major leaders. Typically, this is referring to administrators, but other influential gatekeepers (e.g., the principal's secretary, a senior teacher, the curriculum specialist, guidance counselor) are often overlooked and can thwart progress because of their somewhat veiled decisionmaking power and control of resources. Top-down administrative or informal power base support or both must be secured before any hope of school-wide implementation can be expected. Leaders should be informed of the contribution that training staff in cognitive–behavioral methods can make to reducing discipline referrals, improving school climate, and fulfilling the school's obligation to foster the social–emotional development as well as the cognitive development of students. Administrators will also be interested in the "public relations" advantages of such programs, which are generally applauded by parents and other community constituents. It also can be suggested that cognitive–behavioral programs may ultimately reduce "budgetary drain" by reducing referrals and placements to special education, the budget of which is rarely fully funded by federal dollars. These attempts to "sell" the program to administrators and other gatekeepers take into account the major concerns of building principals: money, resource and personnel allocation, and public relations.

Once administrative support is assured, a somewhat formal contract should be drafted that outlines the goals, delineates a rough timeline, establishes a coordinate structure at the top that represents key gatekeepers and student services support staff, and articulates the procedures for establishing the program. Among critical issues to address in contract negotiation, the consultant should ascertain the extent to which the administration will (1) give a long-term commitment to project implementation, (2) support intensive staff training during school hours or on dedicated inservice days, (3) allocate resources for materials and incentives, (4) allow curriculum time within the school day for formal student training, (5) allow time for coordinating and follow-up consultation meetings among key project teams, and (6) play an active role in planning and implementation efforts. The administrator also can act as a collaborator with the consultant in securing district-level support for the above considerations.

Staff Level Entry and Piloting

Step two in the process involves reentering the system at the staff level and orienting everyone to the concepts, rationale, advantages, and strategies of the program. This can be accomplished in relatively brief inservice meetings. Again, all personnel should be included at this point. Do not discount maintenance staff, cafeteria workers, bus drivers, etc., who may have personal characteristics and backgrounds that ultimately make them excellent trainers and models for at-risk children. Research shows that nonprofessionals can deliver cognitive–behavioral interventions with a level of success equal to or surpassing that of professionals (Durlak, 1982). Sometimes at-risk children relate better to and are more likely to model nonprofessionals who come from backgrounds similar to their own. One of the first author's most effective training resources in a dropout prevention program for "incorrigible" secondary students was the head plant operator.

The staff orientation offers an opportunity to identify the first key implementation group—volunteers from the staff who show the highest level of acceptance and enthusiasm for the proposed project. This key group generally should include grade-level teacher representation and any of the other constituents already mentioned. Rather than proceeding to full, building-level implementation at this point, our experience indicates that an initial small-scale pilot project may provide a better foundation for eventual success. Several staff from the key group are trained by the consultant in social–cognitive curriculum delivery and generalization enhancement methods in intense, hands-on inservice workshops. The school psychologist consultant has his or her heaviest direct involvement in student training following the key group workshops. He or she acts as the facilitator, and the teacher or staff as cofacilitator, in pilot group training until the regular school staff feel comfortable in taking the role of primary trainers. By piloting the training model within a few select classrooms or with small pull-out groups, the consultant can offer more focused support to the pilot personnel, thus maximizing staff treatment integrity, skill, and confidence. Significantly, the same principles of generalization apply in adult learning as were presented regarding student training. The pilot group requires opportunities to try training skills under safe, controlled conditions, with frequent constructive feedback and reinforcement, followed by sequenced increases in responsibility. The school psychologist gradually fades direct involvement in group training and serves as a clinical consultant thereafter—conducting observations and giving the new trainers constructive feedback, aiding in troubleshooting implementation problems, and collecting outcome data to show the efficacy of the pilot program. The pilot project helps to identify and solve building- or population-specific problems and create innovative ideas for training, usually resulting in enthusiastic and well-trained staff who can be used to promote the school-wide program and help train the rest of the staff, and provides "hard data" to present to administrators and the remaining staff to further convince them of the efficacy of the program.

Planning, Training, and Implementation at the Building Level

Logically, step three in the process starts with a report to the administration and staff regarding the outcomes of the pilot project and discussion of the potential for building-wide implementation. Critically, a full and anonymous staff vote should be conducted at this point. It is recommended that the program should not be initiated unless at least 80% of the staff are in favor of proceeding. Moreover, if it can be discerned that the dissenting percentage includes any key gatekeepers, there is still major reason for concern. As a colleague succinctly put it, "Don't try to launch a ground war without air support." Following the preceding steps should reduce the likelihood of a negative vote.

Next, an intense planning phase is initiated by a volunteer coordinate group at the staff/community level. This group includes members of the pilot team but should be representative of all internal and external stakeholders and grade levels. Among the many purposes of this planning phase are conducting needs assessments and an analysis of helping and hindering factors at the school level, selecting skills for training, deciding on order of skill presentation, establishing infusion and incentive systems to support generalization, soliciting community and business support and designing parent involvement programs, and planning school-wide training for the full staff. The final product of the planning phase should be clearly operationalized goals and substeps for training, implementation, and evaluation, and action plans delineating timelines and persons responsible for each step.

Training those staff members with primary responsibility for conducting formal skills training with students follows the same format as described for the pilot group. The difference is that the school psychologist now has the pilot group as an additional training resource. These personnel are highly involved in the initial inservice workshops by providing concrete examples of skill training steps, sharing innovative ideas, and assuaging concerns voiced by trainees. Moreover, the pilot group members can serve as "master teachers" in the collegial supervision of their peers as they begin to implement groups in their own classrooms. Administrative support for team teaching and clinical supervision during this experiential phase of training is critical. Clearly, one-shot inservice workshops do not provide the level of support and feedback necessary to assure that all social–cognitive trainers are exhibiting an adequate level of treatment integrity. The pilot team and the school psychologist continue to conduct periodic treatment integrity observations and trainer feedback sessions as part of ongoing evaluation of the project. A somewhat modified, but similar, training experience is provided to nonteaching support staff who will reinforce and coach students in teaching interactions outside of the classroom (i.e., in the office, cafeteria, buses, hallways). Finally, follow-up meetings of the core planning group, and occasionally the entire staff, should continue throughout implementation to troubleshoot, share ideas, fine-tune programming, and foster enthusiasm. The core group should represent the staff at large by soliciting and bringing issues, ideas, and concerns to the consultant and administration.

Program Evaluation

Space precludes a thorough discussion of the components and processes of program evaluation. In short, formative and summative evaluations are imperative. Formative evaluation refers to the degree to which training procedures are being implemented as planned. The training cycle described above provides the context for formative evaluation. The authors have found checklists of the desired steps in skill training useful, both for staff feedback and as a permanent empirical record of staff development and treatment integrity. These training documents should not identify specific staff members and should be used in summary form only to guide formative modifications in the project. Other formative process measures may include measures of treatment acceptability from teachers, students, parents, and other concerned stakeholders, measures of students' in-group acquisition of target skills, and evidence of generalization of skill use outside of the classroom. If student token reinforcement of skill use is well documented, this may serve as a rough assessment of generalization within the school environment. Ideally, direct observations of students' skill use in various school environments are incorporated in formative evaluations as well.

Summative evaluations are measures of the extent to which outcome goals for the project have been met. The necessary range of data will depend on the age of the student population and the types of problems that the program was supposed to impact. If preventive programming for young children is provided, proximal (e.g., discipline referrals, suspensions, retentions, social skills rating data) and distal/longitudinal (e.g., school continuance, juvenile system involvement, gang-related activity) evaluations may be necessary to get a full picture of the desired outcomes.

☐ Conclusion

Clearly, thorough program planning, implementation, and evaluation as described above takes time, usually more than is initially expected. In reality, making a large organizational change requires that participants adjust their estimates of how long it may take from months to years. Critically, such efforts must be supported by district-level systems (and by association, federal- and state-level systems) that understand and tolerate gradual but systematic change. This will require the elimination of the "use it or lose it" mentality often underlying educational funding patterns. Not only time, but timing, is important. Knoff (1995) points out that planning and funding cycles at the federal, state, district, and school levels often vary tremendously, and these differences must be taken into account when planning a large-scale project.

In the wider view, the processes reviewed here hold promise for dealing with larger aspects of gang-related problems in schools and the community. Given the escalating intensity, deadliness, mobility, and ubiquity of the gang problem, it will be necessary to abandon unidimensional, "magic bullet" approaches to intervention. It is now more imperative than ever that we design prescriptive and comprehensive approaches that account for the variety of motivations behind gang participation, the wide diversity among potential and actual gang members, and the degree of gang presence in the community. Comprehensive programs will require major, well-planned, systems-level change.

All in all, the potential components for effective, comprehensive, well-implemented, and appropriately evaluated gang intervention efforts already exist. The larger question is whether and when our society will place priority on, and subsequent funding and mobilization toward, intensive, integrative, and comprehensive gang intervention programming. While there is some justification for guarded optimism to be derived from an analysis of what has worked and what has not in isolated cases, our society's inefficient responses to other social crises (e.g., homelessness, public assistance, health care, and mental illness) inhibits complete confidence in hopes of a positive future for the majority of our disenfranchised gang youths. However, the cogent and diligent application of the processes of organizational change will increase the odds for success.

Mental health interventions can be of help to gang adolescents and their families in their quest for a better quality of life. Cognitive behavioral interventions have the potential of teaching social skills that can be transferred to other settings. In the process of learning the new skills the adolescent will develop new insights into his or her behavior and decide to change other things about how they interact with the world as well. This process of self-examination has been called introspection. What is perhaps more basic than the client thinking about his behavior is that the professional conducting the interventions will also raise questions about what they are doing and the reasons why. Are the mental health and programmatic interventions created in an attempt to normalize otherwise unacceptable behavior? Or do organized programs simply ignore the developmental contexts in which adolescents function and pathologize attempts at negotiating developmental hurdles that may fall outside of prevailing middle-class attempts at solving the identity questions? Put another way, one should wonder if attempts at *helping* gang adolescents are well-intentioned efforts that normalize pathology or if they making normal developmental processes pathognomic. This is the question addressed by Branch in the following chapter in this volume.

☐ References

Arbuthnot, J., & Gordon, D. A. (1986). Behavior and cognitive effects on moral reasoning development intervention for high-risk, behavior-disordered adolescents. *Journal of Clinical Psychology, 34*, 208–216.

Atwater, E. (1988). *Adolescence* (2nd ed.). New Jersey: Prentice–Hall.

Baittle, B., & Kobrin, S. (1964). On the relationship of a characterological type of delinquent to the milieu. *Psychiatry, 27*, 6–16.

Bandura, A., & Walters, R. H. (1963). *Social learning and personality development*. New York: Holt, Rinehart & Winston.

Berland, D. I., Homlish, J. S., & Blotcky, M. J. (1989). Adolescent gangs in the hospital. *Bulletin of the Menninger Clinic, 53*(1), 31–43.

Bernard, T. J. (1990). Angry aggression among the truly disadvantaged. *Criminology, 28*, 73–95.

Bernardio, J. (1994, July 14). Federal Bureau of Investigation, personal communication.

Campbell, A., Munce, S., & Galea, J. (1982). American gangs and British subcultures: A comparison. *International Journal of Offender Therapy and Comparative Criminology, 26*, 76–89.

Cartledge, G., & Milburn, J. (1986). *Teaching social skills to children: Innovative approaches* (2nd ed.). New York: Pergamon.

Chalmers, J. B., & Townsend, M. A. R. (1990). The effects of training in social perspective taking on socially maladjusted girls. *Child Development, 61*, 178–190.

Christenson, S. L., Rounds, T., & Franklin, M. J. (1992). Home-school collaboration: Effects, issues, and opportunities. In S. L. Christenson & J. C. Conoley (Eds.), *Home-school collaboration: Enhancing children's academic and social competence* (pp. 19–52). Silver Spring, MD: National Association of School Psychologists.

Clark, C. M. (1992). Deviant adolescent subcultures: Assessment strategies and clinical interventions. *Adolescence, 27*, 283–293.

Clements, C. B. (1988). Delinquency prevention and treatment: A community-centered perspective. *Criminal Justice and Behavior, 152*, 286–305.

Corsica, J. Y. (1993). Employment training interventions. In A. P. Goldstein & C. R. Huff (Eds.), *The gang intervention handbook* (pp. 301–317). Champaign, IL: Research Press.

Crick, N. R., & Dodge, K. A. (1994). A review and reformulation of social information processing mechanisms in children's social adjustment. *Psychological Bulletin, 115*, 74–101.

Crick, N. R., & Ladd, G. W. (1993). Children's perceptions of their experiences: Attributions, loneliness, social anxiety, and social avoidance. *Developmental Psychology, 29*, 244–254.

DeLeon, D. (1986). *The prevention of mental-emotional disabilities: Report of the National Mental Health Association Commission on the Prevention of Mental-Emotional Disabilities.* Alexandria, VA: NMHA.

Dowd, T., & Tierney, J. (1992). *Teaching social skills to youth.* Boys Town, NE: Boys Town Press.

Dryfoos, J. G. (1990). *Adolescents at risk: Prevalence and prevention.* New York: Oxford University Press.

Durlak, J. A. (1982). Use of cognitive-behavioral interventions by paraprofessionals in the schools. *School Psychology Review, 11,* 64–66.

Feindler, E. L., Marriott, S. A., & Iwata, M. (1984). Group anger control training for junior high school delinquents. *Cognitive Therapy and Research, 8,* 299–311.

Fox, J. J., & Savelle, S. (1987). Social interaction research with families of behaviorally disordered children: A critical review and forward look. *Behavioral Disorders, 12,* 276–291.

Furlong, M. J., & Morrison, G. M. (1994). Introduction to miniseries: School violence and safety in perspective. *School Psychology Review, 23,* 139–150.

Goldfreid, M. R., & Merbaum, M. A. (1973). A perspective on self-control. In M. R. Goldfried & M. Merbaum (Eds.), *Behavior change through self-control* (pp. 3–36). New York: Holt, Rinehart & Winston.

Goldstein, A. P. (1993). Issues and opportunities. In A. P. Goldstein & C. R. Huff (Eds.), *The gang intervention handbook.* Champaign, IL: Research Press.

Goldstein, A. P., & Glick, B. (1987). *Aggression replacement training: A comprehensive intervention for aggressive youth.* Champaign, IL: Research Press.

Goldstein, A. P., Glick, B., Carthan, W., & Blancero, D. A. (1994). *The prosocial gang: Implementing aggression replacement training.* Thousand Oaks, CA: Sage.

Greene, M. B. (1993). Chronic exposure to violence and poverty: Interventions that work for youth. *Violence and Poverty, 39,* 106–124.

Gross, A. M., Brigham, T. A., Hopper, C., & Bologna, N. C. (1980). Self-management and social skills training: A study of predelinquent and delinquent youths. *Criminal Justice and Behavior, 7,* 161–184.

Guerra, N. G., & Slaby, R. G. (1990). Cognitive mediators of aggression in adolescent offenders: 2. Intervention. *Developmental Psychology, 26,* 269–277.

Hirschi, T. (1969). *Causes of delinquency.* Berkeley: University of California Press.

Hollin, C. R. (1993). Cognitive-behavioral interventions. In A. P. Goldstein & C. R. Huff (Eds.), *The gang intervention handbook.* Champaign, IL: Research Press.

Huff, C. R., & McBride, W. D. (1993). Gangs and police. In A. P. Goldstein & C. R. Huff (Eds.), *The gang intervention handbook.* Champaign, IL: Research Press.

Izo, R. L., & Ross, R. R. (1990). Meta-analysis of rehabilitation programs for juvenile delinquents: A brief report. *Criminal Justice and Behavior, 17,* 134–142.

Jones, R. N., Sheridan, S. M., & Binns, W. R. (1993). Schoolwide social skills training: Providing preventive services to students at-risk. *School Psychology Quarterly, 8,* 57–80.

Kanfer, F. H. (1973). Self-regulation—Research, issues, and speculation. In M. R. Goldfried & M. Merbaum (Eds.), *Behavior change through self-control* (pp. 397–430). New York: Holt, Rienhart & Winston.

Kennedy, L. W., & Baron, S. W. (1993). Routine activities and a subculture of violence: A study of violence on the street. *Journal of Research in Crime and Delinquency, 30,* 88–112.

Klein, M. W. (1968). The Ladino Hills Project (Final report to the Office of Juvenile Delinquency and Youth Development). Washington, DC: Office of Juvenile Delinquency and Youth Development.

Knoff, H. M. (1995). Best practices in facilitating school-based organizational change and strategic planning. In A. Thomas & J. Grimes (Eds.), *Best practices in school psychology-III.* Washington, DC: National Association of School Psychologists.

Knoff, H. M., & Batsche, G. M. (1995). Project ACHIEVE: Analyzing a school reform process for at-risk and underachieving students. *School Psychology Review, 24,* 579–603.

Kohlberg, L. (1969). Stage and sequence: The cognitive-developmental approach to socialization. In D. A. Goslin (Ed.), *Handbook of socialization theory and research* (pp. 347–480). Chicago: Rand McNally.

Kovaleski, J. F., Tucker, J. A., & Duffy, D. J. (1995, June). School reform through instructional support: The Pennsylvania Initiative (part 1). *Communique, 23,* (insert).

Malmquist, C. P. (1978). *Handbook of adolescence.* New York: Aronson.

McConnell, S. R. (1987). Entrapment effects and the generalization and maintenance of social skills training for elementary school students with behavioral disorders. *Behavioral Disorders, 12,* 252–263.

McGinnis, E., Goldstein, A. P., Sprafkin, R. P., & Gershaw, N. J. (1984). *Skillstreaming the elementary school child: A guide to teaching prosocial skills.* Champaign, IL: Research Press.

Miller, W. (1982). Youth gangs: A look at the numbers. *Children Today, 11,* 10–11.

Rinsley, D. B. (1980). *Treatment of the severely disturbed adolescent.* New York: Aronson.

Rogers, C. (1993). Gang-related homicides in Los Angeles County. *Journal of Forensic Sciences, 38,* 753–834.

Serna, L. A., Schumaker, J. B., Hazel, J. S., & Sheldon, J. B. (1986). Teaching reciprocal social skills to parents and their delinquent adolescents. *Journal of Clinical Child Psychology, 15,* 64–77.

Skinner, B. F. (1953). *Science and human behavior.* New York: The Free Press.

Spergel, I. A. (1990). Youth gangs: Continuity and change. In M. Tonry & N. Morris (Eds.), *Crime and justice: A review of the research* (Vol. 12). Chicago: University of Chicago Press.

Spergel, I. A. (1992). Youth gangs: An essay review. *Social Service Review, 66,* 121–140.

Spergel, I. A., & Curry, G. D. (1993). The national youth gang survey: A research and development process. In A. P. Goldstein & C. R. Huff, *The gang intervention handbook.* Champaign, IL: Research Press.

Stephens, R. D. (1993). School-based interventions: Safety and security. In A. P. Goldstein & C. R. Huff (Eds.), *The gang intervention handbook.* Champaign, IL: Research Press.

Stokes, T. F., & Osnes, P. G. (1986). Programming the generalization of children's social behavior. In P. S. Strain, M. J. Guralnick, & H. M. Walker (Eds.), *Children's social behavior: Development, assessment, and modification.* Orlando, FL: Academic Press.

Taylor, C. (1990). *Dangerous society.* East Lansing: Michigan State University Press.

Thompson, D. W., & Jason, L. A. (1988). Street gangs and preventive interventions. *Criminal Justice and Behavior, 15,* 323–333.

Thoresen, C. E., & Mahoney, M. J. (1974). *Behavioral self-control.* New York: Holt, Rinehart & Winston.

Thornberry, T. P., Krohn, M. D., Lizotte, A. J., & Chard-Wierschem, D. (1993). The role of juvenile gangs in facilitating delinquent behavior. *Journal of Research in Crime and Delinquency, 30,* 55–87.

Thrasher, F. M. (1936). *The gang: A study of 1313 gangs in Chicago.* Chicago: University of Chicago Press.

Valentine, E. P. (1991). *Strategic management in education: A focus on strategic planning.* Boston: Allyn and Bacon.

Wright, F., & Wright, P. (1982). Violent groups. *Group, 6,* 25–34.

Curtis Branch

Pathologizing Normality or Normalizing Pathology?

Adolescence is generally regarded as the developmental period when questions of identity are resolved. The importance of the peer group in matters of social etiquette and behaviors is unmatched by other institutions and individuals in the lives of adolescents. Because of the high level of peer pressure in early and middle adolescence (12–16 years) affiliation with groups (i.e., cliques, clubs, gangs) is most likely to occur during this period. It is frequently true that adolescents seek to get their affiliation needs met in a variety of settings, finally settling for contexts in which they perceive that they are accepted without conditions. Branch (1997) reports that many adolescents who claim gang membership identity the "feeling of camaraderie" and "blind acceptance" as the conditions that led them to join the gang. "They are like family." is the way several gang members seen in counseling by Branch described the relationship with the gang.

Other scholars and clinicians have documented similar attributions by gang members. What remains undocumented about these familial-like relationships, however, is the qualitative assessments of the relationships. Do gang members have a healthy sense of allegiance to other gang members, as is often the characteristic of families, which remains constant across good and bad situations? Or are the relationships reported to be "like family," filled with an unusual amount of distrust and contention? Or do the gang members overestimate the strength of their relationships with each other as a cognitive dissonance reduction ploy? That is, do they simply say the relationships are close, in the absence of objective data to substantiate the claim, as a way to mask the fact that they have no truly close relationships with anyone? The answers to these and related questions are likely to be as diverse as the reasons individuals join gangs.

Despite the absence of a consistent set of reasons for joining and remaining in gangs, it is clear that being in the gang does meet a need. The need itself may not be obvious to the gang member in a way that she or he can discuss openly with an "outsider." Rather, they know that they feel good about being in the gang, but may not be able to explain "what" they get as a result of being in the gang. It could be the case that the member is responding to an internal psychological barometer that drives them to get certain needs met, even if it means engaging in high-risk self-destructive behaviors intermittently. Such an arrangement might be construed as high-risk unhealthy behavior being pursued in the quest for a sense of purpose or an identity. Put another way, it could be thought of as being pathological in an attempt to be "normal."

This chapter will explore such oximoronic behavior and thinking by examining the proposition that joining gangs is often a pathogenic attempt to get normal developmental needs met. More precisely, the question of how scholars, program planners, and mental health clinicians have interpreted gang membership among adolescents will be explored. Are gangs seen as pathologizing of normal behavior or as normalizing of pathological behavior? The emphases here will be placed on how gangs and gang membership have been treated in the literature, as well as how policymakers and other adults have responded to gang members themselves.

Before turning to the substantive question, a brief review of some basics appears to be in order. Lets start with the definition of a gang. In Chapter 1 of this volume the Jankowski operational definition of a gang is given. It forms the basis of all subsequent conceptualizations of gangs used in this text. The definition indicates that gangs are highly structured organizations that place demands on their members (i.e., require that they follow the social codes of the group, hold the personal agendas in abeyance in deference to the groups plans, and often require members to participate in illegal acts). Internalizing all of these requirements can be a daunting task for an adolescent. It is not a task that an out-of-control callous person is able to master.

☐ Pathologizing Normality: "Just Wanna Be Respected"

The limits to which individuals will go to have their psychological needs met are considerable. The case of adolescents and gangs is a good example. The tendency to congregate with others who one believes to be like himself or herself is well documented in the psychological literature. The perceived similarity between self and others is often the basis of attributions that are made to others and sometimes function as a way to reduce anxiety. For example, when given a choice of persons with whom one can work or play most individuals will opt for a person with whom they feel comfortable. In this case comfortable can be translated to mean "someone like me." This pattern of self-selection toward persons like oneself is nowhere more evident than among adolescents.

Springthall and Collins (1995) note that before adolescence, children spend more time with adults than with other children. With the onset of adolescence, however, they spend more time with friends and classmates and also more time alone than with their families (Csikeszentmihalyi & Larson, 1984; Larson, Kubey, & Coletti, 1989). The shift from an adult-focused social world to one that is dominated by peers also parallels the fluctuations in peer pressure and influence experienced by most adolescents. It is precisely this shift in peer influence and pressure that might partially explain the high appeal of gangs to adolescents who are in the midst of trying to find a place for themselves in the complex and sometimes overwhelming social world to which they are starting to become exposed.

There is a great deal of variety of types of groups from which adolescents have to choose—cliques, crowds, and gangs. Springthall and Collins (1995) note that there are multiple ways of classifying youth groups, including the *interactions* between their members. Groups formed by people who simply "hang around together" have been called cliques (Dunphy, 1963; Springthall & Collins, 1995). Relatively small in numbers, cliques are formed because the members are engaged in the same activity or because members are all actually friends from another context.

Dunphy (1963) describes cliques as being "small enough to allow for regular interaction of all members, to ensure that all members understand and appreciate one another better than do people outside the clique, and to permit members to regard the clique as their primary base of interaction with groups of age mates" (p. 177). Many adolescents and adults view cliques as being exclusionary and thus undesirable. The appeal of cliques declines in later adolescence. Among most adolescents, by the senior year of high school they are involved in a variety of groups and types of relationships, each meeting different psychological needs. It is at about the same time that susceptibility to pressure (parental and peer) declines dramatically. Membership in cliques is maintained by active interaction with others. Clique members must "do something" to sustain their status as a member in good standing. This is not true, in an absolute sense, in a crowd, another type of group to which many adolescents belong.

Classification as a member of a crowd is made on the basis of certain attitudes, of others, and attributions made to the adolescent. *Social reputation* is what becomes the foundation for crowd membership. Labels like "jocks," "nerds," and "potheads" are examples of crowd names. It should be remembered that crowds are not interactional groups. Rather, they are stereotypes that others, adolescents and adults alike, invoke as a way to group individuals on the basis of assumed shared qualities. Even social deviants and shy, withdrawn, otherwise unaffiliated, adolescents are placed into crowds.

Crowd labels serve the purpose of helping others know how to respond to an adolescent, wrongly or rightly. Another somewhat extreme type of group common among adolescents is gangs. Membership in gangs is a volitional decision, unlike being relegated to a crowd, and often follows an initiation. The complexity of sociological and psychological issues, which may prompt a young person to feel the need to join a gang, is considerable. Recent changes in social demography and the proliferation of drugs and violence among adolescents have altered the rosters of gangs tremendously. Springthall and Collins (1995, p. 299) report, "Whereas much gang activity was once identified with protecting a group's turf from encroachments by gangs from other areas, the activities of such groups today are more associated with crimes such as the sale of illegal drugs." Another shift in gang behavior, which has not been fully embraced by scholars and the general public, concerns the location of gangs. At one time gangs were thought to be exclusively an inner-city problem, found only in poor neighborhoods populated by people of color. Branch (1997) reports that this is no longer true. He comments that various levels of gang activity have recently been reported to exist in hitherto middle-class White neighborhoods, a pattern also reported by Mydans (1990a, 1990b) and Monti (1994).

The big question about gangs is often why would anyone chooses to join a gang in view of the safety risks associated with joining. Unlike cliques and crowds most gangs are not viewed as having any prosocial qualities in which members can share. It has been suggested by some scholars that the proliferation of gangs is the result of fewer satisfactory relationships in family, school, and community. The need for psychological validation is expressed within the group. The bond among gang members is sometimes viewed as a substitute for the close, protective relationships previously associated with families (Springthall & Collins, 1995). Still another viewpoint sees gang activities as the result of frustration over persistent obstacles to economic and social progress in many people of color communities. Whatever the reasons for gangs, it is clear that young people get, or at least report that they get, some of their needs met through them.

The three types of groups noted here are forums in which many adolescents function. Crowds are different from the others in that adolescents are *placed* into them by others. In all of the group settings mentioned here, the member behaves in ways that maintains his or her status within the group. The result is that a significant part of his or her socialization experience comes through the filter of the group. How meaningful the group is to the adolescent or how his or her life is shaped, long term, by having been in the group may not be readily apparent. Of the three groups discussed here, gangs are overwhelmingly considered to be the most risky and damaging to the adolescent. That may or may not be the case, especially if cliques are defined by drug abusing or other illegal behaviors. It is quite possible to have a clique that resembles a gang in many ways but is without a formal code of behavior or organizational rules.

What psychological needs of adolescents are met through gang affiliation? This question has the potential of also answering the quintessential question of what young people find so attractive about gang membership. Again, the responses are likely to be as varied as the lives of the young people who join gangs. Different people get different things from gangs, knowingly and unknowingly. The assumption that some need is being met by gang membership is unquestioned here. The exact nature of that product is, however, the object of interest here. Researchers seem to think that the act of affiliating with the gang itself is rewarding to some adolescents. Others disagree and posit instead that the meaningfulness of the membership is only forthcoming when the member becomes actively involved in the program of the gang. Let's examine these two positions.

Proponents of the first position think that the act of affiliating with the gang, alone, is satisfying to many youngsters. The sense of psychological connection, which is engendered by the gang membership, is regarded as being highly rewarding. This system of logic also holds that in adolescence the need for affiliation with peers increases as the young person starts to individuate from parents and family of origin. Joining cliques and other groups (e.g., athletic teams, fraternities, sororities, etc.) populated by peers is concrete evidence of the inverse relationship between closeness to family and level of involvement with peers. Silverberg and Steinberg (1987) and other developmentalists have cautioned that involvements with peers and out-of-family activities should not be interpreted as genuine emotional autonomy from the family and its influence. They suggest, instead, that as adolescents appear to be moving away from the family, based on their overt behaviors, they maintain a level of respect and emotional bonding with parents and family, which may not be readily apparent to others. Hill and Holmbeck (1986) offer empirical evidence that strengthens this argument. Specifically they show that autonomy is not a unitary personality dimension that consistently comes out in all behaviors. Now back to the issue of affiliation, gangs, and psychological needs.

The pressure for connection with peers (i.e., peer pressure to be with other adolescents) may be a partial explanation for why some adolescents join gangs. Society quietly requires that youngsters move away from the family of origin. The psychological need is that they move to a place where they can still get their "needs" (i.e., being valued, personal safety, nurturance) met. For some young people gangs become a viable option as a group that might meet many of their needs. It should be kept in mind that in some neighborhoods gangs are not thought of as being deviant or pathological in any ways. They are merely organizations that exist in the community, often with an implicit *contract* with the community residents. So, as the young person seeks to find himself, joining the gang looms as a viable option for accomplishing that goal, This pattern is very pronounced in economically poor neighborhoods where the residents are at high risk for feeling marginalized by the larger society. The rationale of joining because it is an integral part of the community and an option for "normal" individuation from the family of origin, however, does not apply in many situations. Earlier in this decade there were reports of gangs in middle-class suburban communities (Mydans, 1990a, 1990b). Obviously the interpretation of gangs being a historic part of the community fiber would not be true in such cases.

Mydans (1990a, 1990b) and Branch (1997) suggest that the appeal of gangs to middle-class suburban adolescents may be related to a romanticized notion of life in inner-city 'hoods and the stereotypic images of adolescents of color. By mimicking the behavior of inner-city residents, adolescents who live in the suburbs are getting a need met. What could it be? Likewise, inner-city residents who join gangs also are getting a need met by doing so. What could it be? It appears that affiliation with a gang, real or imaginary, has the capacity to satisfy an adolescent's need to belong to something. Maslow and Murphy (1954) identified this need for affiliation as a basic human need that must be satisfied before higher-order needs can be met. In affiliating with the gang some adolescents produce a temporary answer to the "Who am I" question. But the authenticity or level of internalization of their newfound identity is suspect. In extreme cases it may even be characterized as a high level of ambivalence about belonging to the gang. Behavioral manifestations of ambivalence may take the form of gang members who "freeze" and "falter" when they are asked to carry out antisocial acts. Still, being a part of the group, in name if not in spirit, causes some adolescents to experience a sense of identification they might not know otherwise.

Being a part of a gang then seems to make adolescents who are in transition (i.e., from nuclear family identification to a sense of independence and autonomy) feel that they have arrived at an identity. In common vernacular they think they have "found themselves." The gang provides a sense of refuge from isolation, confusion about how to individuate from family, and impending confusion about self-identity questions. On a psychological level these appear to be outcomes associated with aligning oneself with the structure and program of the gang. The dissonance and big questions about the utility of gangs arise when the qualitative aspects of the gang are considered. Most gangs participate in flagrantly illegal and antisocial activities. Can good come from being associated with such negatively oriented organizations? Many adolescents and adults would respond affirmatively.

The act of affiliating with gangs should be seen as a matter separate from assessments of the gang itself. The literature contains many accounts of young people who semi-innocently joined gangs because they appeared to be "like a family" (i.e., devoted to each other, tightly knit, etc.). Once they were involved in the gang another image started to emerge. The idealized image of the gang was shattered. In many cases the disillusioned adolescent suddenly realized that the decision that he had made to improve his status with others had served to fracture his relationship with his family of origin, the community, and society in general. A common occurrence at this stage is that the new gang member comes to be in a state of "conflict" about which voice he should follow—the old family values or the new imperatives of the gang. All of this internal conflict can frequently lead to depression which coexists with conduct disordered behavior (Branch, 1997; Moffit, 1993; Wasserman, Miller, Pinner, & Jaramillo, 1996). Despite new conflicts about being in the gang and remaining in good standing, the question of what the adolescent thought he would get by joining continues, often unanswered.

Anticipation of the benefits to be derived from joining a gang often interferes with an adolescent's capacity to assess the merits of his decision to join. What he "wanted" unduly influenced his pull toward the gang, so much so that he couldn't say "no." Movement toward the gang also clouded the adolescent's ability to objectively review the decision to join. Perhaps even more basic than that, some adolescents are unsure of what they need. They know that they don't like the feelings of isolation that they often experience when they review the quality of their relationships. Remember that the adolescent is individuating from family of origin at the same time that he is having to choose between multiple cliques and special interest groups who are bombarding him with intense peer pressure. Most adolescents also recognize that the increasing implicit pressure to "find themselves" forces them to associate with someone or something where they can be validated. Why then the gang? Why not the gang?

In neighborhoods where gangs are a way of life, socialization into gang culture is considered a viable option, just as deciding which college to attend may be a major adolescent issue in another community. The complete story about gang life or the dangers and risks associated with it are minimalized, if not outright denied, by recruiters and would-be recruits. Instead, the gang is seen as a way out of a liminal state of identity.

Jankowski (1991) purports that joining a gang is seen as a search for "respect." The respect that is sought by gang members allows them to blindly accept a life characterized by risk and danger. Unfortunately they don't acknowledge the risks associated with membership. They see the other benefits of gang membership, respect among them, as outweighing the dangers and risks.

Respect of course is defined variously by gang members. Reduced to its most basic array of denominators, respect is usually defined as a feeling that others acknowledge your existence and accept you as an important person. It is debatable whether gang members are really craving respect or if they are wanting others to be deferential to, no, afraid of, them. Again, the "need" for approval and acceptance seems to be at the core of the "respect motif" that adolescents verbalize as a reason for joining gangs.

Another position concerning the value of gang membership posits that members gain a sense of importance and value by *doing* something within the gang. Simply joining and being a member of the family by association does not satisfy the criteria of doing. Rather, members must be engaged in the actions of the group with other gang members or outsiders. Just any action won't do. It must be action that gang members consider to be dangerous and worthy of the *praise* of other gang members. Perhaps the first level of doing this occurs at the initiation.

Different gangs use various types of initiation. The common denominator among most initiations is aggression against the outside community. Examples of such behaviors include having a fight with one's parents, committing an act of antisocial behavior such as a robbery, physically attacking an innocent bystander, or staging a conflict with members of a rival gang. In New York City, for example, during 1997, there was a rash of scissor attacks on women in midtown Manhattan locations. The media reported these random acts of violence to be part of the initiation ritual of girl gangs that were thriving in Harlem.

A more common course of action during the initiation process is for gang members to subject themselves to acts of violence perpetrated by other gang members. Two types of acts have been described extensively in television documentaries about gangs and in autobiographical reflections of gang members. The first type, gang assault, requires that the members be "jumped in" as a way to join the gang. A second type of initiation ritual requires that girls have sex with several male gang members in rapid succession.

In both of the aforementioned initiation rituals the objective is to test the new recruit to see if he or she measures up to the implicit toughness index of the gang. Recruits who don't show "heart" during the "jumpin' in" fight are not permitted to join the gang. Likewise, girls who cry or otherwise can't withstand the gang rape are rejected from the class of recruits. Both routines have been the object of much discussion and debate among scholars of gangs and gang members themselves. It has been suggested that recruits who survive the initiation rituals, without appearing timid or cowardly, are elevated in the eyes of the other gang members. They are "respected" more than a member who exhibits any signs of ambivalence or weakness during the initiation rite. It appears that the respect accorded newly initiated members elevates their status within the group. This upgrading allows them to participate in gang activities (i.e., drive-by shootings, etc.) and to make demands of new recruits. The upgraded member comes to have a new "respect quotient."

The quest for respect that led many adolescents to come to the gang in the beginning continues to drive their behavior even after they have been accepted into the gang. There is a culture of constant and changing demands of gang members. Failing at any of the tests required of them decreases the level of respect given to the members. In this revolving door type of scenario the respect sought by some members is never fully realized. When opportunities to bolster one's perceived level of respect are not forthcoming because the gang doesn't assign a task to the member, a unique conflict exists. The gang member wants to be respected, but the gang doesn't assign him anything to do that enhance his respect level. There are a number of ways in which this dilemma can be resolved. Most often gang members not challenged and given a chance to earn respect create situations, often with innocent bystanders and rival gang members, unprovoked attacks on others or heinous crimes that far exceed the seriousness of the offenses that may have prompted them. Again, both of these behaviors are often described by gang members as an attempt to command respect from others.

Respect can be defined in multiple ways. The way in which it is used by some gang members appears to be idiosyncratic to their situation. In a very fundamental way respect, as used by gang members, seems to suggest that others must bestow it in response to something done by the gang member. General public use of the word respect refers to positive regard given to someone because he or she has presented himself or herself in an exemplary way and as a result commands the attention and accolades of others. In other words, the public had little or no choice but to acknowledge the gang member in a positive way because their behavior has been stellar. The concept seems to be used differently in gang culture. Respect is not limited to positive regard for exemplary behavior but also appears to connote recognition of behavior that others note as being significant, positive or negative. The need for respect and affirmation that many gang members had in their pregang days is brought with them into the gang. One of the problems with their quest for respect in the gang undermines their attempts to get the outside world to respect them. Let me explain.

The adolescent has a need to be respected. He believes that the environs in which he lives are not giving him any respect. To change this situation, he joins a gang. When he becomes a member of the gang, the need for respect increases exponentially. Now the new gang member seeks to earn the respect of the older gang members and the outside world (i.e., family of origin, community). As a new gang member the recruit must constantly review his behavior and ways in which he can increase his "respect quotient." Antisocial acts within the context of the gang are seen as ways to command the respect of other gang members. The same behavior, however, acts to distance the new recruit from the larger society. Behaving in an antisocial manner causes others (i.e., family members) to move away from the recruit. The complexity of the situation can be summarized thusly: wanting to get respect the adolescent joins a gang. In so doing he comes to believe he has to continue to earn the respect of fellow gang members by being tough and engaging, sometimes, in unprovoked antisocial acts. The more he succumbs to the implicit demands of antisocial behavior that exists within the gang, the less respect he receives from the others outside the gang. Members of gangs exist in two systems simultaneously: the world of the gang and the community at large. The codes of behavior and the values of the two systems seem to be at odds with each other. Closer examination of the value systems of the gang and the communities in which they reside may show that the differences are not as polarized as is commonly believed.

Jankowski (1991) argues this position as he proposes that gangs are about economic gain. According to him gangs exist as a way for gang members to attempt to share in the wealth of neighborhoods by selling drugs and participating in other entrepreneurial activities that place them on par with the rest of the community. The more economic loot the gang can amass, says Jankowski, the more respect they garner in the community. This seems somewhat ironic. The gang engages in socially condemned behavior (i.e., selling drugs) in an attempt to cause others to respect them as people who reside in the community, perhaps. Another way to think about the behavior of gangs and gang members along the respect continuum is that gangs and their members are involved in adversarial relationships with the communities in which they reside. The purpose of their negative behaviors, some researchers contend, is to articulate their recalcitrent attitudes and anger at the larger community. This type of reasoning fits with the widely held public view that no matter what gang members say to the contrary the groups are really designed for the proliferation of illegal and antisocial behavior, for the gratification of narcissistic needs of members. Believers of this position are not swayed by gang members' professions of their desire for respect. Instead, gang members are actually wanting others to fear them. Their entry into the gang is punctuated by their feeling good about themselves. The decision to join the gang often represents the latest accomplishment of which they are proud. Pride among gang members has occasionally been discussed as a dimension along the respect continuum also.

Jankowski (1991) has elevated the discussion of the role of pride in the lives of gang members to a new level by noting that there is also the issue of honor, alongside pride, which often drives much of the behavior of gang members. "While respect and honor are pivotal values in the identity/ethical development of the individual gang members I studied throughout the United States, they do not hold the same meaning from one place to another, and they produce different behavior patterns. Except for Chicano gangs, all the gangs studied used the concept of respect as a fundamental code in their interpersonal relations. The Chicano gangs used the concept of honor as the fundamental code governing the interpersonal relations" (Jankowski, 1991, p. 142).

The overarching issue in thinking about gangs as the functions they play in the lives of gang members has to do with the question of whether there is anything redemptive about belonging to a gang. Put another way one could think of it as asking if joining a gang is pathological, separate and apart from the question of what happens within the gang. Do gangs add a pathological quality to adolescent attempts at individuation and identity development? Remember that in adolescence it is quite normal that a young person would move away from the family, psychologically and physically, in an attempt to become an authentic and autonomous being. Where and how they go about this quest to find themselves is driven by the options that the adolescent perceives to be available to him or her. In some neighborhoods gangs are such a pervasive and integral part of the lives of residents that they are considered a legitimate and reasonable choice that a young person must make. That is, joining or not joining the gang becomes a major decision in the young person's life. Affiliation with the gang is not done for any devious or sociopathic reason but merely as a part of the complex set of questions that the young person must answer. This is a point that has been lost in much of the social science and criminology research. Rather, scholars have missed the possibility that a young person joined a gang because he felt that there were few other options available to him. This type of one-sided report has resulted in what Garbarino (1996) refers to as the "demonization of young people." The focus of that line of research has been on pointing out the destructive and negative outcomes associated with gang membership, with little or no regard for the possibility that there could be another side to the story.

Focusing only on the exotic and sociopath elements involved in gang activities seems to have the effect of pathologizing the larger issue of attempting to get psychological needs met within the context of the gang. Indeed, the common theme in many young people's defense of their decision to join a gang is an acknowledgment that the gang is about more than illegal acts and violence. Granted that is generally what the public sees of gangs, but that doesn't mean that it is an accurate or complete picture of the whole story. The definition of a gang that we have used throughout this text notes that there is a public and a semiprivate dimension to gang life.

Perhaps the semiprivate part includes social benefits that are not obvious to those who are outsiders.

Gangs may be a microcosm of the larger world in which many gang members have functioned earlier in life, or they may be the fantasy creation of what a gang member's world may come to be. Either way, gangs represent attempts on the parts of their members to have some semblance of predictability and order in their lives. The unanswered question, from the perspective of this writer, is whether gang membership is an attempt to pathologize normality.

Joining gangs has been pathologized by confusing "why" young people join gangs with what they do once they are actively involved with the gang. The distinction that needs to be made is what a person was seeking when they joined the gang and what they actually do after joining. The issue of what was being sought seems to point to joining a gang as a fairly normal activity driven by a "need to belong" or "seeking affirmation" through association with others. Who the others are and what types of behavior they emit should not be factored in at this point. Unfortunately many scholars and the general public do not make those distinctions. Everything about joining the gang gets reduced to one single analysis. Gangs do terrible things; therefore, there could not possibly be anything good about them, at any level of analysis. Gangs are also pathologized by focusing only on the acts of the gang, losing perspective on individual gang members in the process. There is a critical need to separate the organization from the individual. It is logically possible that there could be normal and benign relationships within the context of antisocial organizations. The compartmentalizing of gangs and gang members is necessary to help us remain cognizant of how groups often act in ways that are not reflective of the internal values of their members. In the current state of scholarship gangs and gang members get treated as synonymous entities, both pathognomic because of periodic participation in destructive and violent acts.

The selective and partial reporting on the life of gangs contributes considerably to the pathological image of gangs and gang members. This is driven by a pervasive social belief that there are only negatives associated with gangs. Scholars and journalists conduct their professional activities through the filter of their personal development and beliefs. If that community of writers only sees gangs as pathological units, then that is what will come through loudly and clearly in the writings about gangs. In a similar way gangs are presented as pathological units when writers fail to acknowledge the developmental aspects of gang membership or the fact that *many* gang members have some type of epiphany that causes them to reassess their gang-banging activity. Branch (1997) describes several such cases and raises the question of how it was possible for the gang bangers to shift their world-view, even as they were still participating in gang-banging activities of the most negative and pejorative type.

Changes that occur among gangstas and their organizations are often related to other developmental changes that are sometimes referred to as *maturation*. Some young men report that they simply grow out of the gang and turn their energies toward more socially appropriate and acceptable projects. Whether leaving a gang is just so simple and straightforward is an issue that has been hotly debated. There are two sides of the issue, which have been verbalized. Some insist that one can never leave a gang; when you join it is a lifetime commitment. On the other end of the spectrum is the view that members grow beyond the program of the group and move on to other activities. Getting married, having a family, and becoming a social activist who is concerned about children and adolescents is a commonly reported scenario for gang members who graduate.

Arguments that contend that gangs are subjected to attempts to normalize them have also been articulated. The author recalls an incident that stimulated him thinking about whether adolescents who join gangs are behaving in a pathological manner and whether gangs themselves are attempts to normalize (i.e., distort) pathology. In a graduate class discussion of gang adolescents and their realities a student became very agitated and perplexed at the tenor of the discussion. The graduate student lashed out and complained, "professor, . . . you're talking about them like they're normal people." How could that be? Or was the student missing the larger points of the discussion? Let's briefly turn our attention to the question of whether gangs are an attempt to normalize pathology.

The first evidence for an argument for normalization of pathology comes from the gang members themselves. Rationalizations and justifications of antisocial behavior are often found in how gang members defend their decision for being involved in destructive behaviors with the gang. Explanations rooted in political activism are often offered to justify otherwise unacceptable social behaviors. For example, when questioned as to why they sell drugs or steal from others some gang members will say it is because they are "marginalized" by the larger society or that such behaviors are their way of "sending a message" to the society. Of course the folly of such reasoning is that many of the criminal acts of gangs are perpetrated against members of their own residential communities. In some ways they are acting aggressively against their own relatives, family friends, and neighbors while the supposed culprits remain unscathed. The argument of political reasoning also becomes a concrete representation of the will of the gang superseding the goals and objectives of individual gang members. Put another way, the will of the gang overrides the rights of others, and the gang shows no regard for how others are hurt as they attempt to carry out their own goals. Narcissistic thinking and behavior reigns supreme!

Another way in which gangs have tried to intellectually defend their behavior is found in the tendency of some gangs to harm others by "testing them" to see if they measure up to the tough standards of the gang. The building of respect and honor requires that those aspiring to the elevated and desirable status of gang membership be violated and disrespected in the process of becoming a gang member in good standing. The gang claims to respect its members and initiates but routinely abuses them in the process of accepting them into the fold. Once the initiation process is ended suddenly the new member is respected because he is perceived to be worthy of respect and also to embrace the values and behaviors of the gang, all on the basis of having withstood the initiation ritual.

Perhaps the most direct evidence of the gang's attempts to normalize pathogenic behavior revolves around its relationship with the larger community in which it is located. Being outside of the community psychologically but at the same time aspiring to most of the things that are held in disdain (i.e., social status, material goods, etc.) seems to be self-contradictory. It's a bit oximoronic, wanting to be in the gang but acting in ways that push them further away from the community.

☐ Conclusion

Scholars who sometimes want to give an alternate view of gangs are overly zealous in their portrayals of gangs as being "normal" in the sense that it is a venue that many adolescents explore in an attempt to answer the "Who am I" question. The psychological benefits of gang membership are articulated to the exclusion of the negatives that are just as prominent in the gang's repertoire. This behavior is analogous to writers who only report the negatives of gang membership.

Are gangs an attempt for adolescents to pathologize normal behavior (i.e., individuation and separation, identity development, exploration of multiple life roles) and to rationalize the same? Or are gangs really an attempt to "normalize" otherwise unacceptable behavior? The answer appears not to be a simple yes or no to either. Rather, it seems to be nested in an understanding of the process of joining gangs as being distinct from continuing involvements within the gang culture. Good intentions, loosely defined, may have led an adolescent to the gang, but the greater index of the gang experience should be what the member does once he or she is in the gang. Remember, good intentions alone don't explain why something continues to be. Actions, after the good intentions have been exercised, I think, are a more valuable index of the meaning of gang membership. Finally, remember that a certain road is paved with good intentions.

☐ References

Branch, C. (1997). *Clinical interventions with gang adolescents and their families.* Boulder, CO: Westview Press.

Csikeszentmihalyi, M., & Larson, R. (1984). *Being adolescent.* New York: Basic Books.

Dunphy, D. (1963). The social structure of urban adolescent peer groups. *Sociometry, 26,* 230–246.

Garbarino, J. (1996). Personal communication.

Hill, J., & Holmbeck, G. (1986). Attachment and autonomy during adolescence. *Annals of Child Development, 3,* 145–189.

Jankowski, M. (1991). *Islands in the street.* Berkeley, CA: University of California Press.

Larson, R., Kubey, R., & Coletti, J. (1989). Changing channels: Early adolescent media choices and shifting investments. *Journal of Youth and Adolescence, 18,* 583–599.

Maslow, A., & Murphy, G. (1954). *Motivation and personality.* New York: Harper.

Moffit, T. (1993). Adolescence-limited and life course persitient antisocial behavior: A developmental taxonomy. *Psychological Review, 100,* 674–701.

Monti, D. (1994). *Wannabe: Gangs in suburbs and schools.* Cambridge, MA: Blackwell.

Mydans, S. (1990a, January 29). Life in a girls' gang: Colors and bloody. *New York Times,* pp. 1, 12.

Mydans, S. (1990b, April 10). Not just the inner city: Well-to-do join gangs. *New York Times National Magazine,* pp. A–F.

Silverberg, S., & Steinberg, L. (1987). Psychological well-being of parents of early adolescents. *Developmental Psychology, 26,* 658–666.

Springthall, N., & Collins, W. (1995). *Adolescent psychology—A developmental view.* New York: McGraw–Hill.

Wasserman, G., Miller, L. Pinner, E., & Jaramillo, B. (1996). Parenting predictors of early conduct problems in urban, high risk boys. *American Journal of Child and Adolescent Psychiatry, 35,* 1227–1236.

IV

SUMMARY, CONCLUSIONS, AND RECOMMENDATIONS

The range of opinions expressed by the authors in this volume illustrates the diversity of thought concerning gangs and what must be done to be responsive to them in a way which produces positive outcomes for all concerned. Historically, responses to gangs have been articulated from the perspective of reducing their presence in communities. Specifically, incarceration and "wars on gangs" have been approaches heavily endorsed. The result is a proliferation of gangs and a continuation of all the "problems" associated with gangs and gang members. It appears that one factor that has contributed to this cyclical pattern has been that program planners and policymakers have been reluctant to be creative and revolutionary in their service delivery to gangs. Instead, old tried and unsuccessful approaches have continued to be employed, with no new outcomes. There are several explanations for this recidivistic programming, including the following:

1. Violence and social disruption are the dimensions of gang life that are most problematic for the larger society. Hence, containment of gangs, most notably through suppression, is the logical response.
2. Gangs have been associated with poor and people of color communities. The result of this pairing is that responses to gangs take on racialized overtones, which drive the program planner's actions into benign neglect, paternalistic attitudes, or hostile intolerance.
3. Preventive interventions have not occurred very often. Instead, efforts to "help" have been reactionary and "after the fact" rather than *before* young people get involved in gangs.
4. Enactment of new approaches not steeped in law enforcement philosophies are frequently criticized as being "soft" and "ineffective," even before they are tried.
5. Deficit model thinking is applied to young people and communities who do not conform to the model approach to thinking and behaving.

The chapters in this volume represent the beginning of some new ideas that may shift the paradigm of what must be done to create new and effective ways of working with gang members. Most of the ideas articulated here are built on the premise that gangs themselves are only symptomatic of a larger set of social issues and developmental needs. To effectively identify which things are gang member issues and which are social order/community issues we must engage in an intense process of analysis of the components. That frequently doesn't happen because of the negative associations made with gangs. Instead, interventions are planned as if the only and desirable outcome is to crush the gangs. One of the problems with that approach of course is that the members of the gang, often young and salvageable community residents, are crushed in the process also.

Gonzalez's chapter offers some insights into how communities can be built and strengthened by harnessing the energy that has started to be generated around gang membership. Community building can be brought about at several levels, but it requires that gang members and all others with an interest in the community be included in the dialogue about the future of the community. Special efforts should be made to assure that organizers do not conclude that one's behaviors are indicative of their values or levels of commitment to the community. Sometimes individuals behave in what appears to be socially irresponsible manners simply because they don't know any better or don't have any other behaviors available in their repertoire. For example, some young people who engage in theft and petty larceny types of behaviors may be assessed to be unsympathetic to the community and its residents. This appraisal is poignant in that most of their offenses are against fellow community residents and small businesses. When questioned about their behaviors many thieves and their accomplices will insist that economic poverty and hardships are what led them to such acts.

In trying to defend their antisocial behaviors they are overlooking two critical facts: their thefts hurt others community residents and businesses, possibly hastening their departure from the community, and that poverty alone does not justify antisocial behaviors. Other community residents suffer through poverty but do not ultimately decide to steal from neighbors. There is, of course, beneath the veneer of stealing behavior and reckless antisocial presentations a sense of caring and concern, perhaps even pride, in one's neighborhood which may go unexpressed. The community may be valued, but its members may not know how to express the same. At risk in situations like this is the possibility that community residents who behave improperly may be dismissed as devaluing the community. Gonzalez suggests that a similar type of analysis should be made when trying to understand the motivations and behaviors of gang members. The episodic participation of gang members in violent and destructive behaviors should be contextualized.

Gangs are not out of control collections of sociopaths who are habitually consumed by thoughts of violence and anarchy. Rather, gangs represent human capital awaiting rescue and development. The interest of the community is not served by having random acts of violence and destruction committed by gang members. On the other hand we must constantly remind ourselves that gangs do not spontaneously occur. They are the by-product of young people having psychological needs that they perceive as only being met through gang affiliation. To engage in such logic, I suggest, is an indictment of the service provider agencies in a community (i.e., families, schools, faith communities, etc.) as well as of the young people themselves.

The human capital that exists in all communities potentially can lead to dramatic improvements in the quality of communities. Continuing to believe that gang members represent "social throwaway" potentially dilutes the resources of a community. Specific strategies that will work in building communities vary according to the ethnic/racial and economic makeup of the communities. A common denominator in all communities is school. From within the parameters of school communities strategies for building the community can be made. The real value of public educational communities like schools is that they interact with every constituent group within the community. Quamina offers his range of observations from the perspective of an educational practitioner. He suggests that there has been a major sociological shift in the African American community that places young males at risk for psychological disengagement.

The role of the media in creating pop culture images that serve as the basis of social relationship roles should not be underestimated. Quamina thinks the evolving pattern of young African American males being less and less available for sustained interpersonal relationships can be attributed in part to the impact of the media. Within school settings, he thinks, myths of jocks and players are reinforced by larger real-world examples of professional athletes making enormous salaries has not helped the situation. At the core of the disengagement movement is a devaluing of formal education in favor of more quick results and short-term gratification outcomes. These dramatic changes have manifested themselves in more and more youngsters doing less and less in the area of organized and structured prosocial activities, which demand interpersonal relating. Gangs appear to benefit from disengagement cycles in communities because they come to have a larger pool of people from whom to recruit, says conventional wisdom. One major problem with this logic is that active participation within gangs requires that members "relate" to the leadership and to fellow members. Loners and detached types are a serious threat to the integrity of the group.

No one knows for certain why the pattern of disengagement and detachment noted by Quamina and others exists. A range of explanations for the trend has been offered: it is a by-product of social and media technology; individualism versus collectivism is an ideology within communities; communities have been realigned such that boundaries are more porous than before; and the culture of narcissism has become an American society reality. Another less optimistic interpretation of the disengagement is the possibility that many young people are fatalistic, believing that they have no future (i.e., I will die very young); therefore, they should engage in self-serving hedonistic activity today because they will have no years beyond the present. A glimpse of this lack of vision and hope is found in the empirical work of Doucette-Gates.

One of the significant findings reported by Doucette-Gates is that many of the subjects in her research had an extremely limited vision of the future. Because they anticipated short lives they did not make long range plans nor did they engage in activities which required a significant delay of gratification. Rewards for which they were willing to work were by definition intrinsic and immediately available. Membership in gangs modified this relationship somewhat but did not eliminate it. Doucette-Gates points out how academic achievement and mastery of simple matters necessary for daily living were adversely impacted by such pejorative and pessimistic views of life.

Participation in gangs, for many adolescents, is an attempt to get many of their needs met, and quickly. Concerns about personal safety or the value of the lives and property of others are often secondary to the pressing goal of acquisition of material things. Perhaps even more interesting is the observation that many new gang recruits don't anticipate the level of psychological demands associated with gang membership. Blind allegiance, fidelity, and acceptance of group goals are examples of some requirements that are frequently problematic for new and overly naive gang members. An inability to resolve the demands of the gang and their capabilities of new members often leads to internal conflicts. The new recruit wants to be in the group but finds himself or herself unable to "get with the program." This mismatch often leads to ambivalence, which gets expressed by verbalizing a commitment to the group but privately seeking the help of family-of-origin members and social service agencies.

Appeals for help are often disguised and presented in veiled manners that defy easy detection. Confiding in an outsider, hoping all the while that he will do something to help the new recruit resolve the dilemma, and engaging in risky behavior that is certain to get the rookie gang member caught, are common behavioral expressions of ambivalence. It should be kept in mind that all of this is subconscious and not obvious even to the person who is emitting the behavior.

Noting the levels of disclosure that occurs when a young gang member is brought to the attention of a helping professional is fascinating. On the one hand they appear to be recalcitrent and uncooperative but on the other hand their behavior betrays them. Take for example situations in which gang members continue to show up for appointments with probation officers even after emphatically announcing that they "don't have no problems." One has to wonder about the psychological benefits being derived from the ongoing contact with the probation officer. An even more transparent example occurs when the psychologically unsophisticated gang member engages in arguments with adults with whom he is suppose to be working. Each round of the argument is characterized by the adolescent sharing more and more vital information about himself and his colleagues' behaviors. These types of scenarios become complicated when the disclosures are of a variety that goes beyond the service delivery capability of the professional to whom they are being disclosed. In some instances professionals can readily identify the mismatch and seek consultations from colleagues in other professional disciplines. Other situations are less obvious, and the gang member's pleas for assistance may go without a direct response. The specialized services provided by an agency reflect the professional biases and expertise of the persons employed by the agency. Unfortunately many troubled adolescents don't make the distinction. When they are ready to talk or to engage in a psychological game of "catch me if you can" they anticipate that they will get a positive response from the adult with whom they are relating. The absence of the same is likely to be interpreted as insensitivity or, worse yet, dismissal.

Abdullah and Branch demonstrate how the Denver Juvenile Courts responded to families with multiple problems by enlisting the collaboration of a group of mental health professionals to assist in providing services to gang adolescents and their families. The approach was novel in several ways. First, some of the programming involved the families of gang members. That was a bold departure from the often articulated belief that families of gang members are not available or interested in trying to help their troubled adolescent.

Second, the inclusion of mental health professionals in a collaborative and collegial relationship that was ongoing created a new paradigm. Historically mental health professionals had been used by the court as consultants. Their work was done away from the court and in settings unfamiliar to the probationers and their families. The FIP presented another model. Last, the range of programs attempted by the juvenile courts provided structured opportunities for probation officers and others to see the families in action, concurrently. This rare setup revealed strengths and weaknesses of families. Secondhand reports, often relied upon heavily by court systems, were eliminated.

The law enforcement perspectives on gangs and delinquent behavior are critical. However, Abdullah and Branch show that it is not the only perspective that can be helpful in intervening in the lives of gang adolescents and their families. One of the examples of new discoveries that grew out of the courts' experimental programs was a rethinking of recidivism as an index of the effectiveness of diversionary activities. It was concluded that recidivism rates are only part of the story. They simply report who gets apprehended for subsequent offenses, not a true statement of who is a repeat offender. Families were instrumental in pointing out that often offenses occur but they go undetected because the offender becomes very skillful in soliciting the support of others in not reporting the crime. Offenders often develop a larger corp of enablers with the passage of time. This is nowhere more evident than in school where academic and behavior problems may go unreported for a variety of reasons, none of them facilitative of the gang members psychological or educational maturation.

Lorita Foster extends the axiom further by noting that much of the difficulty many troubled adolescents experience in school may not be the result of willful defiant behavior. Rather, she believes, many behavior problems exhibited by students may be psychiatric disturbances in the early stages of development. PTSD is highlighted in her work as a specific clinical syndrome likely to manifest itself among adolescents who have been exposed to violence over a protracted period of time. Foster points out that classroom teachers, because of their extensive exposure to students, should develop some skills in early detection of clinical syndromes like PTSD.

It is not enough to assume that the business of early identification of emotional problems should be handled by trained mental health professionals. In most school settings there are simply not enough clinicians to do all of the early detection work that is needed. Foster suggests that teachers can be valuable resources in the area of early identification because of the multitude of circumstances under which they see students operate. Academic mastery is only one area in which problems in the early stages of development may appear. Interpersonal relationships with peers, teachers, and administrators, as well as how new and stressful situations are approached, are other sources of data about students' emotional stability.

PTSD has been documented to occur in school-age children and adolescents who have been exposed to violence for extended periods of time. It should be considered as a possible explanation for some of the behavior difficulties reported in schools. An awareness of the developmental course of the illness may help teachers and parents recognize it as a clinical manifestation that exists in schools and homes. Recognizing the illness as one that occurs among groups other then Vietnam veterans also allows communities to think about the possibility that some gang members may also be suffering from the disorder. That is a somewhat disquieting thought when one considers the easy access that many adolescents have to guns and drugs. Perhaps an appropriate response to this possibility should be that communities should act to inoculate themselves from troubled adolescents who are manifesting evidence of psychiatric impairment. The inoculation of a community can come in many forms, ranging from basic factual information about gangs, drugs, and youth violence, to the creation of community action plans for times of crisis.

Strategies for energizing communities are delineated by Norman Randolph. He thinks the school community should play a vital role in helping the rest of the community identify and activate resources for responding to gangs. The Randolph Plan also presupposes a level of communication and connection within the community that would facilitate intense work relationships. Embedded in Randolph's approach to energizing communities is the idea that the skills and resources necessary to respond effectively to gang issues are already present in most communities. The work of the organizers is to activate those resources. In so doing new partnerships will emerge and a spirit of community will pervade the work and future work assignments.

Schools are central to Randolph's strategies. He thinks the presence of a school building, even in the economically poorest of neighborhoods, is a common denominator that bodes well for empowerment of community residents. The school building represents a neutral site in the community and a place to which nearly all residents have some level of ongoing attachment. Perhaps at an even more basic level schools can be thought of as the place where many community aspirations are born. When gang members make their presence felt in a community, schools can play an important role in providing "education" to potential gang recruits, a preventative strategy that often does not get performed.

Last is the issue of mental health and its relevance as an intervention for working with gang-affiliated adolescents and their families. Mental health is an area that has been sorely overlooked in the literature about what to do relative to gangs in communities. There are several reasons that support the paucity of mental health literature relative to gangs, but none of them is without serious fault. In the current volume the Vargas and DiPilato chapter offers a refreshingly direct and clear statement of one approach for working with gang adolescents. They describe a program of group psychotherapy in which cultural experiences are the focus of the group work. There are two things, at least, to be said about this approach that make it worthy of possible replication. The modality of choice for doing clinical work with gang adolescents does not appear to be well documented in the literature primarily because mental health professionals have not spent a lot of time attempting to "treat" gang adolescents. There is a huge literature on treating conduct disordered individuals, of which many gang members number, but a narrow focus dealing mostly with acknowledged gang members has not emerged. Despite this dubious history it appears that group work does offer some advantages over the traditional medical model individual treatment approach.

Gangs, by definition, are collections of young people who are bonded together in search of fulfilling some superordinate goal. Group psychotherapy provides a similar opportunity for individuals to be connected to each other around an issue that was represented among all of them. Vargas and DiPilato have chosen cultural experiences as the issue that potentially connects gang members across boundaries of turf and individual differences. Their work as articulated here suggests that cultural experiences are something that all adolescents have and with some prompting will be able to share without fear of failure or rejection.

At a more basic level the Vargas and DiPilato chapter presents the idea that mental health professionals do have something of significance to offer gang adolescents. The mental health community has not been particularly interested in deviant adolescents except as a part of resocialization in residential therapeutic settings or as extensions of the criminal justice system. The group therapy approach articulated by Vargas and DiPilato offers some hope that such limited applications of mental health concepts can be changed. The work with gangs as they have outlined it in this volume can be implemented in the context of other programs without mental health or group work being treated as something "special."

Group psychotherapy is very rooted in the psychodynamic tradition. It supposes that within the context of the group new and novel experiences will cause the client to relive an old experience. The action within the group will be catalytic in that it will prompt the client to recall some hitherto forgotten event or feelings. This associational hypothesis is such a pronounced part of psychological thinking and the general public's image of therapy that it is often accepted as being canonical. It is a psychoanalytic concept. In many places there is an unchallenged assumption that all psychotherapy is psychoanalytic in nature. Nothing could be further from the truth. Indeed in this volume the chapter by Carylon and Jones offers another theoretical orientation, which may have utility in its application to work with gang adolescents. Carylon and Jones' use of cognitive behavioral interventions suggests that restructuring the thinking and behaviors of gang adolescents offers some hope for producing long-term changes in their behaviors. The setting of schools described by the authors makes the cognitive behavioral orientation especially rich in that schools are a setting in which most adolescents have some history.

An especially important concept presented in the Carylon and Jones chapter is the idea that the entire school community can be involved in structuring a cognitive–behavioral intervention program. The authors note that the boundaries of the school community should include everyone who has a presence (i.e., maintenance workers, teacher assistants, etc.) in the school building. An overarching idea of the cognitive–behavioral intervention philosophy is that there should be major changes within the system and that no targeting of individuals should occur.

The final chapter in this volume raises the question of whether gangs are an attempt at meeting developmental needs that has gone awry. To pursue that logic theoretically Branch offers the provocative question of whether gangs are an attempt to normalize pathology or are they a disguised effort to pathologize identity-seeking activities? He offers some insights into how adolescent gang members attempt to explain away the antisocial behavior of their gangs by suggesting that being a member of a gang is like being "in family." The other extreme of the dichotomy is that researchers have pathologized efforts that adolescents have made to define themselves, especially if those activities have taken them through a phase of gang involvement. Transient stops in gangs provide many adolescents with valuable information that will be helpful to them in answering the "Who am I" question. It is not patently clear that the answer to the pathologizing normality question is either/or. Rather, it is one about which policymakers will have to think very carefully before venturing to design intervention programs. The nature of intervention programs is that they are inherently rooted in the belief in the goodness or badness of the system that is being altered. While we can all decry the violence and social disruption caused by gangs, very little energy has been invested in thinking about the human capital that is potentially lost as a result of gang involvement. The matter really seems to be whether people can get healthy milestones met in unhealthy environs.

The temptation in creating a volume such as this one is to end with a set of stark recommendations about what needs to happen to overcome the problem. In closing this volume the temptation to succumb to that urge is also present. However, I think it would be nonsensical to attempt to reduce the issue of gangs and their presence in communities into a simple-minded formula that is responsive to linear interventions. Rather, I would like to leave the reader with the idea that gangs are a very complex issue. In many communities they have long-standing histories, borne out of feelings of marginalization and racial prejudice in bygone years of American history. More recent changes in international community boundaries have made gangs an issue that spreads across international lines with an amazing level of consistency of form. I am of the opinion that no single intervention program has "the" answer. Because of that, I think, a multimethod interdisciplinary approach is necessary. There is strength in numbers and diversity of approach.

INDEX